Civic Life Online

D1397155

This book was made possible by grants from the John D. and Catherine T. MacArthur Foundation in connection with its grant making initiative on Digital Media and Learning. For more information on the initiative visit www.macfound.org.

The John D. and Catherine T. MacArthur Foundation Series on Digital Media and Learning

Civic Life Online: Learning How Digital Media Can Engage Youth, edited by W. Lance Bennett

Digital Media, Youth, and Credibility, edited by Miriam J. Metzger and Andrew J. Flanagin

The Ecology of Games: Connecting Youth, Games, and Learning, edited by Katie Salen

Digital Youth, Innovation, and the Unexpected, edited by Tara McPherson

Learning Race and Ethnicity: Youth and Digital Media, edited by Anna Everett

Youth, Identity, and Digital Media, edited by David Buckingham

Civic Life Online

Learning How Digital Media Can Engage Youth

Edited by W. Lance Bennett

The MIT Press
Cambridge, Massachusetts
London, England

For information about special quantity discounts, please email special_sales@mitpress.mit.edu.

This book was set in Stone sans and Stone serif by Aptara, Inc.

Printed and bound in the United States of America.

Library of Congress Cataloging-in-Publication Data

Civic life online : learning how digital media can engage youth / edited by W. Lance Bennett.
        p.   cm.—(The John D. and Catherine T. Macarthur Foundation series on digital media and learning)
    Includes bibliographical references.
    ISBN 978-0-262-02634-5 (hardcover : alk. paper)—ISBN 978-0-262-52482-7 (pbk. : alk. paper)
    1. Youth—Political activity.   2. Political participation.   3. Mass media and youth.
    4. Digital media—Social aspects.   I. Bennett, W. Lance.
HQ799.2.P6C58   2008
320.40835—dc22   2007029041

10 9 8 7 6 5 4 3 2 1

CONTENTS

Foreword   vii
Series Advisors

Changing Citizenship in the Digital Age   1
W. Lance Bennett

Youth and Digital Democracy: Intersections of Practice, Policy, and the Marketplace   25
Kathryn C. Montgomery

Not Your Father's Internet: The Generation Gap in Online Politics   51
Michael Xenos and Kirsten Foot

Contesting Cultural Control: Youth Culture and Online Petitioning   71
Jennifer Earl and Alan Schussman

Using Participatory Media and Public Voice to Encourage Civic Engagement   97
Howard Rheingold

A Public Voice for Youth: The Audience Problem in Digital Media and Civic Education   119
Peter Levine

Civic Identities, Online Technologies: From Designing Civics Curriculum to Supporting Civic Experiences   139
Marina Umaschi Bers

Our Space: Online Civic Engagement Tools for Youth   161
Kate Raynes-Goldie and Luke Walker

Doing IT for Themselves: Management versus Autonomy in Youth E-Citizenship   189
Stephen Coleman

Foreword

In recent years, digital media and networks have become embedded in our everyday lives, and are part of broad-based changes to how we engage in knowledge production, communication, and creative expression. Unlike the early years in the development of computers and computer-based media, digital media are now *commonplace* and *pervasive*, having been taken up by a wide range of individuals and institutions in all walks of life. Digital media have escaped the boundaries of professional and formal practice, and the academic, governmental, and industry homes that initially fostered their development. Now they have been taken up by diverse populations and non-institutionalized practices, including the peer activities of youth. Although specific forms of technology uptake are highly diverse, a generation is growing up in an era where digital media are part of the taken-for-granted social and cultural fabric of learning, play, and social communication.

In 2005, The John D. and Catherine T. MacArthur Foundation began a new grant-making initiative in the area of digital media and learning. An initial set of exploratory grants in the study of youth practices and the development of digital literacy programs has expanded into a major initiative spanning research, educational reform, and technology development. One component of this effort is the support of this book series. As part of the broader MacArthur Foundation initiative, this series is aimed at timely dissemination of new scholarship, fostering an interdisciplinary conversation, and archiving the best research in this emerging field. Through the course of producing the six initial volumes, the foundation convened a set of meetings to discuss the framing issues for this book series. As a result of these discussions we identified a set of shared commitments and areas of focus. Although we recognize that the terrain is being reshaped even as we seek to identify it, we see these as initial frames for the ongoing work to be put forward by this series.

This book series is founded upon the working hypothesis that those immersed in new digital tools and networks are engaged in an unprecedented exploration of language, games, social interaction, problem solving, and self-directed activity that leads to diverse forms of learning. These diverse forms of learning are reflected in expressions of identity, how individuals express independence and creativity, and in their ability to learn, exercise judgment, and think systematically.

The defining frame for this series is not a particular theoretical or disciplinary approach, nor is it a fixed set of topics. Rather, the series revolves around a constellation of topics investigated from multiple disciplinary and practical frames. The series as a whole looks at the relation between youth, learning, and digital media, but each book or essay might deal with only a subset of this constellation. Erecting strict topical boundaries can exclude some of the most important work in the field. For example, restricting the content of the series only to people of a certain age means artificially reifying an age boundary when the phenomenon demands otherwise. This becomes particularly problematic with new forms of online participation where one important outcome is the mixing of participants of different ages. The same goes for digital media, which are increasingly inseparable from analog and earlier media forms.

In the case of learning, digital media are part of the redefinition and broadening of existing boundaries of practice and our understanding of what learning means. The term *learning* was chosen rather than *education* in order to flag an interest in settings both within and outside the classroom. Many of the more radical challenges to existing learning agendas are happening in domains such as gaming, online networks, and amateur production that usually occur in informal and non-institutional settings. This does not mean we are prejudiced against learning as it happens in the classroom or other formal educational settings. Rather, we hope to initiate a dialog about learning as it spans settings that are more explicitly educational and those that are not.

The series and the MacArthur Foundation initiative respond to certain changes in our media ecology that have important implications for learning. Specifically, these are new forms of media *literacy* and changes in the modes of media *participation*. Digital media are part of a convergence between interactive media (most notably gaming), online networks, and existing media forms. Navigating this media ecology involves a palette of literacies that are being defined through practice but require more scholarly scrutiny before they can be fully incorporated pervasively into educational initiatives. Media literacy involves not only ways of understanding, interpreting, and critiquing media, but also the means for creative and social expression, online search and navigation, and a host of new technical skills. The potential gap in literacies and participation skills creates new challenges for educators who struggle to bridge media engagement inside and outside the classroom.

The shift toward interactive media, peer-to-peer forms of media communication, and many-to-many forms of distribution relate to types of participation that are more bottom-up and driven by the "user" or "consumer" of media. Audiences have always had the opportunity to "talk back" to corporate media or to create their own local media forms. However, the growing dominance of gaming as a media format, the advent of low-cost digital production tools, and online distribution means a much more dynamic range in who participates and how they participate in the production and distribution of media. Gamers expect that media are subject to player control. Add to this the fact that all forms of media are increasingly being contextualized in an online communication ecology where creative production and expression is inseparable from social communication. Finally, new low-cost digital production tools mean that amateur and casual media creators can author, edit, and distribute video and other rich media forms that were once prohibitively expensive to produce and share with others.

We value the term *participation* for the ways in which it draws attention to situated learning theory, social media literacies, and mobilized forms of media engagement. Digital media networks support existing forms of mass media distribution as well as smaller publics and collectivities that might center on peer groups or specialized niche interests. The presence of social communication, professional media, and amateur niche media in shared online spaces introduces a kind of leveling effect, where small media players gain new visibility and the position of previously authoritative media is challenged. The clash between more socially driven or niche publics and the publics defined by professional forms of media is playing out in high-profile battles in domains such as intellectual property law, journalism, entertainment, and government. For our purposes, the questions surrounding knowledge and credibility and young people's use of digital media to circumvent adult authority are particularly salient.

The emerging power shift, where smaller and edge players are gaining more visibility and voice, is particularly important to children and youth. If we look at children and youth through the lens of digital media, we have a population that has been historically subject to a high degree of systematic and institutional control in the kinds of information and social communication to which they have access. This is one reason why the alchemy between youth and digital media has been distinctive; it disrupts the existing set of power relations between adult authority and youth voice. While many studies of children, youth, and media have for decades stressed the status of young people as competent and full social subjects, digital media increasingly insist that we acknowledge this viewpoint. Not only must we see youth as legitimate social and political actors, but we must also recognize them as potential innovators and drivers of new media change.

This does not mean that we are uncritical of youth practices or that we believe that digital media necessarily hold the key to empowerment. Rather, we argue against technological determinism, stressing the need for balanced scholarship that recognizes the importance of our current moment within the context of existing structures and unfolding histories. This means placing contemporary changes within a historical context as well as working to highlight the diversity in the landscape of media and media uptake. Neither youth nor digital media are monolithic categories; documenting how specific youth take up particular forms of media with diverse learning outcomes is critical to this series as a whole. Digital media take the form they do because they are created by existing social and cultural contexts, contexts that are diverse and stratified.

As with earlier shifts in media environments, this current turn toward digital media and networks has been accompanied by fear and panic as well as elevated hopes. This is particularly true of adult perception of children and youth who are at the forefront of experimentation with new media forms, and who mobilize digital media to push back at existing structures of power and authority. While some see "digital kids" as our best hope for the future, others worry that new media are part of a generational rift and a dangerous turn away from existing standards for knowledge, literacy, and civic engagement. Careful, socially engaged, and accessible scholarship is crucial to informing this public debate and related policy decisions. Our need to understand the relation between digital media and learning is urgent because of the scale and the speed of the changes that are afoot. The shape and uses of digital media are still very much in flux, and this book series seeks to be part of the definition of our sociotechnical future.

Mizuko Ito
Cathy Davidson
Henry Jenkins
Carol Lee
Michael Eisenberg
Joanne Weiss
Series Advisors

Changing Citizenship in the Digital Age

W. Lance Bennett

University of Washington, Seattle, Center for Communication and Civic Engagement

Democracy is not a sure thing. Governments and party systems often strain against changes in societies, and some fall prey to corruption and bad policies. Under the right conditions, people may reassert their rights to govern, and produce remarkable periods of creative reform, realignment, and change. In these times, politics becomes a focus of personal life itself, restoring the sense that participation makes a difference. The challenges of influencing the course of nations and addressing global issues may inspire creative solutions from the generations of young citizens who have access to digital communication tools. The cascading advance of media platforms and social software enables unprecedented levels of production and distribution of ideas, public deliberation, and network organization.

It is clear that many young citizens of this digital and global age have demonstrated interests in making contributions to society. Yet the challenge of engaging effectively with politics that are linked to spheres of government remains, for most, a daunting prospect. The reasons are numerous. A casual look at world democracies suggests that many of the most established ones are showing signs of wear. Parties are trying to reinvent themselves while awkwardly staying the course that keeps them in power. In the press, in everyday conversation, and often from the mouths of politicians, politics has become a dirty word rather than a commonly accepted vocabulary for personal expression.[1] Perhaps most notably, younger generations have disconnected from conventional politics and government in alarming numbers. These trends in youth dissatisfaction with conventional political engagement are not just occurring in the United States, but have parallels in other democracies as well, including Germany, Sweden, and the United Kingdom.[2] The pathways to disconnection from government are many: adults are frequently negative about politics, the tone of the press is often cynical, candidates seldom appeal directly to young voters on their own terms about their concerns, politicians have poisoned the public well (particularly in the United States) with vitriol and negative campaigning, and young people see the media filled with inauthentic performances from officials who are staged by professional communication managers.[3] Paralleling these developments has been a notable turning away from public life into online friendship networks, gaming and entertainment environments, and consumer

The author would like to thank Peter Levine, Alan Schussman, Cathy Davidson, and Chris Wells for their helpful comments on this chapter. In addition, the lively discussions both on- and offline among all the authors in this volume have informed and changed my thinking on many aspects of citizenship and digital learning. The online discussions with an impressive group of participants further added to the intellectual stimulation of this project. Thanks to everyone who so generously shared their time and creative spirits.

pursuits. Where political activity occurs, it is often related to lifestyle concerns that seem outside the realm of government.[4]

Many observers properly note that there are impressive signs of youth civic engagement in these nongovernmental areas, including increases in community volunteer work, high levels of consumer activism, and impressive involvement in social causes from the environment to economic injustice in local and global arenas.[5] Some even ascribe civic engagement qualities to many activities that occur in online social networking and entertainment communities. For example, Henry Jenkins, Cathy Davidson, Mimi Ito, and Jochai Benkler argue that many forms of shared activity online (from blogging, to conflict and protest behavior in gaming, fan and entertainment sites) represent forms of civic or media engagement.[6] The chapter by Earl and Schussman in this volume makes a good case that online petitions to entertainment and media corporations constitute a kind of social activism that displays skills mirroring social movement repertoires of action.

Many of the spontaneous and creative forms of collective expression online seem more appealing than the options typically offered in youth engagement sites sponsored by governments and nongovernmental organizations (NGOs) in efforts to invigorate public life for young people. In Coleman's concluding chapter in this volume we learn that many well-intentioned youth engagement sites have clear ideas about what constitute proper citizen activities. As a result, these *managed* environments seem inauthentic and irrelevant to many young people. Indeed, Coleman's survey of *managed* (government- and NGO-built and -operated) and *autonomous* (youth-built and -operated) sites in the U.K. suggests that young citizens find more authentic experiences in edgier political sites and in entertainment media and games. The dilemma is that many of the political sites that young people build and operate themselves may avoid formal government channels for communication and action and may lack the resources needed to sustain and grow them.

A key question thus becomes how to nurture the creative and expressive actions of a generation in change, while continuing to keep some positive engagement with government on their screens.

Two Paradigms of Youth Engagement

One goal of this chapter is to note and explore the sharply differing views of what constitutes civic engagement and citizenship for young people both on and off line. Indeed, there seem to be two different paradigms that contrast young citizens (roughly in the fifteen to twenty-five age range) as either reasonably active and *engaged* or relatively passive and *disengaged*. Like all paradigms, each foregrounds different core organizing values and principles, prompting proponents to weigh and select different sets of supporting facts and reasons. Each paradigm thus comes equipped with its own arguments and evidence, making it convincing to adherents and elusive and often maddening to those operating from the other constructed reality.[7]

The *engaged youth* paradigm implicitly emphasizes generational changes in social identity that have resulted in the growing importance of peer networks and online communities. In this view, if there is an attendant decline in the credibility or authenticity of many public institutions and discourses that define conventional political life, the fault lies more with the government performances and news narratives than with citizens who cannot engage with them.[8] In an important sense, this paradigm emphasizes the empowerment of youth as expressive individuals and symbolically frees young people to make their own creative choices. In the bargain, the engaged youth paradigm also eases the overriding duty to participate in conventional government-centered activities. In many cases, researchers in this school are only dimly aware of (and may tend to discount) research on declines and deficits in more conventional political participation among young citizens. As a result, the *engaged youth* paradigm opens the door to a new spectrum of civic actions in online arenas from MySpace to *World of Warcraft*. By contrast, the *disengaged youth* paradigm may acknowledge the rise of more autonomous forms of public expression such as consumer politics, or the occasional protest in MySpace, while keeping the focus on the generational decline in connections to government (e.g., voting patterns) and general civic involvement (e.g., following public affairs in the news) as threats to the health of democracy itself.

A typical exchange in a series of online discussions that accompanied the development of this volume found Jochai Benkler listing a variety of sites as examples of engaged youth, including the Harry Potter fan publication of the fictional wizard newspaper, the *Daily Prophet*. He also offered as evidence a Pew study showing that a majority of bloggers are under thirty, and roughly one third of them think of what they are doing as journalism. In his view, a faculty-student network for providing medicines to poor countries "must have missed the memo about lack of political engagement in today's youth."[9] In response, Ulises Mejias acknowledged the existence of some forms of civic life on the Web but expressed the following concerns: "If voting and reading the newspaper are deemed antiquated forms of civic participation, what kind of public sphere is being created by new forms of participation such as blogging, news aggregating, etc.? . . . the question is: what participant interests mold democracy's new architecture of participation? . . . Yes, there are important alternative spaces, but as the Pew study that Yochai cites points out, while a minority is interested in exploiting these uses for pro-social political action, the majority of users are content to view the technologies as means for individual expression (articulated through consumer choices)."[10]

This exchange, along with many others, show that the same evidence can be interpreted differently when placed in different paradigm frames. One root of the difference is that the two paradigms reflect different normative views of what the good citizen ought to do when she grows up. The *engaged youth* viewpoint, in a sense, empowers young people by recognizing personal expression and their capacity to project identities in collective spaces. As Cathy Davidson noted in the online discussions, ". . . I think we have a unique opportunity to take advantage of peer-to-peer sites for creative, imaginative, activist learning purposes. That is a lot harder mission than critiquing the young. . . . I want to be attuned to what youth themselves say about the alternative forms of learning and social networking afforded by Web 2.0."[11]

By contrast, those who lean toward the disengaged youth perspective often worry about this very personalization or privatization of the political sphere and focus more on how to promote public actions that link to government as the center of democratic politics, and to other social groups and institutions as the foundations of civic life. As David Buckingham (editor of the MacArthur series volume on identity) put it:

Part of me would agree that we do need to be worried, although I would accept that disengagement is a fairly understandable response to what currently seems to count as "public affairs." Yes, new media may be offering new possibilities for civic participation, at least for some—although we need to know if this is just for the "usual suspects." . . .

But the point that worries me a little is the Harry Potter anecdote. OK, young people may well be participating and engaging in all sorts of very active and interesting ways online; and we could probably think of many other examples. But in what ways is this CIVIC engagement? . . . "media engagement" is not necessarily the same as "civic engagement." I would accept other people's comments to the effect that this term "civic" is a little worthy and moralistic... but how, in the end, are we defining what counts as "civic," and what doesn't?

I would suggest that "civic" implies some notion of the public (the polis or the public sphere, even)— by which I suppose I mean an open debate about issues of general social concern between people who may not agree with each other. In this respect, there are certainly tendencies in the internet towards an individualisation, or at least a fragmentation, of social/political debate (a settling into established niche groups). So there may be ways in which the internet promotes participation, but undermines the "civic.". . . [12]

And so the debate goes, often with real consequences in the worlds in which young people work, play, learn, and vote. As Cathy Davidson, Peter Levine, Howard Rheingold, and Henry Jenkins, among others, have pointed out, the disengaged youth viewpoint leads to something of a narrative of despair or decline about young citizens, one that travels all to easily in the news and leads to overlooking the many innovations that young people have brought to our public communication spaces.[13] At the same time, Lew Friedland, Michael Delli Carpini, Zephyr Teachout, Peter Levine, and others have noted that traditional activities such as voting continue to matter, and young people hold the future of our democratic life insofar as citizens can still shape their political institutions. Some of these observers, including this author, straddle the two perspectives while seeking to bridge and transcend them. For example, Peter Levine has contrasted the core elements of the two narratives about young people, beginning with what the decline story often leaves out:

1   The narrative of decline overlooks creative developments, often led by youth, that may be building the foundations of civil society in the twenty-first century.

2   The decline story overlooks ways that various subpopulations engage on issues of special concern to them. For example, African American youth may be well informed about Katrina. (. . . African American youth are generally more politically engaged than White American youth, across the board).

3   It overlooks certain positive trends in youth engagement, such as a steep rise in the volunteering rate in the United States.

4   It focuses narrowly on youth, without recognizing that many declines in participation are evident among all age groups.

5   It treats a withdrawal from major institutions (such as elections and the press) as a decline, when these trends may actually reflect growing sophistication. Perhaps youth are deliberately and wisely choosing not to endorse forms of participation that are flawed.

The last point underlines the fact that "civic engagement" is a deeply normative concept. It is impossible to decide whether recent trends in engagement are good or bad—or important or meaningless—without developing a full-blown political theory.

I think that there is a problem with youth civic engagement, but it is not located inside young people's heads. Institutions are also at fault. Telling young people to participate in bad institutions is mere propaganda. On the other hand, young people need to be taught and encouraged to take part in reform efforts and other aspects of politics. Political participation does not come naturally, nor do powerful institutions have incentives to encourage it. In short, we must not only prepare citizens for politics but also improve politics for citizens.

From my perspective, several trends in youth civic engagement are troubling. These trends are symptoms of institutional failure, poor civic education, and cultural forces that work against democratic participation. Selected survey results (see box for details) for U.S. residents, age eighteen to twenty-five show:

1 A decline in face-to-face, local participation—except volunteering. This decline precedes the rise of the Internet. The increase in volunteering is often attributed to service programs and requirements in high schools and colleges.

2 A big decline in all forms of election-related participation and protest until 2004, when there was a substantial increase.

3 A big decline in interest in the news and public affairs, accompanied by falling trust in the press—both of which occurred before the rise of the Internet. (I would blame the press, rather than youth, for this trend.)

4 A big decline in trust for other people, but no change in beliefs about government's responsiveness. (Also, young adults are somewhat more confident in the government than their elders.)[14]

These divergent views of youth engagement shape the thinking of policymakers and educators concerned about getting young people involved in civic life. When set side by side, the broader picture seems to point to changing the institutional and communication environments in which young people encounter politics, rather than somehow fixing the attitudes of youth themselves. Yet the institutional and communication environments themselves are politically contested, and often produce anemic and restricted (what Coleman would call heavily managed) experiences with credible or authentic politics. How many textbooks (or classroom teachers, who are monitored by school officials and parents) acknowledge that it makes sense for young people to follow the political lead of a rock star, such as Coldplay's Chris Martin, who encouraged concert goers to join Oxfam's *Make Trade Fair* campaign? Yet many Coldplay fans actually connected with government on their own: the band's 2003 U.S. tour included Oxfam workers at concerts gathering some 10,000 postcards to send to President Bush, asking him to stop dumping subsidized exports such as rice on poor countries where farmers could no longer profit from growing the same crops.[15] For those who were not at the concerts, a visit to the band's Web site contained a link off the home page to the fair trade campaign materials.

Such pathways to political engagement are often not accommodated in traditional civic education and or government sponsored e-citizen sites, leaving many young citizens at odds with brittle conceptions of proper citizenship imposed upon them by educators, public officials, and other institutional authorities. Even when more creative civic education and engagement approaches enable young people to trace their own personal concerns through the governmental process, the end result may crash against the palpable failure of governments, parties, and candidates to recognize the communication and identity preferences of young citizens, as illustrated so clearly in the chapter by Xenos and Foot in this volume.

An important task of this chapter and the volume as a whole is to clarify the different assumptions about citizenship and engagement that underlie the often-competing views of the political and civic lives of young citizens. Clarifying and building bridges between the paradigms is necessary in order to better promote constructive dialogue among researchers and clearer policy and practice among educators, youth workers, parties, campaigns, and public officials.

Engagement Patterns of Young Citizens, Age 18–25

I. Participation in civil society, mostly local

Attend a club meeting (DDB Life Style survey): down from 49 percent in 1976 to 23 percent in 2005, with most of the decline in the 1980s.

Member of at least one organization (General Social Survey [GSS]): down from 63.5 percent in 1976 to 54 percent in 2004.

Work on a community project (DDB) down from 29 percent in 1976 to 21 percent in 2005. (The decline among older people is much steeper.)

Volunteer (DDB): up from 39 percent in 1976 to 41 percent in 2005.

Membership in extracurricular school groups such as student governments, school newspapers, and music clubs: down between 1972 and 1992, according to four waves of federal adolescent longitudinal studies.

II. Social trust

Believe that other people are generally honest (DDB): down from 64 percent in 1976 to 38 percent in 2005, with most of the decline in the 1980s.

Believe that most people can be trusted (GSS): down from 37 percent in 1976 to 25 percent in 2004.

III. News consumption/interest

Follow what's going on in government and public affairs most of the time (National Election Survey [NES]): down from 24 percent in 1976 to seven percent in 2000, then slightly up to 10 percent in 2004.

Read a daily newspaper (GSS): down from 44 percent in 1975 to 19 percent in 2002, but then back up to 28 percent in 2004.

Watch the TV news at least twice a week (NES): down from 79 percent in 1980 to 44 percent in 2004.

IV. Knowledge about government (or confidence in one's knowledge)

Feel that you can understand government (NES): up from 26 percent in 1976 to 34 percent in 2004.

Able to identify Republicans as the more conservative national party (NES): up from 49 percent in 1976 to 78 percent in 2004 (all the increase is recent).

Know the name of your own candidates for U.S. House (NES): down from 25 percent in 1978 to 16 percent in 2000.

V. Political participation

Vote in presidential election (Census surveys, self-report): basically unchanged from 43 percent in 1976 to 42 percent in 2004, but there was a deep decline in the 1980s and 1990s.

Been contacted by a party or candidate (NES): up from 49.5 percent in 1984 to 66 percent in 2004.

Persuade other people to vote a certain way (NES): up from 37 percent in 1976 to 56 percent in 2004, but the big increase in 2004 followed decades of modest decline.

Protests involving young people: down by about 50 percent according to Soule and Condo, using a database of news articles.

VI. Efficacy/trust in institutions

My vote matters (NES): basically unchanged from 88 percent in 1976 to 84 percent in 2000.

People like me have a say in government (NES): basically unchanged from 58 percent in 1976 to 55 percent in 2004 (with modest changes in between).

Trust the government in Washington to do the right thing most of the time (NES): basically unchanged from 42 percent in 1976 to 36 percent in 2004, with 45 percent recorded in 2000.

Confidence in the press (GSS): down from 32 percent in 1976 to 13 percent in 2004.

VII. New media

In 2005, according to the DDB Life Style survey, 20 percent of 18–25s had read a blog at least several times during the past year, compared to 32 percent of the whole population.

Thirty-three percent of 18–25s had regularly participated in online forums or chatrooms, compared to 36 percent of the whole population.

Source: Peter Levine, from MacArthur Online Discussions on Civic Engagement (http://spotlight.macfound.org/resources/Civic_Engagement-Online_Discussions'06.pdf, pp. 16–18. See also http://depts.washington.edu/ccce/civiceducation/mdlp.html).

(Mis)Communicating with Young Citizens

Perhaps one of the most obvious factors contributing to the relatively passive, disengaged stance of many young people toward government and formal elements of politics is the withering away of civic education in schools. Not only have civics offerings been in decline, notably the United States, but, where offered, the curriculum is often stripped of independent opportunities for young people to embrace and communicate about politics on their own terms. (I shall return to this important problem later in the chapter.) The result is that there is often little connection between the academic presentation of politics and the acquisition of skills that might help develop engaged citizens. A massive International Education Association (IEA) survey of 90,000 fourteen-year-olds in twenty-eight nations suggested that civic education, where it is offered, remains largely a textbook based experience, largely severed from the vibrant experiences of politics that might help young people engage with public life.[16]

Even in nations that do reasonably well at imparting some basic civic knowledge to young citizens, there are signs of relatively little carryover to participation in public life. For example, a study of Australian civic education in the late 1990s concluded that "the importance of civic knowledge has been well established. . . Yet knowledge itself will be of little relevance if it does not lead to action in the civic sphere. . . ."[17] What emerges from different national surveys is something of a generational shift in which young citizens tend to express areas of interest and concern but often see those interests as unconnected, or even negatively related, to government. For example, the Australian survey associated with the IEA project assessed the political and social attitudes of 3,000 students in 150 high schools. The students were largely disinterested in government, while interested in a brand of civic engagement that the researchers described as a "social movement citizenship." Youth orientations defined under the category "conventional citizenship" were not encouraging: 83 percent who felt that is was not important to join a political party, only 55 percent thought it was important for a citizen to know about the country's history, a bare 50 percent though it important to follow issues in the media, and fully 66 percent found it unimportant for citizens to engage in political discussions. The "social movement" citizen profile presented an interesting contrast: 80 percent regarded participating in activities to benefit others as important, 74 percent regarded it important to act to protect the environment, and 68 percent were concerned about human rights.[18]

Broadly similar patterns were found among young people in a survey of political attitudes of Americans at the turn of the millennium.[19] Beyond the mixed attitudes toward political engagement, the American sample revealed interesting signs of generational cohesion among those immersed in digital media. The so-called *dotnet* generation (born between 1977 and 1987, ages fifteen to twenty-five at the time of the survey) expressed a strong sense of generational identification, in contrast to so-called generation X (1965–1976, ages twenty-six to thirty-seven) who came of age amidst the social and economic turbulence of the global economy of the 1980s and 1990s, but did not find their early social bearings online as did the *dotnets*.[20] A subsequent survey released in 2006 indicated that while levels of *dotnet* identification had declined as the shock of 9/11 faded (from 69 to 56 percent of the same cohort indicating strong generational identification), the level of generational coherence remained strong.[21]

We know that digital media provide those young people who have access to it an important set of tools to build social and personal identity and to create the on- and offline environments in which they spend their time. However, as Howard Rheingold notes in this volume, many young people live online, but they may lack the skills to communicate their common concerns in effective ways to larger (public) audiences. Rheingold suggests building a public communication digital media skill set. Peter Levine then discusses the importance of finding audiences that recognize those public expressions once the communication skills have been sharpened.

Perhaps the major puzzle running through all of this is how to create the media environments in which online communities can build the kinds of social capital—those bonds of trust and commitment to shared values—that lead to participation in civic life and the political world beyond. Every chapter in this volume explores some aspect of this puzzle, from the online environments available in elections (Xenos and Foot), youth engagement sites (Montgomery, Raynes-Goldie and Walker, Coleman), civic education programs (Rheingold, Levine, Bers), and entertainment sites (Earl and Schussman) to the overarching policy issues that may keep the internet free and viable for noncommercial civic spaces to continue to emerge (Montgomery).

As suggested by the two paradigms of youth engagement, there is a distinct possibility that the entire question of civic engagement is confounded by how one chooses to define citizenship itself. Should young citizens be like the generations before and have an ingrained sense of duty to participate in forms such as voting? But what if young people have grown up under conditions that simply do not produce and reinforce such dispositions? These children of the new millennium may well come to politics, but through different routes than their parents and grandparents did. Their brands of civic engagement may seem unfamiliar. Above all, their sense of how to reform creaky political processes may not yet be imaginable. What may be most important for politicians, educators, and young people themselves to learn is how to use the media that are now so richly developed for social and entertainment purposes to build civic and political communities. The lessons involved here are likely to strain, and ultimately expand, political comprehension within and across generations. The learning required to encourage the creative involvement of young people in politics will be the most difficult for those older gatekeepers who continue to live in different political, social, and media worlds. Yet all of those involved with processes that affect involvement with public life must be encouraged to learn a few lessons in common. Researchers play an important part in documenting what those common lessons are and demonstrating why they matter. In this process of designing research and policy that address and reconcile the different stories about young citizens, the competing paradigms may be transcended.

Signs of Political Life in the Digital Age

The future of democracy is in the hands of these young citizens of the so-called digital age. Many young citizens in more economically prosperous societies already have in their hands the tools of change: digital media, from laptops, pagers, and cell phones to the convergences of the next new things. These new media reposition their users in society, making them both producers and consumers of information. Perhaps more important, they enable rapid formation of large-scale networks that may focus their energies in critical moments, as Rheingold has discussed in describing what he calls Smart Mobs that used cell phones and pagers and other digital devices to coordinate decisive protests that sped the fall of corrupt regimes in the Philippines and elsewhere.[22]

Sometimes those technologies enable large and more sustained political networks, as in the formation of Indymedia, a global political information network. Indymedia was created through the distribution of open source software enabling the production and sharing of information by young activists under the motto: Be the Media. This network began during the now iconic Battle of Seattle protests against the World Trade Organization in 1999 as a means for protesters to communicate among themselves and produce their own news coverage to counter what they perceived as the filtering of corporate media aligned with the targets of protest. Other, more issue-specific networks have emerged via the application of networking technologies to spark protests such as those that emerged around the world against war in Iraq on February 12, 2003. Estimated at between thirteen and twenty million participants, they were the largest coordinated protests in human history. They were organized in a matter of months through the integrated use of on- and offline network mobilization.

Digital media also show signs of successful adaptation to the work of conventional politics, as happened with the American presidential primary campaign of Howard Dean, whose early followers (many of whom were not so young) organized online networks to share their perceptions of the candidate. They eventually created unprecedented levels of bottom-up communication within the notoriously centralized *war room* communication model of election campaigns. However, the growth of semiautonomous supporter networks, with their pressures for some degree of bottom-up steering of the campaign ultimately clashed with the centralized bureaucracy of the professionally managed campaign. The cautionary tale here is that the integration of horizontal digital networks with other organizational forms is not always seamless.

In other cases, applications of digital media do seem to bridge, and at times, transcend the conventional boundaries between different kinds of political organizations such as parties, interest groups, and social movements.[23] This boundary jumping happened, for example, when the (mostly) online networking operation MoveOn.org became involved in Democratic Party politics in the United States, acting as a check on the party, and even running its own commercials. In other configurations, MoveOn acts more as an interest organization, mobilizing pressure on specific issues moving through legislative processes. In other moments, the organization joins many issue constituencies in protest actions as might happen in a social movement. The attractiveness of these loosely tied organizational forms to young people has not been lost on many conventional political organizations as they witness the graying of their conventional membership rosters.[24]

Despite these and other signs of potential to revive and perhaps reinvent politics among next generation citizens, two overall trends seem to hold:

- The majority of those communicating with young people about conventional politics continue to do so in tired top-down, highly managed ways that most young people find inauthentic and largely irrelevant.

- What young people do online tends to be largely social and entertainment oriented, with only tangential pathways leading to the conventional civic and political worlds.

These two patterns are most likely related to each other. For example, in order to learn how to expand youth involvement in aspects of public life pertaining to governance, politicians, policymakers, and educators need to communicate differently with young citizens. And in order for young citizens to feel comfortable engaging in more conventional politics, they need to feel invited to participate on their own terms, and to learn how to use their digital tools to better express their public voices. This chapter and the book as a whole explore what young people are doing online, why social and political authorities often misperceive these activities, and what all parties can learn that might help better integrate young people in all aspects of politics. Resolving dissonant perceptions of proper citizenship and participation, while suggesting ways in which digital media may help better connect young people to public life, may enable future generations to reinvent their democracies.

Where Are They? What Are They Doing?

The news headlines signaled a battle raging between television networks and Nielsen, the company that provided the audience ratings on which their income depended. In releasing their fall ratings sweeps for 2005, Nielsen reported a shocking trend. It was so shocking that the TV networks disputed it, as it seemed to make no sense to them. Moreover, they would lose huge amounts of ad revenues for their fall programs. The young male demographic was missing. The much sought after eighteen- to twenty-four-year-old male demographic (only 12 percent of the total audience, yet accounting for $4.1 billion in ad revenues) had dropped nearly 8 percent from TV viewing the year before, with an even larger drop in prime time. Every minute less TV watched by this group meant a $77 million loss in revenues across broadcast and cable. It was a trend that had been developing slowly for a dozen years, but suddenly soared to crisis levels for the television industry. Where did the young men go? It turned out that many of them were still watching TV, but they were more likely to be playing an Xbox on it. This same demographic group accounted for more than half of video game sales in a booming multibillion dollar market.[25] Creating and interacting with one's entertainment programming was just more interesting than watching it passively.

Gamers are joined by even more young people who gravitate to social network environments that change almost as quickly as adults can learn their names: Friendster, Facebook, MySpace. When media mogul Rupert Murdoch saw the writing on the wall, he hedged his bets on the television networks that had been aimed at young audiences and bought MySpace, then the largest recorded social networking site, attracting upwards of sixty million youth. Early on, large online communities also formed around music file-sharing sites that indicated the creativity with which young people approached digital media, all because, as Benkler put it, "a few teenagers and twenty-something-year-olds were able to write software and protocols."[26] Montgomery in this volume discusses the potential for social communities such as MySpace to incorporate more central civic aspects, while cautioning that heavily commercialized online communities may be at odds with public interest content.

A quick visit to any of the social sites suggests that what happens there mainly revolves around the formation of loosely connected networks dedicated to sharing music, movies, photos, and, above all, current and prospective friends. In what may be an eternal generational response, many older observers look disapprovingly on all this, seeing these environments as dangerous magnets for sexual predators, and as outlets for young people to indulge in inappropriate and edgy displays. The dangers of regulating and restricting these sites based on poor understandings of their importance are explored by Montgomery in Chapter 2. Regulators must proceed with caution in attempting to control the online experiences of young people. The importance of these networks for forging generational identity and solidarity cannot be underestimated. Moreover, lurking just beneath the surface is the potential for vast networks of public voice on contemporary issues. This potential has barely been tapped. Surprisingly large demonstrations against congressional immigration legislation in the spring of 2006 spread through organizing networks within MySpace. And, the recognition by the Dean campaign that supporters were gathering in Meetups quickly moved the Dean network (which attracted a broad age demographic) past Chihuahua owners and Elvis fans to become the most populous Meetup. Presidential candidates in 2008 gathered friends in MySpace.

A challenging question is how to better integrate the social and public worlds of young people online. Unlike classic accounts of civil society in which social bonds strengthened political participation in the golden age of dutiful citizens,[27] the separation of the social and the civic in the youth online world often seems stark. There are, however, some curious signs of the integration of politics and social experience within these virtual worlds. For example, there have been reports of political protest in game environments. *World of Warcraft* was disrupted by demonstrations over vaguely defined class issues facing the warriors, resulting in protesters being banned under game rules established by Blizzard Entertainment, owner of the game.[28] Benkler discusses a "tax revolt" that occurred in *Second Life*, as players stacked tea crates around an image of the Washington monument to protest rate increases.[29] And, early on, music file sharers raised property ownership and copyright issues that eventually brought legal sanctions, and in many ways changed how file sharing was regulated and used. And Earl and Schussman in this volume raise interesting questions about the adaptation of behaviors from the social movement repertoire by young people pressuring entertainment corporations about the management and distribution of products.

As noted by Lessig and Benkler, among others, the very ways in which people use digital media present fundamental challenges to established understandings of property, which in turn, lie at the foundation of the political order.[30] For these and other reasons, it is important to expand our conception of politics and the political, as young people, both wittingly and unwittingly, push those bounds through their applications of digital technologies. In what ways are these activities political? Do the communication skills involved transfer to more conventional areas of politics? Do political and legal responses concerning ownership and copyright enforcement make for formative early contacts between young people and the often distant world of power and government? These are among the important questions that abound in the grey zones of digital life.

Yet for all the tangential incursions of politics into the social and play environments of digital media, the sphere of more explicitly youth-oriented politics remains comparatively isolated and underdeveloped. Youth sites often seem less social, more moderated, less open to posting and sharing media content, and more top-down compared to those pertaining to dating, friends, games, music, or video. There are, of course notable exceptions, including TakingITGlobal, as discussed by Raynes-Goldie and Walker in this volume, along with examples discussed by Montgomery both here and elsewhere.[31] Many questions arise when contrasting youth politics sites with more social or entertainment sites: How much traffic do they really get? Can they be sustained in the absence of commercial or equally restrictive foundation or government subsidies? Are they likely to grow and become connected in large and stable enough networks to stimulate effective political behavior? The problems and prospects of this youth political Web sphere are central to the chapters by Xenos and Foot, Montgomery, Coleman, Levine, and Raynes-Goldie and Walker in this book.

Finding productive answers to the many questions about better integrating the public and private worlds of youth involves different kinds of learning for different kinds of players:

1   The politicians and public officials who represent the official world of politics to young people must learn more about their citizenship and communication preferences and how to engage with them.

2   The educators and other youth workers who design civic education programs, often based on unexamined assumptions about what citizenship should be, can benefit from learning how generational social identities and political preference formation are changing so they can design more engaging civic education models.

3   The government agencies, foundations, and NGOs that design and operate youth engagement communities online can benefit from learning more about how those sites may be networked and how they may be opened to partnership with young people who must see them as authentic if they are to participate in them.

4   News organizations and other public information producers can learn how to develop information formats that appeal to the young citizen's interest in interacting and coproducing digital content and in better integrating the information and action dimensions of citizenship.

5   Young people themselves can better learn how to use information and media skills in ways that give them stronger and more effective public voices.

6   And academic researchers can learn how to bridge the paradigms in order to better motivate and inform all of these players.

Understanding Changing Citizenship across Paradigms

Learning about communities, networks, and civic life can take place at different levels and in different ways among the groups of key players in youth civic engagement identified above: politicians and public officials, educators and youth workers, operators of youth engagement communities, information producers, young people searching for public voice, and researchers trying to understand how these players can interact more effectively to promote engagement that is both personally satisfying and mindful of democracy.

A starting point for civic learning among all of these groups is to recognize the shifts in social and political identity processes resulting from the last several decades of global economic and social change. The story here is a familiar one, so I will keep it short. (The reader may also want to consult the version offered by David Buckingham in the introduction to the identity volume in this series.) The collection of nations once known as the industrial democracies have gone through a period of rapid and, in some cases, wrenching economic change, with the result that they may now more properly be called postindustrial democracies. Manufacturing is moving to the periphery of economic focus, as design, distribution, marketing, and management of information have come to the fore. Several results of this process, among others, include careers have changed from relatively secure life-long bonds with a single employer and type of work to several different employers and kinds of work; women have become fully engaged in the work force, changing the organization of family life; more work and more working parents means less discretionary time and more stress for most members of families. As a result, the experiences of childhood and transitions to adulthood are different for recent generations. One casualty associated with these changes is that the group based society that was the foundation of Putnam's fabled pluralist civic life[32] has transformed into a network society in which individuals seek various kinds of support and recognition based on different conceptions of membership, identification, and commitment.

In the network society, individuals may belong to many loosely tied associational chains that connect them to their social and occupational worlds. A major consequence of the uprooting from the broad social influence of groups is that individuals have become more responsible for the production and management of their own social and political identities. Contemporary young people enjoy unprecedented levels of freedom to define and manage their self-identities in contrast with earlier generations' experiences with stronger groups (denominational church, labor, class, party) that essentially assigned broad social identities to their members. This transformation of the relationship between individual and society places increasing strains on parties and governments to appeal to highly personalized political preferences that are more difficult to address, much less satisfy, than the broad group or class interests of an earlier era. At the same time, individual citizens—particularly younger generations who have grown up in this new social and economic matrix—feel that their personalized expectations of politics are perfectly reasonable (reflecting who they are) and often find that politics and politicians either ignore them or are far off the mark in their communication appeals.

As politicians and parties use marketing techniques to target ever more refined demographics, the democratic result is that ever larger groups of citizens are excluded from the discourses of elections and policy as they are deemed unnecessary by consultants. Young citizens are among those most blatantly excluded from the public discourses of government, policy arenas and elections. The result is that the world of politics and government seems distant, irrelevant, and inauthentic to many citizens, particularly younger demographics.

Table 1
The Changing Citizenry: The Traditional Civic Education Ideal of the Dutiful Citizen (DC) versus the Emerging Youth Experience of Self-Actualizing Citizenship (AC)

Actualizing Citizen (AC)	Dutiful Citizen (DC)
Diminished sense of government obligation—higher sense of individual purpose	Obligation to participate in government centered activities
Voting is less meaningful than other, more personally defined acts such as consumerism, community volunteering, or transnational activism	Voting is the core democratic act
Mistrust of media and politicians is reinforced by negative mass media environment	Becomes informed about issues and government by following mass media
Favors loose networks of community action—often established or sustained through friendships and peer relations and thin social ties maintained by interactive information technologies	Joins civil society organizations and/or expresses interests through parties that typically employ one-way conventional communication to mobilize supporters

The challenge for civic education and engagement here is to begin by recognizing the profound generational shift in citizenship styles that seems to be occurring to varying degrees in most of the postindustrial democracies. The core of the shift is that young people are far less willing to subscribe to the notion held by earlier generations that citizenship is a matter of duty and obligation. This earlier sense of common commitment to participate at some level in public affairs was supported, indeed forged, within a group- and class-based civil society. The underlying sense of citizenship has shifted in societies in which individuals are more responsible for defining their own identities, using the various tools offered by social networks and communication media.

In short, there is a broad, cross-national generational shift in the postindustrial democracies from a *dutiful citizen* model (still adhered to by older generations and many young people who are positioned in more traditional social settings) to an *actualizing citizen* model favoring loosely networked activism to address issues that reflect personal values.[33] In some cases, this brand of politics may be tangential to government and conventional political organization, and may even emerge in parallel cyberspaces such as games. This citizenship transformation is by no means uniform within societies. Where traditional institutions of church or labor remain strong, more conventional patterns of civic engagement prevail, and moral conflict may erupt. Other citizens lack the skills and background to engage civic life at either the group or the individual level, and actively avoid politics altogether.[34] However, two broad patterns do seem to mark a change in citizenship among younger demographics coming of age in the recent decades of globalization. Table 1 illustrates some of the defining qualities of this shift in citizenship styles.

Bridging the Paradigms: Six Learning Scenarios

The tendency to either explicitly or implicitly anchor political opportunities and offerings to young people in one conception of citizenship or the other helps to explain the rise of the two paradigms of youth engagement discussed earlier. Those paradigms support our dissonant public conversation about whether young people are engaged or disengaged. Given their value premises and empirical references, the paradigms are (by definition) both right, but they are also equally responsible for confounding much of our theoretical, empirical and practical approaches to youth engagement in the digital age.

Trying to keep both the actualizing citizen (AC) and dutiful citizen (DC) clusters of citizenship qualities in mind when we discuss learning goals for different players may help bridge the paradigms, while helping all of the players in the civic engagement process think about youth engagement in a more holistic way. In other words, recognizing the shift in emphasis from DC to AC citizenship among younger citizens, and then deciding how to accommodate both dimensions of citizenship in theory and practice may have important implications for what the various players in citizenship production can (and, dare I say, should?) learn about youth civic engagement in the digital age.

What Can Politicians and Government Officials Learn?

Politicians often appear to be faking it in the eyes of young citizens, who are finely tuned to media performances. Indeed, there is reason to think that some of the popularity of reality TV shows over news and other political fare may have something to do with the blatantly staged and marketed aspects of politics. By contrast, reality programs often involve young people in emotionally resonant situations.[35] Not only is the heavily marketed and staged nature of politics off-putting but the even deeper problem is that much formal political communication seems to ignore young people, as discussed in the chapter by Xenos and Foot in this book. Young voters are generally regarded by consultants as a poor investment of communication budgets because they tend not to vote, and they are hard to reach through common media channels (recall the earlier discussion of the lost demographic). The result is that there has developed a political culture in many nations in which young people are not asked to participate, and, when they are asked, the language and issues are not convincingly presented. An exceptional case here proves the rule: the 2004 presidential election in the United States witnessed one of the largest mobilization efforts ever aimed at young voters, and turnout in the difficult eighteen- to twenty-four-year-old bracket was up dramatically over previous elections.

The deeper implication of a political culture in which rituals and discourse are managed increasingly by professional communications consultants is that the importance of broad and inclusive communication for democracy has all but been pushed aside.[36] A case in point involves an address I gave to a convention of international political consultants. The time was just at the turn of the millennium, when digital media strategies were becoming recognized as useful means of targeting hard to reach demographics. I spoke about the growing fragmentation of societies and the resulting democratic dilemma of communication strategies that exclude particular demographic groups, most notably young people. During the question period following the talk, the first person to stand was one of the founders of professional political communication consulting going back several decades. He remarked that most of what I said about targeting and exclusion was true but that I had missed a crucial point: the obligation of hired consultants was not to promote democracy but to get the client elected, or win the client's policy battles.

Governments that continue to exclude future citizens through their communication strategies only perpetuate the divided sense of citizen identity that leads young people to find political outlets outside government. Given the low costs and potentially broad reach of digital media, there is much that could be done to improve the daily communication outreach of politicians. As Foot and Xenos observe in this book, the design of campaign Web sites and the presentation of issues on them could be much more tuned to take advantage of the interactivity, networking capacity, and other affordances of digital media that young people experience in social networking sites, blogs and games. The ultimate dilemma, as noted earlier, is the reluctance to yield some degree of control over political communication content to the audience. The top-down, one-way model of communication was much more in tune with the DC citizenship style. It simply does not work with AC citizens. This is the central point of Coleman's concluding chapter.

In addition, public officials must move beyond the posturing that brands youth social sites as magnets for predators, and showcases for other undesirable behaviors. Such positions may make news, but they stigmatize young people and undermine the authenticity of the places where they gather online. As Montgomery notes in the next chapter, a more productive policy concern is to ensure what has become known as "net neutrality." The very future of public information traveling over digital networks is threatened if service providers can impose restrictions on categories of noncommercial content.

What Can Educators, Policymakers, and Community Youth Workers Learn?
The groups that may be both the most important and the most out of touch with the shifting citizen identity patterns of youth are educators and education policymakers. Most of those who preside over curriculum decisions and policies continue to be older-generation DC citizens who assume that their model of citizenship needs to be acquired by future generations. Added to this common misperception are the intense political battles over the moral and political content of school curricula of recent years. The politicization of education on many fronts reinforces a conservative and actively off-putting approach to civic education found in many and perhaps most public schools, particularly in America. Indeed, it is probably not too big a stretch to propose that the majority of school civics experiences for those coming of age in contemporary society fall into one of two categories: (1) little or no civics content or (2) courses that stick to academic coverage of basic government functions and present unappealing perspectives on the subject. Most courses in public schools are thoroughly cleansed of the kinds of political issues and active learning experiences that young people might find authentic and motivating.

Consider some evidence for these generalizations.[37] A study of the top three high school civics texts indicated that they contained references to few political issues. Moreover, protest politics was presented as an historical throwback to days before people won their civil rights. And government was idealized in terms of its representative and responsive capacities.[38] One could not design an experience less likely to be believed, and less likely to engage with the preferences of AC citizens for personal contact with important issues and shared peer-to-peer communication about them.

The alternative to such ideologically rigid DC education appears to be no civics education at all. It is noteworthy that No Child Left Behind has left citizenship standards far behind math and reading in the priorities of schools. Many school systems have no standards for civic knowledge, much less, guidelines for the acquisition of citizen skills that might aid participation later in life. This trend has developed over the last several decades. A Carnegie/CIRCLE report on the Civic Mission of the Schools noted that in 1949, a course called "problems of democracy" appeared on 41.5 percent of high school transcripts. Students in those courses typically learned about government by discussing contemporary issues, often supplemented by newspaper reading assignments. That course appeared on fewer than 9 percent of transcripts by the early 1970s, and has by now almost completely disappeared.[39]

Another telling sign of educational policy neglect and misdirection is that the principal national assessment guide for civics (National Assessment of Educational Progress) almost exclusively measures historical and constitutional knowledge. There is little or no attention to student civic orientations, engagement levels, or skills that might enable the discussion of real political issues. As Peter Levine has noted, the predominant approach of government civic education policy and funding is to avoid controversy, active student engagement, and even voter registration.[40]

This profile of contemporary civic education is bleak, particularly in light of the information and communication opportunities afforded by digital media technologies that are already familiar to most young people. In many cases, it is unclear whether having no curriculum is better or worse than having one that actively clashes with young people's sense of political reality and meaningful personal expression. There are, of course notable exceptions to these trends, and many foundations and progressive educators are experimenting with creative alternatives. The chapters in this volume by Bers and Rheingold illuminate the kinds of interactive, communication-driven curricula that might better engage the political identities of young citizens.

There is need for caution and considerable creativity in thinking about implementing more creative approaches to engage young people in communication with each other about real political concerns. For example, a civic education project that I operated in Seattle aimed to offer young people direct experiences with issues in their communities.[41] The idea was to combine community issue surveys and face-to-face meetings with policy officials, while introducing students to communication skills such as classroom deliberation, all in the context of an information rich online news environment. Students were also invited to participate in chats and to design other networked communication applications to develop a public voice about their newly defined issues. It soon became apparent that the more progressive private schools were already doing much of this in one way or another, and most of their students even had their own laptops. At the other extreme, the poorest of the public schools presented infrastructure obstacles for even getting a single computer in some classrooms. In addition, many teachers faced pressures to teach conservatively from textbooks, due to the lack of time and resources needed to fashion community projects for their classes. In settings less progressive than Seattle (and, not infrequently, even there), teachers also face added pressures from parents who are suspicious of bringing many public issues into the schools. To top it off, students in the lowest achieving schools typically had the strongest antipathy toward politics and government, many having experienced them only in negative ways involving law and social service encounters. Yet the at-risk students and their teachers who managed to navigate these obstacles typically produced some of the most powerful projects proposing actions to address their community issues. These students developed impressive public voices using a variety of digital media, from interactive Web sites to streamed video public affairs programming.

In subsequent years I have followed the Student Voices project as it has been put on self-sustaining footing in the schools. What seems to stick for all but the most dedicated teachers are the free curriculum downloads. The core community project and peer-to-peer communication experiences have withered due to lack of time, technology resources, and other support. The encouraging lesson from this project is that it is possible to engage even the most challenging at-risk populations, and raise civic skill levels. The discouraging lesson is that the obstacles facing those populations and their schools often prove hard to overcome.

The lesson of formal civic education is often that the civically rich get richer and the poor become discouraged. These realities make the kinds of civic communication skill sets recommended by Rheingold in this volume seem flexible and relatively low-cost additions to current educational approaches. They also make it wise to attend to the cautionary notes sounded by Levine. Even if young people are given the skills and resources to build networks for themselves, there is the important question of "if they build it, will they come?" Levine discusses the potential for discouragement among young people who develop blogs and other networking technologies only to discover that they receive little reaction from the outer world. At the same time, this possibility must be weighed against the distributed and hyperlinked properties of digital networks that Benkler regards as keeping even potentially isolated nodes in easy range of activation and inclusion. The capacity for broad linking of content gives even obscure sites the potential to reach large numbers of people and to jump media strata, sometimes, even pushing content from the personal level to large audience media. Still, we need to learn how to help the majority of solitary young bloggers and content producers join their voices more effectively with others.

What Can Operators of Youth Engagement Networks Learn?
An early survey of youth electoral engagement sites in the United States found that the often well-intentioned operations funded by foundations and other public interest organizations suffered several notable digital deficits: the sites tended to be sticky rather than encouraging networking, the kinds of interactive affordances lagged far behind what was then available outside the political media sphere, and perhaps most notably, there was a disconnection between the often vibrant youth sites and the election candidate and campaign sites that lay disturbingly out of reach.[42] Some of these problems have been remedied, as demonstrated in the far greater networking among youth sites in recent elections. However, the curious disconnect between the youth engagement sphere and the sphere of elections and government remains a stubborn problem. In part, the problem is due to the earlier mentioned combination of neglect and misapprehension of young people and their communication preferences by politicians and government. Perhaps until politicians and governments find ways to communicate a politics that seems authentic and inviting to young citizens these disconnections will persist.

These concerns aside, there is a growing and, in many ways, thriving collection of youth political engagement opportunities online. Montgomery and her colleagues have documented the evolution of many of these sites and networks here and elsewhere.[43] However, there are important issues that remain to be addressed so that those who design and operate the youth engagement sphere may better learn what works and what doesn't. To begin with, there remains an often alarming gap between government and foundation operations and youth-built networks in terms of the communication affordances, the content, and the degree of control offered to youth. This is the focus of Coleman's chapter in this volume. The key seems to be recognizing the changed citizenship styles of young people, and their growing preference for relatively nonhierarchical networks that enable free exploration of ideas. Government and foundation sponsored sites are often reluctant to allow young visitors to define and expand the bounds of politics.

When success models for youth civic networks are identified, they need to be studied and shared. This book includes a detailed look at one of the largest and most successful youth civic networking and communication operations, TakingITGlobal. In their chapter Raynes-Goldie and Walker discuss various youth engagement sites in contrast to social sites such as MySpace, and discuss issues of sustainability, growth, mission, and limits on control and content in a successful youth engagement network.

What Can News Organizations and Information Producers Learn?

Surely one place to begin reconnecting AC citizens to government is rethinking the learning process surrounding the uses of political information. In this digital society, the axiom that information is power is more appropriate than ever. Yet, given prevailing AC attitudes about conventional *dutiful citizen* politics, it is not surprising that there is correspondingly little interest among young citizens in following current issues and events in the news—at least as the news is typically constructed and presented. Most young people simply do not believe that following and learning about various issues will translate into the power to help decide them. Strong (daily) levels of interest in politics are expressed by barely 13 percent of eighteen- to twenty-four-year-olds, compared to more than twice that level among those over fifty-five. Interest levels in the news reflect interest levels in politics.[44] Only 17 percent of eighteen- to twenty-four-year-old women say they follow what is going on in government and public affairs most of the time, compared to nearly half of women over fifty.[45] Twenty-eight percent of men in the younger demographic bracket claim to follow political news, but more than 60 percent of men over fifty say they actively follow politics. The important point here is not just that there is a generation gap in connecting to conventional politics but also that it has grown steadily over the past several decades.[46] Young people are more tuned out than were their corresponding peers at any point in the last half century. Even in political systems with strong commitments to high quality public service radio and TV news, and cultures of strong adult engagement, the arrival of commercial television—with its cheap news formulas of mayhem, scandal, and crime—quickly drew young audiences. And those young commercial news viewers put politics and government affairs near the bottom of their attention ladders, well below crime, accidents, sports, and weather.[47]

Part of the problem here is surely that conventional news is designed for DC citizens. At its best, it is generally information rich, but also filled with the views of officials and government authorities, and it generally lacks much in the way of citizen voices or action ideas. The DC citizen is the "informed citizen," an ideal that dates from the progressive model of objective reporting and informed citizenship that emerged in the United States nearly a century ago.[48] The informed citizen is supposed to take abstract, impartial information and then decide how to apply it. This model simply doesn't work for AC citizens. They are skeptical of official versions of events. They prefer to help assemble and deliberate about information. And above all, they seek information that is attached to values and activities they know and trust. The AC citizen is more inclined to seek integrated information that comes with action options, and to participate in the evaluation of information on which decisions about action are based.

There are many lessons to be learned about how to create news and information for AC citizens, and they tend to begin with involving the audience in the information process itself. Part of the solution is to make information interactive, and to involve the audience in the rating, editing, evaluation, and commentary processes. There are models from the early days of Internet news suggesting that this can be done effectively within narrow communities of interest and among activist networks: Slashdot uses a collective editorial and rating technology that produces high-quality information as viewed by its audience; Plastic pioneered a blog-driven news format; and Indymedia introduced an audience-produced, but generally unedited, news-commentary-action format. Many experiments now exist with collective editing and quality control involving the audience in the information production process. Many of these information experiments raise issues of credibility that are explored in the volume edited by Metzger and Flanagin on that subject in this series.

The paramount issue in assessing the credibility of more engaging news formats should not be to compare them to the current DC standard of balanced, politically neutral, "objective" news that is disconnected from action opportunities. That standard, like the style of citizenship on which it is based, is fading. News of the future is more likely to follow the logic of the BBC experiment I*Can*, which anchors the news in civic networks organized around issues as defined by news audiences themselves.[49] The resources of the news organization in this model are aimed at helping citizens organize effectively on issues they care about. Perhaps much of the news agenda of the future will be driven by such audience affinity networks. On the downside, the BBC project tends to be aimed at connecting citizens to government, and it is not particularly well suited to the more diffuse kinds of activities that may cluster in AC politics. Moreover, there is little specific communication with younger citizens on their own terms, making it unclear whether such information formats can help young people engage effectively with conventional political processes. Perhaps the ultimate question in this chain of possibilities is whether those who hold power in government and business will be receptive to sharing power when younger citizens eventually challenge it, as they probably will.

What Can Young People Learn?

A theme running through many of the chapters in this volume is that young people can better learn how to transfer skills they are already using in other online experiences to more conventional arenas of politics. They can also be encouraged to acquire additional skills that actively enable the formation of public voice both in their social networks and in more explicitly political contexts. Given even minimal learning opportunities, the core AC citizenship concerns seem strong enough among enough young people to motivate the continued creation and growth of impressive youth engagement networks focused on issues such as environment, global justice, and human rights. The connections to conventional politics and government, however, may continue to be thin. The embrace of the traditional core of politics—elections and interest representation in policy processes—may not come easily for generations with such deep skepticism toward politicians and parties. It might help if those offering DC approaches to civic education, community participation, or news more often included protest, governmental reform, and activism as legitimate considerations.

Young people may be right in sensing that politics in nations such as the United States is an insider game requiring money and connections, and, thus, not for them. However, the opportunities to apply considerable political pressure for reforms are now available through digital media networks. Perhaps those networks can be dedicated to the task of political reform. The next social movement may well launch demonstrations from desktops and cellular phones. It may write its own news and gain large audiences for it. Indeed, early efforts to mobilize large-scale protests targeting particular governmental actions (war, media deregulation, and immigration reform) have shown the power of networks in action. The question is whether generations as distant from government as recent ones will find the time, energy or relevance to reform the system.

What Can Scholars Learn?

Many scholars have discovered a shift in value patterns in postindustrial democracies in which people (particularly younger citizens) are more inclined to become interested in personally meaningful, lifestyle-related political issues, rather than party or ideological programs. These AC citizens seek public commitments and issues that fit with the values at the center of personal lifestyles, giving rise to sharp trends in consumer politics, for example.[50] Not surprisingly, scholars and researchers who tend to focus on more personally expressive aspects of youth politics tend to resonate with the engaged youth paradigm. Meanwhile, scholars who continue to emphasize the importance of various government-centered activities such as voting and following public affairs tend to embrace the disengaged citizen paradigm, even as they may recognize the rise of alternative forms of political action among young people.

What is needed is research that combines principles underlying both citizenship styles. That is, research aimed at identifying and assessing strategies of engagement that appeal to AC citizens while creating connections to government that help promote DC democratic ideals. Research that leans too heavily on one side or another of the citizenship divide will only contribute to sustaining the paradigm conflicts that cloud our understanding of civic engagement.

Conclusion: Two Scenarios of Youth Engagement

Depending on how the above learning scenarios play out, there are several different scenarios for future youth engagement. It is important to understand that these developments need not be left to their own evolution or devolution. In the process of synthesizing what we know about youth engagement we—academics, educators, educational policymakers, NGOs, journalists, foundations, public officials, and young people—can make choices about what outcomes are desirable and how to nurture them.

If nothing is done to bridge the paradigms, the default scenario will likely be persistent youth disconnection from conventional politics, with little reconciliation of the gap between AC and DC citizenship styles, and continuing unproductive paradigm battles in the academic world. The flip side of this scenario is the continued growth of youth (AC) politics "by other means": political consumerism, pressures on entertainment product ownership and distribution, and issue networks spanning local and global concerns. This scenario will do little to bring young citizens meaningfully back to government, and it will continue to provoke unproductive debates about engagement and disengagement that talk past each other in academia, education, foundations, and government policy circles.

A second scenario utilizes the possibilities for convergence of technologies and political practices to bring vibrant experiences of politics into classrooms, youth programs, and yes, even elections, showing young people how their concerns can gain public voice within the conventional arenas of power and decision making. This scenario requires more creative research paradigms that combine AC and DC citizen qualities into realistic scenarios for engagement that can be implemented and assessed.

The most important question before us is: What kind of democratic experiences would we choose for future generations? This is a properly political question, yet it is one that often chills creativity among government officials, educators, and NGOs—the very players with the capacity to make a difference in the political futures of young people. The outcomes for youth engagement, insofar as they involve the restoration of positive engagement with government alongside creative and expressive personal communication, depend importantly on the adults who shape the early political impressions of young people. Are politicians, parents, educators, policymakers, and curriculum developers willing to allow young citizens to more fully explore, experience, and expand democracy, or will they continue to force them to just read all about it?

Notes

1. Nina Eliasoph, *Avoiding Politics: How Americans Produce Apathy in Everyday Life* (New York: Cambridge University Press, 1998).

2. W. Lance Bennett, Civic Learning in Changing Democracies: Challenges for Citizenship and Civic Education, in *Young Citizens and New Media: Learning and Democratic Engagement*, ed. Peter Dahlgren (New York: Routledge, 2008).

3. Stephen Coleman, From Big Brother to Big Brother: Two Faces of Interactive Engagement, in *Young Citizens and New Media: Learning and Democratic Engagement*, ed. Peter Dahlgren (New York: Routledge, 2008).

4. See Anthony Giddens, *Modernity and Self-Identity: Self and Society in the Late Modern Age* (Stanford: Stanford University Press, 1991); Ronald Inglehart, *Modernization and Postmodernization: Cultural, Economic, and Political Change in 43 Societies* (Princeton, NJ: Princeton University Press, 1997); W. Lance Bennett, The UnCivic Culture: Communication, Identity and the Rise of Lifestyle Politics, *P.S.: Political Science and Politics*, 31 (December 1998): 741–61.

5. See, for examples, Marc Hugo Lopez et al., The 2006 Civic and Political Health of the Nation: A Detailed Look at How Youth Participate in Politics and Communities. Center for Information and Research on Civic Learning and Engagement. 2006. Retrieved February 15, 2007. http://www.civicyouth.org.

6. See comments by Jenkins, Ito, Davidson, and Benkler in the MacArthur Online Discussions on Civic Engagement 2006, http://spotlight.macfound.org/resources/CivicEngagement-Online_Discussions'06.pdf.

7. Note the recurrent bumping of these paradigms in the exchanges in the MacArthur Online Discussions (2006).

8. Coleman (this volume). See also the recurring discussions of these themes in the MacArthur Online Discussions, pp. 1–15.

9. MacArthur Online Discussions on Civic Engagement, pp. 9–10.

10. MacArthur Online Discussions on Civic Engagement, p. 11.

11. MacArthur Online Discussions on Civic Engagement, p. 6.

12. MacArthur Online Discussions on Civic Engagement, pp. 22–23.

13. MacArthur Online Discussions on Civic Engagement, pp. 1–15.

14. Peter Levine in the MacArthur Online Discussions on Civic Engagement (2006, pp. 15–16).

15. http://www.oxfamamerica.org/newsandpublications/news_updates/archive2003/art5892.html. Retrieved January 27, 2007.

16. Judith Torney-Purta et al., Citizenship and Civic Education in Twenty-eight Countries: Civic Knowledge and Engagement at Age Fourteen. International Association for the Evaluation of Educational Achievement. 2001. Retrieved July 19, 2004. http://www.wam.umd.edu/~iea/.

17. Suzanne Mellor et al., Citizenship and Democracy: Students' Knowledge and Beliefs. Australian Fourteen Year Olds and the IEA Civic Education Study. Report to the Department of Education, Training, and Youth Affairs by the Australian Council of Education Research, 2001, p. 160. Retrieved August 20, 2007. http://www.dest.gov.au/sectors/school_education/publications_resources/profiles/citizenship_democracy_students_knowledge.htm.

18. Mellor et al. (2001), p. 160.

19. Scott Keeter et al., The Civic and Political Health of the Nation: A Generational Portrait. Center for Information and Research on Civic Learning and Engagement. 2002. Retrieved September 12, 2003. http://www.civicyouth.org.

20. Ibid.

21. Lopez et al. (2006), p. 29.

22. Howard Rheingold, *Smart Mobs: The Next Social Revolution* (Cambridge MA: Perseus, 2002).

23. Bruce Bimber et al., Reconceptualizing Collective Action in the Contemporary Media Environment, *Communication Theory,* 15 (2005): 389–413; Andrew J. Flanagin et al., Modeling the Structure of Collective Action, *Communication Monographs,* 73, no. 1 (2006): 29–54.

24. Ibid.

25. Christopher Reynolds, The Lost Demo. *Chief Marketer,* 2006. Retrieved February 15, 2007. http://chiefmarketer.com/media360/broadcast_cable/marketing_lost_demo/index.html.

26. Jochai Benkler, *The Wealth of Networks: How Social Production Transforms Markets and Freedom* (New Haven, CT: Yale University Press, 2006). Also available through wikipedia at http://www.benkler.org/wealth_of_networks/index.php/Download_PDFs_of_the_book, p. 85. Retrieved May 12, 2007.

27. See Robert D Putnam, *Bowling Alone: The Collapse and Revival of American Community* (New York: Simon and Schuster, 2000).

28. See accounts, for example, at http://www.joystiq.com/2005/02/01/world-of-warcraft-causes-riots-in-the-streets/. Retrieved February 15, 2007.

29. Benkler, p. 87.

30. Lawrence Lessig, *Code and Other Laws of Cyberspace* (New York: Basic Books, 1999); Benkler, *The Wealth of Networks,* 2006.

31. Kathryn Montgomery et al., Youth as E-Citizens: Engaging the Digital Generation. Center for Social Media, 2004. Retrieved February 15, 2007. http://www.centerforsocialmedia.org/ecitizens/project.htm.

32. Putnam (2000).

33. For a more developed version of this argument, see Sharareh Frouzesh Bennett, An Analysis of the Depiction of Democratic Participation in American Civics Textbooks, Paper presented at the German-American conference on Responsible Citizenship, Education, and the Constitution, Freiberg, Germany (September 2005): 12–15.

34. Eliasoph (1998).

35. Coleman, this volume.

36. Jay Blumler and Dennis Kavanagh, The Third Age of Political Communication: Influences and Features, *Political Communication* 16 (1999): 209–230.

37. I am indebted to Peter Levine for providing these references.

38. Bennett (2005).

39. Courtesy of Peter Levine, cf. Civic Mission of the Schools (2003). Carnegie Corporation of New York and CIRCLE. Retrieved February 15, 2007. http://www.civicyouth.org/PopUps/CivicMissionof Schools.pdf.

40. Peter Levine, personal communication.

41. Seattle Student Voices, a branch of the national Student Voices program of The Annenberg Policy Center. See W. Lance Bennett et al., Seattle Student Voices: Comprehensive Executive Summary. Center for Communication and Civic Engagement, 2002. Retrieved February 15, 2007. http://depts.washington.edu/ccce/assets/documents/pdf/SeattleStudentVoicesExecSummaryFINAL.pdf.

42. W. Lance Bennett and Mike Xenos, Young Voters and the Web of Politics: Pathways to Participation in the Youth Engagement and Electoral Campaign Web Spheres. Center for Information and Research on Civic Learning and Engagement, 2004. Retrieved June 27, 2007, at http://www.civicyouth.org/PopUps/WorkingPapers/WP20Bennett.pdf.

43. Montgomery et al. (2004).

44. David T. Z. Mindich, *Tuned Out: Why Americans Under 40 Don't Follow the News* (New York: Oxford University Press, 2005), p. 21.

45. James T. Hamilton, *All the News That's Fit to Sell: How the Market Transforms Information into News* (Princeton, NJ: Princeton University Press, 2004), p. 85.

46. Putnam (2000).

47. For sample news trends in Germany, see Bennett (2008).

48. Michael Schudson, *The Good Citizen: A History of American Civic Life* (New York: Free Press, 1998).

49. Retrieved February 15, 2007. http://www.bbc.co.uk/dna/actionnetwork/.

50. Inglehart (1997); Giddens (1991); Bennett (1998).

Youth and Digital Democracy: Intersections of Practice, Policy, and the Marketplace

Kathryn C. Montgomery

American University, School of Communication

Since the advent of the World Wide Web in the early nineties, the so-called Digital Generation has been at the epicenter of major tectonic shifts that are transforming the media landscape. The more than 70 million individuals born in the United States during the last two decades of the twentieth century represent the largest cohort of young people in the nation's history, and the first to grow up in a world saturated with networks of information, digital devices, and the promise of perpetual connectivity. Youth are in many ways the defining users of the new media. As active creators of a new digital culture, they are developing their own Web sites, diaries, and blogs; launching their own online enterprises; and forging a new set of cultural practices.[1] A study by Forrester Research found that youth incorporate digital media into their lives at a faster rate than any other generation. "All generations adopt devices and Internet technologies, but younger consumers are Net natives," one of the report's coauthors explained to the press. They don't just go online; they "live online."[2]

Foundations, music industry celebrities, corporations, and wealthy donors in the United States have poured large sums of money into a variety of initiatives aimed at using digital media to reach and engage young people in civic and political activities. These ventures are based on the hope that new technologies may be able to help reverse the long-term declines in civic and political participation among youth.[3] Experts such as Michael X. Delli Carpini, Dean of the Annenberg School for Communication at the University of Pennsylvania, have expressed some cautious optimism. Commenting on some of the early Web-based efforts, he has identified several important Internet features that lend themselves to enhanced engagement. These include increased speed with which information can be gathered and transmitted, greater volume of information that is easily accessible, more flexibility in how and when information is accessed, and much greater opportunity to interact with others in a range of contexts (one to one, one to many, many to one, and many to many), using a variety of media types (text, audio, and video). As a result, Delli Carpini notes, the Internet both shifts the nature of community from geographic to interest-based and challenges traditional definitions of information gatekeepers and authoritative voices, of content producers and consumers. He suggests, however, that Internet-based initiatives are likely to be more useful in expanding the activities of youth already engaged in civic life, rather than encouraging those who do not participate to become involved.[4]

The growth and penetration of broadband and the development and distribution of new software applications—such as social networking platforms, blogging tools, and podcasting—have combined to create the next generation of the Internet, often called

"Web 2.0."[5] As legal scholar Yochai Benkler argues in *The Wealth of Networks: How Social Production Transforms Markets and Freedom*, these innovations have enhanced the participatory capabilities of digital media, building on the core features of the Internet to create a new media environment that, by its very nature, is a democratizing force. "We are witnessing a fundamental change in how individuals can interact with their democracy and experience their role as citizens," Benkler explains. "They are no longer constrained to occupy the role of mere readers, viewers, and listeners. They can be, instead, participants in a conversation." Because digital media "shift the locus of content creation from the few professional journalists trolling society for issues and observations, to the people who make up society," the public agenda

can be rooted in the life and experience of individual participants in society – in their observations, experiences, and obsessions. The network allows all citizens to change their relationship to the public sphere. They no longer need to be consumers and passive spectators. They can become creators and primary subjects. It is in this sense that the Internet democratizes.[6]

Digital Communication at the Crossroads

If Benkler's assessment is correct, then the Digital Generation should be among the key beneficiaries of this new democratizing media system. But as with earlier media technologies, the fulfillment of this democratic potential will be determined not only by technological advances but also by political and economic forces. As a public medium, the Internet is really only a little more than a decade old. Its dramatic growth during that period parallels the rapid penetration of television a half century ago. Like television, the Internet has brought about enormous societal changes, many of which we are just beginning to understand. But this new medium is by no means static. The Internet as we know it is undergoing a fundamental transformation. In the United States, the major telephone and cable companies have gained control of 98 percent of residential broadband service. These companies have been engaged in a high-stakes competitive battle over the control of an array of services delivered through digital pathways on a variety of platforms, including computers, digital television, and wireless devices. Mergers and acquisitions in the telecommunication business (e.g., between AT&T and BellSouth, Verizon and MCI) have all been predicated on expectations for explosive growth in the broadband market.[7] As the Internet continues to make its transition into the broadband era, some of its fundamental defining features that have been taken for granted by users will evolve and change.

The emergence of broadband is fueling a new boom in the digital marketplace, with advertising and marketing at its core. Because of the exponential rise in children's spending power during the last several decades of the twentieth century, the Internet emerged as a new mass medium in the midst of a youth media culture that was already highly commercialized.[8] Interactive technologies have created capabilities that alter the media marketing paradigm in significant ways, extending some of the practices that have already been put in place in conventional media but, more important, defining a new set of relationships between young people and corporations. As a consequence, marketing and advertising have become a pervasive presence in youth digital culture, creating new hybrid forms that blend communications, content, and commerce.[9] Market forces are playing a central role in shaping both the online political youth sphere and the new participatory platforms that have come to define Web 2.0.

A constellation of interrelated public policy issues will also play a critical role in determining the nature of the emerging digital media environment. Many of these issues have been inserted into deliberations over revisions of the U.S. telecommunications laws, replaying some of the earlier debates of the nineties. Some have been thrust into the media spotlight, the topic of intense debate that is too often polarized, simplistic, and narrow. Others have been argued primarily in closed-door sessions at the offices of K Street lobbyists, before the Federal Communications Commission, or on Capitol Hill. Discussion of these complex and arcane policies has largely been confined to business and trade reporting, with virtually no consideration of their impact on civic and political discourse. Several scholars, including Benkler, have written persuasively about the importance of these policies to the future of the democratic media.[10] A few issues have generated considerable online discussion and debate in the blogosphere.

All of these developments will have far-reaching impacts on the nature and extent of civic and political discourse in the new digital media culture, not only for youth but also for the public at large. In the following pages, I will explore the promises and perils of the new digital media as a vehicle for renewed youth engagement in public life. First, I will briefly summarize the findings of a study I coauthored in 2004 that examined the emergence of Web sites designed to foster youth civic and political engagement. Second, I will show how innovations in participatory technology were incorporated into the massive youth vote efforts of the 2004 election. Third, I will discuss some of those same get-out-the-vote initiatives to illustrate the ways in which commercial forces have become a pervasive presence in the new civic and political spaces for young people in the digital media. Fourth, I will outline five of the key policy issues whose outcome will significantly impact the participatory potential of the next generation of digital media. Finally, I will offer several recommendations for policy, research, and public education efforts that could help maximize the democratic capacities of the new digital media.

The Youth Civic Web

Beginning in the late nineties, a number of nonprofits began launching Web sites designed with the explicit purpose of engaging adolescents and young adults in civic and political life. A study completed in 2004 by myself and a team of researchers at American University surveyed more than three hundred Web sites created by and for young people.[11] The Web sites reflected a diversity of goals and constituencies. Some were aimed at a broad youth audience, while others were tailored to more specific communities, such as underserved youth, youth in urban or rural areas, and youth of various racial, ethnic, or sexual identities. Although most were rooted in preexisting organizations and institutions, a few were solely creatures of the digital universe. And while many of the Web sites were little more than static "brochureware," the study also found numerous examples of innovative uses of the interactive digital technologies for a variety of civic and political purposes. A brief look at a handful of the sites in the study shows a richness and variety of content and style:

The Community Information Corps (http://www.westsidecic.org/) of St. Paul, Minnesota, enlists teens to develop an "online tour" of public art in St. Paul's West Side, including clickable photos of the individual murals, many of which reflect the neighborhood's immigrant roots, from its large Mexican American community to its more recent Hmong arrivals.

WireTap (http://www.wiretapmag.org/), an online magazine created by the progressive organization AlterNet refers to itself as "youth in pursuit of the dirty truth." WireTap serves up youth-written reporting, analysis, and cultural reviews on a wide range of contemporary issues, from the job market for young people, to politicians' attitudes toward youth, to the importance of hip-hop music in youth culture.

Tolerance.org (http://www.tolerance.org), a Web project of the Southern Poverty Law Center, offers young people information and skills for promoting tolerance and fighting hate, arranging its content according to age level, with separate sections for parents, teachers, teenagers, and children. "Mix It Up," the teen section, promotes an activist approach to fighting self-segregation and "social boundaries" in schools, whether based on race, religion, or school-based cliques.

Out Proud (http://www.outproud.org/), the Web site of the National Coalition for Gay, Lesbian, Bisexual, & Transgender Youth, is rich in resources designed to assist youth in coming to terms with their sexuality. Most notable of these is "Outpath" (http://www.outpath.com/), a searchable archive with hundreds of personal narratives about coming out, which includes an opportunity for visitors, both youth and their families, to add their own stories to the collection.

TakingITGlobal (http://www.takingitglobal.org/) features a set of interrelated online projects that offer young people connections, resources, and opportunities for international dialogue with their peers. Among the site's many features are: message boards, an internal instant messaging system, live moderated chats, and the ability for members to create their own online groups.

Free the Planet! (http://www.freetheplanet.org) provides resources for activists and helps students win campaigns for environmental protection. The group has taken aim at such corporate giants as Ford Motors and Kraft Foods, among others. In each case the Web site offers a "problem," a "solution," and "what you can do"—from sending an email to a corporate or political decision maker to urging colleges to opt for integrated pest management instead of heavy pesticide use.[12]

Though fragmented and not always in the foreground of the emerging media culture, these online ventures are nonetheless a noteworthy development, suggesting the beginnings of an emerging genre on the Internet that could be loosely called "youth civic culture." While the study did not assess the *impact* of these online civic ventures on young people's attitudes or behaviors, it did identify numerous opportunities for youth to acquire some of the key attributes of civic engagement.[13] Civic Web sites offered a variety of tools for youth expression and communication, including online polls and questionnaires; invitations to submit essays, poetry, artwork, and other original materials; and discussion boards that encouraged collaboration and debate. Specific populations, including racial, ethnic, and gender groups, could take advantage of the Web to strengthen their identities, and to build knowledge, pride, and a sense of belonging through a network of contacts and resources. Civic sites also provided youth with the opportunity to hone such important civic skills as fundraising, volunteering, and communicating with political leaders.[14]

Most of these youth civic Web sites were launched with an "if we build it, they will come" strategy, and many of them have struggled for visibility and influence in a highly seductive and engaging online youth media environment.[15] The growth of participatory online platforms has, in many ways, eclipsed some of the early Web-based efforts for engaging youth. The popularity of YouTube, MySpace, and other user-generated content sites suggests that the emerging digital media culture is expanding the opportunities for young people to connect, engage, and create; and large numbers of them are taking advantage of these new outlets. "Young internet users—especially those with broadband at home—are the most likely contributors of content to cyberspace," noted a 2006 report by the Pew Internet & American Life Project. More than half of bloggers are under the age of thirty, and these young people are also "among the most enthusiastic communicators of the modern age, taking advantage of every opportunity to communicate."[16] While the Pew report found that the majority of bloggers view their online communication as vehicles for personal expression rather than civic discourse, there are also clear indications that many youth are using these tools to participate in public conversations. Some have joined the ranks of "citizen journalists."[17] For example, Guerrilla News Network, an online youth media site, offers members a complete toolbox of participatory software through its "GNN 2.0," encouraging young people to "create and disseminate news themselves, through blogs, headlines, original articles, videos, photos, our own customized personal e-mail newsletters and collaborative, ongoing investigations that will allow GNNers to work together to cover important stories the mainstream media is missing."[18] (In another chapter of this volume, Kate Raynes-Goldie and Luke Walker document a variety of ways in which young people are using Web 2.0 to engage in debate and activism.)

Rocking the Vote—Digital Style

Digital software and technology were a central part of many of the orchestrated efforts to promote youth voting during the 2004 presidential election. While the Internet had already begun to play an increasingly prominent role in campaign politics, 2004 marked the first truly high-tech election. Researchers at George Washington University documented a new category of Internet users, which they labeled "Online Political Citizens." Though not exclusively youth, this cohort of Internet-savvy political participants included a significant number of young people, with 36 percent of them between the ages of eighteen and thirty-four, compared to 24 percent of the general public. A large majority of them (44 percent) had not been politically involved before and had never "worked for a campaign, made a campaign donation or attended a campaign event," the study noted. "They visit campaign Web sites, donate money online, join Internet discussion groups, and read and post comments on Web logs." They also "organize local events through Web sites such as Meetup.com or donate money to their causes on sites such as MoveOn.org or Grassfire.org." They "use campaign Web sites as hubs" and "depend heavily on e-mail to stay in touch with the campaigns, receive news stories and muster support."[19] The successful primary campaign of Vermont presidential candidate Howard Dean, which introduced many of these online practices into the election cycle—with extensive involvement of young people—was hailed as a harbinger of a new era in digital politics.[20] But as Michael Xenos and Kirsten Foot point out in the next chapter in this volume, most of the candidates in the 2004 election failed to make full use of digital technologies to effectively engage youth, creating a "generation gap" between the needs and expectations of young people and the practices of political actors.[21]

   In contrast to this pattern, the dozens of nonpartisan get-out-the-vote campaigns targeted at youth showcased a multiplicity of strategies and tactics for using digital media as a tool for political mobilization. Foundations and individual donors invested large sums of money to fund a variety of efforts aimed at various segments of the youth population.[22] Some had colorful and provocative names, such as Smack Down Your Vote and the League of Pissed Off Voters. Others reflected a diversity of constituencies and approaches. The Hip Hop Summit Action Network (HSAN), launched in 2001 by rap music mogul Russell Simmons, orchestrated a series of events headlined by hip-hop musicians and aimed at urban and Hispanic youth.[23] Rap star Sean "P. Diddy" Combs formed Citizen Change, with a compelling slogan that reflected the high-stakes nature of the upcoming election: Vote or Die! L.A.-based Voces del Pueblo (voices of the people) targeted Latino youth "who are most likely to opt out of participating in the electoral process."[24] The Black Youth Vote project partnered with BET for a black college tour, with a budget of $5 million.[25] The Youth Vote Coalition brought in $660,000 for the election cycle, amassing a coalition of 106 national groups.[26]

The Internet played a critical role in all these efforts, not only providing each initiative with a direct means for reaching its target audience but also facilitating collaboration among the groups, forging virtual coalitions through links and cross-promotion strategies, and creating a "youth engagement Web sphere" on the Internet that was far larger and more sophisticated than any before.[27] This online fluidity enabled visitors to travel across Web sites quickly and effortlessly, gathering information, communicating with others, and joining whatever effort matched their interests and passions.

One of the leading groups was Rock the Vote. Founded by the music industry in 1990, the nonprofit had been a pioneer of the youth vote movement for more than a decade. It played a central role in the deployment of digital tools for engaging youth voters during the 2004 election cycle, combining a range of cutting-edge practices and forging new ones. Thus, its campaign can be viewed as a compendium of state-of-the-art strategies that were replicated by other groups and that created a framework for future efforts.

Rock the Vote's Web site served as the hub of this maelstrom of preelection activity, linking with the growing number of youth vote initiatives in a synergistic network of online relationships.[28] A "Register to Vote" tab linked to a pop-up window with a voter registration form that visitors could print and mail to their state elections office, under the slogan "Fill it and print it, lick it and mail it."[29] By registering online, members could join Rock the Vote's "Street Team," connecting with others in their communities to become part of the army of volunteers who were registering new voters at concerts, clubs, and campuses across the country.[30] Donations could be made easily with a click of the mouse.[31] Youth could also participate in the RTV blog, to learn "what Capitol Hill is saying and find young people's response."[32] The nonprofit went to elaborate means to spread the Rock the Vote brand throughout the Web, including free downloads of RTV banners and radio ads, as well as links to its voter registration page. Groups and individuals could also import the Rock the Vote online voter registration tool and brand it for their own Web sites.[33] Rock the Vote forged a partnership with MySpace.com, using the site's social networking platform to encourage members to spread the message among their peers and employing the latest MP3s, photos, and buddy icons "to inspire, organize and mobilize young people to vote."[34]

Other youth vote campaigns developed their own innovative digital strategies. For example, MoveOnStudentAction.org, a youth initiative started by the online group MoveOn.org, created a "Voter Multiplier" page on its Web site, inviting members to upload their friends' names and e-mail addresses—from their Palm, Outlook, or Facebook programs—in order to create their own "personal precincts." With a few strokes of a key, each individual could instantly contact hundreds of friends, e-mailing them personalized messages—from "virtual door hangers" to online voter registration links to election-day reminders to cast their ballot, along with directions to the right polling place.[35] James Hong and Jim Young, creators of the successful online dating site, HotOrNot, launched VoteOrNot. The venture was based on the same principle that friends could do a much better job of influencing each other than could impersonal advertising messages. To attract people to the site, the sponsors offered a $200,000 sweepstakes that would be split between the winner and the person who had referred him or her to the site. Members who joined VoteOrNot would be linked to another Web site where they could register to vote. Launched over Labor Day weekend 2004, VoteOrNot claimed to have signed up more than 100,000 people before the end of October.[36]

It may be difficult to assess what role, if any, these Internet efforts played in the increased youth vote turnout of the 2004 election. According to the Center for Information & Research on Civic Learning & Engagement, it was a combination of factors, including "extensive voter outreach efforts, a close election, and high levels of interest in the 2004 campaign" that worked together "to drive voter turnout among young people to levels not seen since 1992." Nor could predictions be made as to whether the increased turnout constituted a long-term trend.[37] It is notable, however, that the midterm election of 2006 also showed a marked increase in youth voter turnout, with two million more young people voting than in 2002.[38]

Regardless of their ultimate political impact, the youth vote campaigns may be important indicators of future trends in the use of digital media for political mobilization of young people. Based on Rock the Vote's own documentation, its 2004 online efforts were highly successful, bringing an unprecedented number of young people to its Web site, with more than 45 percent of eighteen- to twenty-four-year-olds visiting the site in the months leading up to the election. Online voter registrations totaled 1.2 million.[39] At the very least, the youth vote campaigns of 2004 demonstrate that well-funded massive outreach efforts, combining cutting-edge digital tools and strategies and popular culture venues, may succeed in energizing large numbers of youth, at least in the short run.

The Branding of Political Discourse

To the extent that Rock the Vote may serve as a trendsetter in organizing young people through the Internet, it is important to take a closer look at some of the patterns and partnerships that were formed during the 2004 election. These, in turn, need to be understood against the backdrop of larger economic developments that are underway in the emerging youth digital culture.

One of the hallmarks of Rock the Vote's youth-vote work is its ability to develop strong relationships with corporations. These companies not only provide financial support but also participate in "co-branding" many of the major elements of the nonprofit's campaigns. While a number of other youth vote initiatives have also partnered with popular brands, Rock the Vote has forged a unique model of democratic participation that merges the roles of fan, consumer, and citizen. For example, in 2004, four corporate sponsors—Dr. Pepper/Seven Up, Unilever's Ben & Jerry's Homemade, Motorola, and Cingular Wireless—paid $1 million each to support the Voter Registration Bus and Concert Tour.[40] In partnership with a company called Meca, the nonprofit created "Rock the Vote Communicator," a "branded" version of instant messaging, offering "six available Rock the Vote–themed skins" that were "designed to appeal to the elusive 18–24 voter demographic."[41]

Rock the Vote promoted its campaign, along with its affiliated brands, through software applications, wireless technologies, and commercial Web sites that married activism and advertising. "Rock the Vote Mobile" packaged appeals for political participation into user-friendly pop culture products designed for integration into the busy lives of young people.

According to its Web site, the mobile project was modeled on several successful "smart mob" political efforts in other countries, including campaigns by activists in Spain the night before the March 2004 elections, where "the spread of text messaging mobilized some thousands of people who congregated in front of the political party running the country, Partido Popular, in just a couple of hours."[42] But the youth vote version of these campaigns was an integrated marketing venture with Motorola. To launch the mobile campaign, the company sent e-mails to its thousands of cell phone users, attaching a video that featured Rachel Bilson, star of the popular Fox TV show *The O.C.*, inviting young people to sign up online for the campaign. As an added incentive, the company offered sweepstakes with prizes that included Ben & Jerry's ice cream and Motorola handsets. Youth could be plugged into a constant stream of interactive content and activities through their cell phones.[43] Biweekly polls were able to "take the pulse of 18-30 year-olds on top-of-mind topics from education and economics to job creation and the war on terrorism," campaign materials explained, and a regular feature asked voters which candidate was "likely to get their vote on Election Day."[44] "Celebrity voice mails... explained how to find a polling place through the Web or through an automatic patch-through to 1800MYVOTE1."[45] Users could also receive "wake-up calls" and ring tones from Rock the Vote musicians, enter election-related contests, and participate in a variety of text-messaging surveys. Undecided voters could take the "candidate match" survey. After answering ten questions on issues such as the war, the environment, and the economy, they would receive a text message with the name of the candidate who best fit their own values and interests."[46] According to the nonprofit, more than 120,000 people joined its mobile campaign.

The synergistic relationships between Rock the Vote and its corporate partners are emblematic of the growing practice of "cause marketing," in which companies link their products to causes and issues in order to build customer appreciation and loyalty. Brands seeking youth are particularly interested in aligning with well-known causes, often willing to pay nonprofits considerable sums of money for the association. Many companies have created specific line items in their marketing budgets for cause marketing.[47] Rock the Vote's cause marketing model was the quintessential win–win strategy; the multi-million-dollar corporate investment played a crucial role in providing support and visibility for campaign, underwriting new digital applications that were invented and put in place for the election. And the brands that partnered with Rock the Vote were able to take advantage of the nonprofit's ability to reach a wide spectrum of young people through the "youth engagement Web sphere."

Incorporating social and political messages into the content of youth entertainment has already become a common practice in the social marketing and "entertainment-education" campaigns of public health organizations. Television programs, music, and other popular venues can be effective vehicles for reaching and educating young people about such issues as sexual health, smoking, and drug abuse.[48] Applying similar approaches to civic and political engagement initiatives may help to popularize and extend participation among youth. Given the elusiveness of the youth audience, and its value as a target market, more corporations are likely to partner with these causes, offering their financial largess in return for brand exposure. To the extent that corporate investment can help support such efforts, companies should be encouraged to become involved. However, there is also a danger that intertwining politics with brand marketing could ultimately undermine the potential of these campaigns.

Such practices also have important implications for adolescent development. Teenagers and young adults undergo a critical process as they acquire the necessary civic knowledge, skills, and emotional attachments that are central to their emerging roles as citizens. As scholars Constance Flanagan and Nakesha Faison have pointed out, "the civic identities, political views, and values of young people are rooted in their social relations and the opportunities they have for civic practice."[49] The ubiquitous and integrated nature of marketing in digital political engagement practices could serve to conflate civic identity and brand identity during this key formative stage.

Commercialized Communities

The extension of brands into youth online politics is part of a larger set of trends in the evolution of youth marketing in digital media. The forms of advertising, marketing, and selling that are emerging as part of the new media depart in significant ways from the more familiar types of advertising and promotion in conventional media. Companies can now forge intimate ongoing relationships with individuals. Digital technologies make it possible to track every move, online and off, compiling elaborate personal profiles that combine behavioral, psychological, and social information on individuals and aggregating that data across platforms and over time. Youth marketers have developed a full array of strategies, especially tailored to the needs and interests of youth, aiming to "become part of the communication structure" of their daily lives.[50]

The practices that are becoming commonplace in the digital environment have important implications for the future of democratic discourse. Of particular concern is the increasing presence of marketing in online communities. Many of the same features of Web 2.0 that are so valued for their participatory capabilities are being designed to incorporate marketing applications, as investors seek to "monetize" the newest forms of digital media most popular among youth. According to marketers at a 2006 "Search Engine Strategies" show in Silicon Valley, social networking sites offer one of the most effective means for reaching the highly lucrative, but challenging, youth market segment. One participant advised marketers to track the content of blogs to find out the interests and needs of the bloggers, suggesting that interacting with them and participating in their postings is a great way to get to know them and to build trust. "To be accepted," remarked another panelist, "means to be built into that culture."[51] A marketing conference in London—entitled "What MySpace Means: Lessons for Every Brand"—offered advice to companies for "cultivating communities" in these social networking spaces.[52] Social networking sites have attracted huge investments in advertising dollars. Companies are particularly eager to take advantage of the large, highly detailed user profiles and expanding lists of "friends" on these sites. "The targeting we can do is phenomenal," one industry executive told the press.[53] As companies insert themselves into these new social networks, they are intentionally seeking to blur the lines between advertising and content. Social networks are "breaking down that wall between what is marketing and what isn't," commented one youth marketing expert. "[S]ometimes the marketing is so embedded in the social network sphere that it draws users to interact with the brand as if they were e-mailing friends," explained an article in *Marketing*.[54]

The intrusion of marketing into these digital social spaces does not necessarily mean that youth cannot still use them to engage in political debate and civic discourse—sometimes challenging the very companies that are targeting them. Over the years, young people have launched both online and offline "culture jamming" campaigns against corporate media.[55] In their chapter in this volume, Jennifer Earl and Alan Schussman document a number of online campaigns by youth consumers around the world that have challenged corporations over the content of youth cultural products.[56] Nor has the presence of advertising thwarted free expression on the Internet. For example, a number of bloggers carry advertising on their sites, enabling them to develop viable business models without interfering with their ability to articulate their views and find audiences.[57] And despite the increasing presence of advertising on YouTube, MySpace, and other peer-to-peer, social networking platforms, these venues have continued to spawn an abundance of diverse viewpoints and to serve as a forum for social protest.

However, the nature and extent of direct involvement by marketers into the daily communication and community-building activities of young people is unprecedented. Using sophisticated data mining, research, and targeting tools, companies are able to strategically penetrate MySpace, YouTube, and other social-networking platforms in order to exploit them for commercial purposes. Marketers speak of "recruiting evangelists" by seeking out the "influencing members of each social network" and turning them into "brand breeders" or "brand advocates" for products. Youth are offered incentives to incorporate brands into their user-generated content and distribute their work virally on the Internet, cell phones, and iPods.[58] The rampant commercialization of these nascent digital communities raises serious questions about their future role as sites for political and civic engagement by youth.

Corporate control and commodification of digital platforms could also bring about more fundamental changes in these spaces, especially in the emerging broadband era. The News Corporation's purchase of MySpace for $580 million is a harbinger of further consolidation trends in the online industry, as advertisers continue to seek out the youth market.[59] These trends have prompted some industry observers to predict that accommodating the needs of advertisers will result in a change in the "architecture" of such networks. "Look for them to make each entry into the many groups accessible via a portal for its users," explained one trade article. "Today, the purely linear, viral nature of the MySpace that is so much fun for users is anything but fun for advertisers who require more content security and targeting precision than MySpace can provide for their messages. That seems certain to change soon."[60]

Key Policy Battles

In addition to these changing market practices and ownership patterns, there are several telecommunications policy issues that are particularly relevant to the future of youth democratic communications. Most of these issues have been highly contentious, sparking a series of ongoing political skirmishes, fought inside the beltway and online, part of what Yochai Benkler calls "the battle over the institutional ecology of the digital environment."[61] In the following pages, I briefly discuss four of the most critical policies that are likely to affect the basic structure and operating practices of digital communications—network neutrality, intellectual property, equitable access, and community broadband—including a few accounts of how some youth activists have become involved in the debates. I also address the debate over online safety. While not as directly connected to these "institutional ecology" concerns, this issue is nonetheless significantly related to the continuing role of youth in the public policy arena.

Network Neutrality.   Although the term "network neutrality" is a recent invention (coined by Columbia University law professor Tim Wu in 2005), the concept (which is sometimes also called "open access") has a long history in communications technology and regulation.[62] Telephone monopolies in the United States have operated on a similar principle for many decades, regulated as "common carriers," which are required to offer services to anyone on the basis of nondiscriminatory rates. As *conduits* for communication, the companies are not involved in the *content* of what they carry. This tradition in the regulation of phone lines became a basic underpinning of Internet technology.[63] A combination of government regulation and funding of the basic infrastructure, along with principles of open-source technology, created the Internet as we know it. Even after it was privatized in the 1990s, the Internet has perpetuated many of these traditions that enable end-to-end and many-to-many communication. As Adam Cohen explained in a *New York Times* editorial, Tim Berners-Lee created the World Wide Web (which runs on top of the Internet) "in a decentralized way that allowed anyone with a computer to connect to it and begin receiving and sending information. That open architecture is what has allowed for the growth of Internet commerce and communication." These inherent technological features are also critical underpinnings to newer peer-to-peer applications.[64]

The fundamental principles that underlie Internet architecture have eroded in recent years, owing to a series of regulatory decisions and market trends. In 2005, under lobbying pressure from telephone companies, the Federal Communications Commission eliminated the rules for nondiscrimination, content treatment, and interconnection that had been part of the common carrier paradigm.[65] (Unlike telephone companies, cable companies, which have become major providers of broadband Internet services, have never operated as common carriers.) Most consumers have a choice between one of two broadband providers—the local cable company or the local telephone company. While other technologies such as community broadband might provide viable competition in the future, there is no guarantee that this will be the case. (See discussion of community broadband later.) As a result, the diversity, openness, and competition that characterized the Internet in the dial-up era could be seriously undermined. The distribution policies of phone and cable companies could limit applications considered less financially profitable, favoring instead the content with which they have a financial relationship. Instead of nondiscriminatory carriage, network owners are likely to apply different policies to content they own or in which they invest.[66] (The cable industry has a long tradition of such discrimination, with many multisystem operators—MSOs—rejecting new channels in which they are not themselves invested or insisting on becoming financial partners with new programming ventures.)[67]

The implications for democratic communications are significant. Developments in the business practices of the broadband industry threaten to undermine the archetypal "level playing field" that the Internet has long provided, in which content providers are accorded equal treatment in the online environment, and users enjoy access to any Internet resource, service, or application. Network neutrality could provide new openings for youth participation in emerging digital media platforms, ensuring continuation of the openness and free access that the public has come to expect with the Internet. However, in the absence of an affirmative policy to guarantee network neutrality, civic and political uses of new media could be undermined. Analysis of existing, as well as planned, policies by broadband providers indicate that discriminatory access and distribution could become commonplace in the networks of the future.[68] Internal industry documents from technology companies such as Cisco and Allot Communications have warned cable and phone companies about the need to "limit unprofitable peer-to-peer communications" or, in some cases, ban them altogether.[69]

The political battle over network neutrality could be a precursor to future digital media policy campaigns, in which online users, including large numbers of youth, can be mobilized through the new participatory tools on the Internet. Advocacy groups on both sides of the issue have proactively reached out to the blogging community to advance their arguments.

Bloggers have also been quick to pounce on several statements by industry leaders that have served as a flashpoint for heated online debate. When AT&T Chairman Edward E. Whitacre, Jr., told *Business Week* that he thought companies such as Yahoo! and Google should be charged for using broadband to reach their customers, the remark sparked a storm of protest by bloggers. In a subsequent press article, an executive at BellSouth said that his company would consider charging Apple an additional five to ten cents every time a customer downloaded a song from iTunes. This remark triggered a second wave of turbulence in the blogosphere over concerns that such additional costs would inevitably be passed onto consumers.[70] Increased costs for downloads could affect not only music but also the full range of other content now available through broadband.

The pro–network neutrality Save the Internet Campaign, spearheaded by the nonprofit advocacy group Free Press, has made a strategic effort to enlist the involvement of bloggers. Working with MoveOn.org, Free Press cultivated a following of bloggers who were interested in the issue, using their blogrolls to build a list of more than six thousand bloggers and then providing them with links to the Save the Internet campaign site. The group also organized an exclusive "blogger only" press call, inviting experts to explain the policy issues surrounding network neutrality and to encourage further coverage online.[71] Such efforts are a reflection of the growing importance of bloggers to issue advocates, who now routinely cultivate relationships with influential members of the blogosphere.[72]

Network neutrality advocates also made a special effort to reach out to online youth through popular social networking and video sites. For its MySpace effort, Free Press enlisted the help of organizers who had been involved in the online youth vote mobilization efforts in 2004. The MySpace Save the Internet profile features blurbs, FAQs, cartoons, blog entries, and links to advocacy videos created by young people on the user-generated site YouTube.com. Members who create links to the Save the Internet Campaign on their own profiles can be rewarded with a free "exclusive MP3 download" with information on the issue.[73] As the network neutrality controversy became more prominent in the blogosphere, some individuals began making their own videos and distributing them on YouTube. Free Press quickly decided to take advantage of it, promoting the videos on the Save the Internet Web site and creating a gallery of more than twenty of them, thus spawning a "virtuous circle" as more and more people began viewing the videos on YouTube. Some of the videos became instant online phenomena, distributed virally to millions of individuals, and revealing how the issue resonates with many members of the digital generation.[74] Many reflect a passion and energy about the issue that is quite remarkable, as well as imaginative ways of rendering the complexities of media policy in understandable, visceral terms that other youth can easily grasp. For example, one video begins with a Web site featuring archival footage of old Warner Brothers cartoons. The cartoons are suddenly interrupted by the familiar multicolored bars of a television emergency broadcast. A young man comes on, playing the part of a media company executive, and tells the Web site operator that he is being shut down. But the Web site operator counters with his own threats against the virtual intruder. The video ends with the tag line "It's your Internet."[75] Such messages reflect the feelings of personal ownership that many youth hold about the digital media, as well as a sense of optimism about their ability to counter any threats to their continued use of these tools. However, in the real world of Washington politics, the battle for nondiscriminatory practices in the broadband era faces substantial opposition.

Activists did successfully intervene in the Federal Communications Commission's (FCC's) 2006 approval of the merger of AT&T and BellSouth, winning concessions that the new company would adhere to principles of network neutrality for two years. Members of the new Democratic-controlled Congress also promised to introduce legislation in 2007 to make net neutrality a Federal law.[76] But the ultimate outcome of the issue remains uncertain.

Intellectual Property.   Intellectual property and copyright issues have been front and center in the digital experiences of young people, directly affecting their daily media practices. Much of the public discourse over copyright in the Internet era has been focused on peer-to-peer music file sharing, with youth at the center of the controversy, cast often as opportunistic freeloaders who are taking what they can for their own personal uses. In 2003, the music industry began filing lawsuits against individual users and their families, as well as against popular file sharing companies such as Napster and KaZaa. These efforts have produced significant changes in online business practices, forcing major file-sharing operators either to shut down or to dramatically change how they operate.[77] As the result of these aggressive legal and PR campaigns, as well as the rise in new music downloading pay services such as iTunes, illegal downloading has been on a decline. At the height of the first wave of lawsuits, surveys of young people suggested that many of them had decided to cease the practice, although subsequent studies indicated that a sizable number of youth still believed it both impractical and, in many cases, unfair to expect them to discontinue doing so.[78]

The intense public focus on music and video piracy has obscured the broader impacts of intellectual property policies, especially on public discourse and democratic expression. Press coverage of crucial legislation and regulatory decisions has often been framed as a business issue, with little public knowledge of its wider implications. For example, the Digital Millennium Copyright Act (DMCA) received very little media attention at the time of its passage in 1998. The law criminalizes the production and dissemination of technologies that could circumvent encoded copy protection devices, imposing penalties as high as ten years in prison or $1 million in fines for willful violations of the provision.[79]

In *Free Culture*, legal scholar Lawrence Lessig provides a well-documented set of arguments that the current direction of intellectual property regulation in the United States threatens not only the Internet but also the larger culture.[80] In the digital era, where sharing, critiquing, modifying, and linking to the content created by others have become an expected and essential part of public discourse, digital copyright laws have created complication and confusion, and posed challenges to bloggers and other online content creators. The nonprofit Electronic Frontier Foundation, a leader in many of the legal battles against copyright infringement lawsuits, has created an online resource specifically for bloggers who are uncertain about what they can and cannot do on their own blogs. The site explains a number of important legal concepts, along with the procedures that must be followed if an Internet Service Provider chooses to remove a posting in response to a copyright infringement complaint. As the site points out, the DMCA has made it much easier for an ISP to take content down without risking liability. Although a blogger whose posting has been removed does have recourse, the entire discussion is a reminder of the complex legal framework within which bloggers and other online commentators must operate, whether they realize it or not.[81]

Passage of the DMCA has spawned a movement of intellectuals and nonprofits working to educate the public about the role of copyright law in free and open democratic discourse. The Creative Commons, a nonprofit founded by Lessig, enables copyright holders to create "flexible licenses" that set the terms under which others can use their work, thus providing an alternative to the rigidity of current copyright law.[82] But additional intellectual property measures have been advanced that could have important implications for the future.[83] In the ensuing years, copyright battles will continue to be fought in the courts, in Congress, and at the FCC.

Several youth activist groups have become involved in intellectual property issues, with music as a key touchstone. For example, Downhill Battle, founded by a group of college students in 2003, has used the Web to engage in "digital civil disobedience" over what it sees as repressive copyright laws.[84] One of the group's key tactics is to create "stunt pages," such as "iTunes is Bogus," which is designed to look like the official iTunes home page, but carries a message attacking the company for some of its business practices.[85] Downhill Battle's "Grey Tuesday" Internet campaign earned the group widespread recognition within the online activist community, as well as mainstream press coverage. After EMI and Capitol Records threatened legal action against the creator of the "mash-up" Grey Album, and anyone who distributed it, the activist group staged an online protest, offering free downloads of the album on its Web site, and encouraging 400 Web sites to turn their sites "grey" for a day. Activists at Downhill Battle used the event as a way to publicize their concerns over copyright law, generating attention from major news outlets, including the *New York Times*, MTV, and the BBC.[86] Downhill Battle has established a nonprofit Participatory Culture Foundation, developing and promoting new software applications and technologies for creating a do-it-yourself "free culture."[87] The foundation has launched a new open-source platform for producing and distributing video online, called "the Democracy Internet TV Platform." The activists see this project as part of their mission to "create a television culture that is fluid, diverse, exciting, and beautiful."[88]

Whether these efforts will be effective at changing any of the existing intellectual and copyright policies, or at preventing further privatization of culture in the digital media, remains to be seen. But engaging young people around the policies that directly affect their own media culture may help them to see the larger connections between their everyday experiences with digital media and the political and cultural forces that are shaping the overall new-media environment.

Equitable Access.   Ensuring equitable access to technology is a policy issue that has largely fallen off the public radar, but nonetheless remains important. During the early nineties, as the Internet was beginning to make its way into the mainstream, the federal government made "bridging the digital divide" a national priority. The Clinton administration's 1993 Agenda for Action called for all schools, libraries, and hospitals to be connected to the Internet by the year 2000.[89] Library and education groups lobbied a provision into the 1996 Telecommunications Act that extended the FCC's Universal Service program to advanced telecommunications services. The act established subsidies (often called the "e-rate") for eligible schools and libraries and for rural health care providers to connect to the Internet.[90] This law, combined with a number of public/private initiatives at the local and state levels, has helped to close the digital divide in the nation's schools. Between 1996 and 2002, the number of schools wired to the Internet went from 65 to 99 percent, with the percentage of wired classrooms rising from 14 to 92 percent. Libraries more than tripled their Internet connections, increasing from 28 to 95 percent during those same years.[91] A 2004 report released by the Consortium for School Networking (CoSN) found that 95 percent of all classrooms nationwide had high-speed access.[92]

But while public policies have helped ensure greater access through schools and libraries, they have not yet erased the troubling gap between young people with access at home and those without it.[93] Although teens and young adults are more likely to have Internet access than other age groups, 13 percent of youth between the ages of twelve and seventeen remained disconnected from the digital universe. As a 2005 Pew Internet & American Life report explained, "Those who remain offline are clearly defined by lower levels of income and limited access to technology," with African American youth underrepresented online in disproportionate numbers. These patterns were consistent with overall Internet penetration.[94] A 2004 report by the Leadership Council on Civil Rights found similar racial disparities in Internet access. Blacks and Latinos, the study noted, are "much less likely than whites to have access to home computers than are white, non-Latinos (50.6 and 48.7 percent compared to 74.6 percent). They are also less likely to have Internet access at home (40.5 and 38.1 percent compared to 67.3 percent). Ethnic and racial disparities in home computer and Internet access rates are larger for children than for adults."[95]

A 2006 survey by the Pew Internet & American Life Project presented a somewhat more hopeful prospect for equitable access to broadband, finding that high-speed connections in the United States had jumped in the previous year, due in part to the fact that many people have moved directly to cable or DSL broadband when they go online, skipping dial-up connections altogether. This rapid growth in broadband adoption, the report explained, is "very strong in middle-income households, particularly for African Americans and those with low levels of education."[96] However, further progress is needed before broadband access will be available to all young people, regardless of geography or income. In an article in the *Washington Monthly*, Robert McChesney and John Podesta note that while both President Bush and the FCC have made commitments to ensuring universal access to broadband technology by 2007, progress remains slow, with the United States lagging far behind many other countries, falling from fourth to sixteenth in broadband penetration since 2001. "In the not-so-distant future," the authors explain, "broadband will be an indispensable part of economic, personal, and public life."[97] For the time being at least, many youth—especially those in poorer households—may have to rely on their schools or local libraries to take advantage of high-speed Internet.

Community Broadband. Community broadband (especially wireless, or "WiFi") networks could go a long way to ensuring that universal access becomes a reality. Advocates point out that there is a long tradition of cities and counties operating electricity and other utility systems for their communities. In the contemporary communications era, publicly run telecommunications systems could provide needed competition to the local telephone and cable monopolies. As public services, such systems can ensure not only more affordable rates but also more effective participation by local civic and political organizations. Many of the youth community projects that are using the Internet to interact with their members and with the public could benefit from community broadband. Municipally operated networks could also help guarantee expanded capacity and services for local schools, libraries, and other public institutions. According to a study by the DC-based Media Access Project, "hundreds of local governments have begun exploring how to provide high-speed broadband through municipal or community networks, either directly or in partnership with others."[98]

Despite these promising developments, however, there are a number of obstacles that could thwart efforts to promote community broadband across the country. One of the largest is organized opposition from telephone and cable companies that fear competition from municipalities. Telecommunications industry lobbyists have successfully lobbied in legislation in fourteen states that restrict future public broadband projects, with a number of other states considering such moves.[99] Another obstacle is the lack of usable spectrum. As McChesney and Podesta point out, many existing WiFi networks have to operate in "junk bands" that are "cluttered with signals from cordless phones, microwave ovens, baby monitors, and other consumer devices. At lower frequencies—like the television band—signals travel farther and can go through walls, trees, and mountains. Opening up some of this spectrum would make Community Internet systems much faster and cheaper to deploy."[100] Many of the same non-profits that are fighting for affirmative national network neutrality policies are also leading the community broadband movement, including Media Access Project, Consumers Union, Consumer Federation of America, and Free Press. Prometheus Radio Project—a Philadelphia-based group of young people who have been advocating release of low-power radio spectrum for community purposes and organizing "barnstorming" of new low-power radio stations across the country—has embraced the goal of promoting community broadband.[101]

Online Safety.   Concerns over "cyberporn" and its impact on the safety of children and youth began during the midnineties. The Communications Decency Act (CDA), passed as part of the omnibus Telecommunications Act of 1996, imposed fines and possible jail sentences on anyone found guilty of transmitting obscene or indecent material, knowing that minors under eighteen could receive it. But as Marjorie Heins, one of the lawyers who opposed the CDA, has noted, the wording of the law was "a masterwork of internal confusion," reflecting a failure by Congress to understand fully the nature of the Internet and creating an opening for a legal challenge.[102] Civil liberty groups fought throughout the two years of congressional deliberations to prevent the bill from passing, staging an online day of protest on the eve of the final vote. Failing in this effort, they immediately challenged the CDA in the courts, and the Supreme Court struck it down within a year of its original passage.[103]

Despite this clear victory, numerous bills have been introduced in the ten years since the passage of the CDA, and several have become law. The Child Online Protection Act (COPA), enacted in 1998, would make it a crime for commercial organizations to allow access by minors under seventeen to sexual material deemed "harmful to minors."[104] Because of challenges by civil liberty groups, the law has been blocked in a series of court decisions. In 2004, the U.S. Supreme Court upheld the most recent court injunction but sent the case back down to a lower court, instructing it to evaluate whether technological advances would provide adequate protections and eliminate the need for the law.[105] In contrast to COPA, the Child Internet Protection Act (CIPA), passed in 2000, has been successfully implemented. That law requires libraries and schools receiving Federal discounts and funding for computers and Internet access (under the U.S. government's e-rate program) to install filters on computers used by minors, in order to restrict their access to harmful material on the Internet.[106]

CIPA has created a legal framework for subsequent legislative vehicles specifically focused on social networking software such as MySpace, Friendster, and Facebook. Under the proposed Deleting Online Predators Act (DOPA), which was passed overwhelmingly by the U.S. House of Representatives in July 2006, CIPA would have been extended to require schools and libraries in the e-rate program to limit young peoples' access to social networking sites, blogs, and wiki's.[107] The blog search site Technorati revealed nearly 1,200 mentions of the controversial legislation, including an informative discussion with scholars Henry Jenkins and danah boyd, who pointed out that such a law would be far too broad.[108] As boyd explained, the proposed legislation would have limited "access to any commercial site that allows users to create a profile and communicate with strangers," blocking not only MySpace but also "blogging tools, mailing lists, video and podcast sites, photo sharing sites, and educational sites." boyd and others have also noted that the statistics on online predators are much lower than many in the public may think, with less than .01 percent of all youth abductions nationwide occurring between strangers. Nor is there any evidence as yet that stranger abductions have occurred because of social network services."[109]

But the politics of cultural policy have often skewed the facts in order to promote particular agendas. For policy makers, protecting children is a compelling issue that can easily be exploited. The possibility, however remote, of children being harmed by strangers on MySpace is more palpable than the concept of ensuring a participatory culture for young people in the digital media. Whether or not legislative efforts to regulate social networking sites are ultimately successful, the debate and press coverage surrounding the issue of online safety could have a chilling effect on youth expression in the digital media. For example, school districts and libraries, fearing controversy and parental objections, may decide voluntarily to block youth access to an entire class of new tools for online participation.

These events are also reminders that the Internet's potential as a tool for unfettered political expression by youth is not immune to political forces. The controversy over MySpace is in many ways a replay of earlier debates that have accompanied the growth of the Internet. Since the early nineties, when the Internet began to make its way into mainstream culture, public discourse over the new medium and its role in the lives of children and youth has been dominated by concerns over harms. The persistent public focus on Internet safety has not only dominated much of the public debate over youth and new media but has also created a climate within the government, the educational community, and the industry that positions young people primarily as potential victims in need of protections, rather than productive participants in digital media culture. In addition to repeated attempts to regulate Internet content, ongoing public concern over Internet harms has spawned a spectrum of protective software and technologies, including filtering and blocking services, as well as labeling and rating systems, all aimed at shielding children and youth from harmful online content.[110] But more important, such fears have diverted attention away from developing a broader understanding of the role of digital media as a positive force in the lives of children and youth.

Although government action on some of the policies described in the preceding pages could take place in the near future, most of these issues are likely to remain in play for quite some time, creating opportunities to enlarge the terms of the debate over the future of digital media, and to enlist the involvement of a broader segment of the public.

Reframing the Debate, Fulfilling the Promise

By examining the myriad ways in which youth are engaging in the new media, we can begin to rethink the role of young people in the media culture and in the society as a whole. As other authors in this volume have documented, we already have abundant evidence of the ways in which many youth are seizing the new digital tools to participate more fully in democracy. The hundreds of civic Web sites created in the last decade are helping to provide young people with some of the essential skills for civic and political engagement. Interactive media make it much easier for them to learn about critical issues of the day, insert their own voices into the public discourse, and actively participate in a wide range of political causes. The 2004 youth vote initiatives are powerful illustrations of how the Internet can be harnessed as an effective mobilizing force in electoral politics. The online efforts of Downhill Battle, FreeCulture.org, and other Internet activist groups demonstrate how some young people are not only creating and distributing their own cultural products but are also fighting some of the crucial policy battles over the future of the digital media system.

To the extent that they are indicators of larger trends, these developments give us reason to celebrate. But despite the numerous examples of young people's empowerment through digital media, serious questions remain about whether such forms of participation can be extended to a broader segment of the youth population, and sustained beyond the occasional bursts of activity surrounding extraordinary events, such as high-stakes national elections. There are also opposing tendencies in the new media that could serve both to enhance and to undermine its democratic potential in the lives of young people. For example, the capacity for collective action, community building, and mobilization are unprecedented. But the move toward increasingly personalized media and one-to-one marketing may encourage self-obsession, instant gratification, and impulsive behaviors.

Whether the Internet ultimately becomes a force for civic and political renewal among youth remains to be seen. However, even though many of the business practices are already in place, there is still enough fluidity in the emerging digital media system to enable decisions to be made to help guide its future. With the support of foundations and government agencies in the United States and abroad, some scholars have begun to explore this potential.[111] Hopefully, these efforts will grow into a broader movement. To deepen our understanding of the new media culture, its institutions, and its varied and complex roles in the lives of children and youth, we will need a broader, more comprehensive multidisciplinary effort, combining the contributions of communications researchers, political scientists, historians, sociologists, anthropologists, economists, and young people themselves. In addition to studies of individual uses of new media, there is an urgent need for serious ongoing examination of the institutions that are creating this digital culture, both its commercial and its noncommercial sectors.

As we consider the policy issues for the next phase of the Digital Age, the goal of fostering a healthy, democratic media culture for young people must be a top priority. These policies need to be understood as the building blocks for a framework that will support democratic communications in the future. The exact shape of the policy framework is less important than the key set of principles that must guide it. These include equitable access to technology, open architecture and nondiscrimination for both consumers and producers of digital content, flexible and fair copyright rules that allow for creativity and sharing of cultural content, and open-source applications that will encourage collaboration and innovation.

Finally, we need a series of national and international conversations, informed by research, on how digital technologies can best serve the needs of children and youth. Youth should be involved directly in that dialogue as key stakeholders, innovators, and leaders. If done well, this process could lead to major public and private initiatives that would help ensure that the democratic potential of the Internet is fulfilled and sustained over the long run, benefiting successive generations of young people.

Notes

1. David Buckingham and Rebekah Willett, eds., *Digital Generations: Children, Young People, and New Media* (Mahwah, NJ: Erlbaum, 2006); Sandra Calvert, *Children's Journeys Through the Information Age* (New York: McGraw-Hill, 1999); Amanda Lenhart, Lee Rainie, and Oliver Lewis, *Teenage Life Online: The Rise of the Instant-Message Generation and the Internet's Impact on Friendship and Family Relationships* (Washington, DC: Pew Internet & American Life Project, 2001); Michael Lewis, *NEXT: The Future Just Happened* (New York: Norton, 2001); Sonia Livingstone, *Young People and New Media* (Thousand Oaks, CA: Sage, 2002); Sharon R. Mazzarella, ed., *Girl Wide Web: Girls, the Internet, and the Negotiation of*

Identity (New York: Peter Lang, 2005); Kathryn C. Montgomery, *Generation Digital: Politics, Commerce, and Childhood in the Age of the Internet* (Cambridge, MA: MIT Press, 2007); Don Tapscott, *Growing Up Digital: The Rise of the Net Generation* (New York: McGraw-Hill, 1998).

2. Karen Brown, Study: Young Adults Snapping Up New Tech, *Reed Business Information*, July 31, 2006.

3. See the chapter by Peter Levine in this volume.

4. Michael X. Delli Carpini, Gen.com: Youth, Civic Engagement, and the New Information Environment, *Political Communication* 17, no. 4 (October 1, 2000): 341–49.

5. Tim O'Reilly, What Is Web 2.0: Design Patterns and Business Models for the Next Generation of Software, http://www.oreillynet.com/pub/a/oreilly/tim/news/2005/09/30/what-is-web-20.html (accessed November 1, 2006).

6. Yochai Benkler, *The Wealth of Networks: How Social Production Transforms Markets and Freedom* (New Haven, CT: Yale University Press, 2006), 272.

7. Jeff Chester, The End of the Internet, *TheNation.com*, February 1, 2006, http://www.thenation.com/docprint.mhtml?i=20060213&s=chester (accessed August 10, 2006).

8. See Susan Linn, *Consuming Kids: The Hostile Takeover of Childhood* (New York: The New Press, 2004). See also Juliet B. Schor, *Born to Buy: The Commercialized Child and the New Consumer Culture* (New York: Scribner, 2004).

9. Kathryn C. Montgomery, Digital Kids: The New On-Line Children's Consumer Culture, in Dorothy G. Singer and Jerome L. Singer, eds., *Handbook of Children and the Media* (Thousand Oaks, CA: Sage, 2001), 635–50.

10. For example, see chapter 11, The Battle over the Institutional Ecology of the Digital Environment, and chapter 12, Conclusion: The Stakes of Information Law and Policy, in Benkler, *The Wealth of Networks*.

11. Kathryn Montgomery, Barbara Gottlieb-Robles, and Gary O. Larson, *Youth as E-Citizens: Engaging the Digital Generation* (Washington, DC: American University, 2004), http://www.centerforsocialmedia.org/ecitizens/index2.htm (accessed July 25, 2006).

12. For a full discussion of each of these Web sites, see chapter 2, Mapping the Online Youth Civic Landscape, in Montgomery, Gottlieb-Robles, and Larson, *Youth as E-Citizens*, 13–53.

13. Constance Flanagan and Nakesha Faison, Youth Civic Development: Implications of Research for Social Policy and Programs, *Social Policy Report* 15, no. 1 (2001): 3–16.

14. Kathryn C. Montgomery and Barbara Gottlieb-Robles, Youth as E-Citizens, in Buckingham and Willett, eds., *Digital Generations*, 131–47.

15. Some nonprofits devised techniques for breaking through the clutter of pop culture. For example, with support from major foundations, the international nonprofit Save the Children conducted market research to identify ways to engage teens in a variety of domestic and global political issues—such as violence, child exploitation, hunger, homelessness, HIV/AIDS, and hate crimes. Its project, YouthNOISE.com, launched in 2001, was consciously modeled on the highly popular teen portal BOLT.com. The compelling and colorful site was equipped with many of the standard "sticky features"—quizzes, contests, discussion boards, and the like—of other dot.com sites, inviting young people to communicate with their peers and to contribute their own content to the site. To enhance its visibility and reach, YouthNOISE forged a strategic partnership with AOL Time Warner, and cross-promoted its content through affiliations with *Seventeen Magazine*, Yahoo, and other media vehicles with large teen audiences. For a profile and history of YouthNOISE, see chapter 3, A Tale of Two Sites, in Montgomery, Gottlieb-Robles, and Larson, *Youth as E-Citizens*, 57–74.

16. Amanda Lenhart and Susannah Fox, *Bloggers: A Portrait of the Internet's New Storytellers* (Washington, DC: Pew Internet & American Life Project, July 19, 2006). Retrieved January 22, 2007. http://www.pewinternet.org/PPF/r/186/report_display.asp.

17. See Shayne Bowman, We Media: How Audiences Are Shaping the Future of News and Information. The Media Center at the American Press Institute, www.hypergene.net/wemedia/download/we_media. pdf (accessed January 9, 2007).

18. GNN FAQ, at: http://www.guerrillanews.com/about/faq.php (accessed August 4, 2006).

19. Joseph Graf and Carol Darr, Political Influentials Online in the 2004 Presidential Campaign, Institute for Politics, Democracy, and the Internet, Washington, DC, February 5, 2004, http://www.ipdi.org/UploadedFiles/political%20influentials.pdf (accessed July 12, 2006).

20. Joe Trippi, *The Revolution Will Not Be Televised: Democracy, the Internet, and the Overthrow of Everything* (New York: Regan Books, 2004).

21. Michael Xenos and Kirsten Foot, Not Your Father's Internet: The Generation Gap in Online Politics, in this volume.

22. For a fuller narrative of the 2004 youth vote campaigns, see chapter 7, Peer-to-Peer Politics, in Montgomery, *Generation Digital*, 178–207.

23. Felicia R. Lee, Hip-Hop Is Enlisted in Social Causes, *The New York Times*, June 22, 2002, 7.

24. NALEO Educational Fund, Voces del Pueblo, http://www.naleo.org/vocesdelpueblo.html (accessed January 10, 2007).

25. National Coalition on Black Civic Participation, Programs and Initiatives: Black Youth Vote! http://www.bigvote.org (accessed July 29, 2006).

26. Ibid., New Voters Project, http:www.newvotersproject.org/about-us (accessed March 15, 2005).

27. Lance Bennett and Michael Xenos, Young Voters and the Web of Politics: Pathways to Participation in the Youth Engagement and Electoral Campaign Web Spheres, Working Paper 20, August 2004, Center for Information & Research on Civic Learning & Engagement, http://depts.washington.edu/bennett/about-cv.html (accessed July 25, 2006).

28. Rock the Vote Rocks the Web With Strategic Alliance, *Business Wire*, July 15, 2004.

29. Montgomery, Gottlieb-Robles, and Larson, *Youth as E-Citizens*, 22.

30. Rock the Vote, Join the Street Team Today, http://www.rockthevote.com/cst/index.php (accessed November 26, 2005).

31. Rock the Vote, RTV Gear, http://www.rockthevote.com/rtv_gear.php.

32. Rock the Vote, Blog, http://blog.rockthevote.com (accessed November 26, 2005).

33. Rock the Vote, Partners, http://www.rockthevote.com/partners_rock.php (accessed November 26, 2005).

34. Rock the Vote and MySpace.com Join Forces to Mobilize Young Voters, *PR Newswire*, April 26, 2004.

35. Presentation by Ben Brandzel to Communication 640, Principles of Strategic Communication, American University, Washington, DC, November 17, 2004.

36. Ariana Eunjung Cha, Grass-roots Politics With Click of a Mouse; In Silicon Valley, Tech-Driven Support Groups, *The Washington Post*, October 25, 2004, A3.

37. Mark Hugo Lopez, Emily Kirby, and Jared Sagoff, *The 2004 Youth Vote*, The Center for Information & Research on Civic Learning & Engagement, 2005, http://www.civicyouth.org/quick/youth_voting.htm (accessed April 2, 2006).

38. Youth Voter Turnout Sharply Up in 2006 Midterm Elections, press release, The Center for Information & Research on Civic Learning & Engagement, November 8, 2006, www.civicyouth.org/PopUps/PR_midterm_06.pdf (accessed January 10, 2007).

39. Rock the Vote 2004 Election Campaign, http://www.rockthevote.com/success.php (accessed January 10, 2007).

40. Betsy Spethmann, Playing Politics, *Promo Magazine*, July 1, 2004, 8.

41. According to the online encyclopedia *Wikipedia,* skins are "custom graphical appearances (GUIs) that can be applied to certain software and Web sites in order to suit the different tastes of different users." Retrieved January 22, 2007. http://en.wikipedia.org/wiki/Skin_%28computing%29.

42. About Rock the Vote Mobile, http://www.rtvmo.com/about.htm (accessed January 22, 2005).

43. Todd Wasserman, Moto Rocks Vote Wirelessly, *Adweek*, April 14, 2004.

44. Rock the Vote and Motorola Team to Mobilize Electorate; Youth Market's the Target in Drive to Excite, Educate and Engage for 2004 Election; Mobile Handsets Provide Easy, Anytime-Anywhere Platform for Political Participation, *PR Newswire*, March 2, 2004.

45. Rock the Vote 2004 Election Campaign.

46. Spethmann, 8.

47. Since 1985, the Working Assets nonprofit group has offered Visa or Mastercard credit cards with ten cents of every purchase donated "to nonprofit groups working for peace, human rights, equality, education and the environment—at no extra cost to you." Cause Marketing Forum, Working Assets, http://www.causemarketingforum.com/framemain.asp?ID=132 (accessed July 15, 2006).

48. See Arvind Singhal and Everett M. Rogers, eds., *Entertainment-Education and Social Change: History, Research, and Practice.* (Mahwah, NJ: Erlbaum, 2004). See also *Entertainment Education and Health in the United States – Issue Brief* (Henry J. Kaiser Family Foundation, April 2004). Retrieved July 16, 2006. http://www.kff.org/entmedia/7047.cfm; and *New Media and the Future of Public Service Advertising, Case Studies* (The Henry J. Kaiser Family Foundation, March 2006), http://www.kff.org/entmedia/7469.cfm (accessed August 10, 2006).

49. Flanagan and Faison, 4.

50. Comments of Greg Livingstone, speaking at the "Born to Be Wired" conference, Yahoo headquarters, Sunnyvale, CA, July 24, 2003. The author was a presenter at this conference.

51. Giselle Abramovich, Clicking With Social Media Users Is Key for Marketers, August 8, 2006, http://www.dmnews.com/cms/dm-news/search-marketing/37782.html (accessed August 12, 2006).

52. http://www.whatmyspacemeans.com (accessed August 12, 2006).

53. Annette Bourdeau, The Kids Are Online, *Strategy*, May 1, 2005.

54. For example, to promote its film *The Ringer*, Twentieth Century Fox created special Web pages on MySpace for the fictional characters, as if they were real users. The tactic proved to be successful. Steve, one of the movie's characters, "has more than 11,000 friends," observed the article, "in other words, more than 11,000 consumers who visited his page requested to become a part of it. They respond to

Steve's fictional blog entries and become involved in the story." Michelle Halpern, *Marketing* 111, no. 3 (2006), 5.

55. For example, see Christine Harold, Pranking Rhetoric: "Culture Jamming" as Media Activism, *Critical Studies in Media Communication*, September 2004.

56. Jennifer Earl and Alan Schussman, Contesting Cultural Control: Youth Culture and Online Petitioning, in this volume.

57. For example, Google's AdSense and blog ad networks like Blogads have been set up to facilitate the process. "In a Forrester Research survey last month, 64 percent of marketers expressed interest in advertising on blogs." Brian Morrissey, Blogs Growing Into the Ultimate Focus Group, *Ad Week*, June 20, 2005, 12.

58. For a fuller discussion of these practices, see chapter 5, Born to Be Wired, in Montgomery, *Generation Digital*, 107–139. See also Joseph Turow, *Niche Envy: Marketing Discrimination in the Digital Age* (Cambridge, MA: MIT Press, 2006); and Jeff Chester, *Digital Destiny: New Media and the Future of Democracy* (New York: New Press, 2007).

59. Responding to concerns over online safety on the Web site, NewsCorp officials promised to appoint a "safety czar" to help assuage parents' fears. The company said nothing about marketing safeguards, although it does discuss advertisers' worries about the safety issues affecting their own effectiveness. Julia Angwin and Brian Steinberg, News Corp. Goal: Make MySpace Safer for Teens, *The Wall Street Journal*, February 17, 2006, B1.

60. Mark Naples, MySpace in the Marketing Mix, *United Online*, July 5, 2006, http://www.imediaconnection.com/content/10273.asp (accessed August 14, 2006).

61. Benkler has written a persuasive, well-documented treatise on most of the issues discussed in my chapter, along with other critical policies that will affect the future of democratic media in the digital era. In particular, see chapter 11, The Battle Over the Institutional Ecology of the Digital Environment, in Benkler, *The Wealth of Networks*.

62. Tim Wu, Network Neutrality, Broadband Discrimination, *Journal of Telecommunications and High Technology Law*, vol. 2, 141 (2003).

63. Mark Cooper, The Public Interest in Open Communications Networks, Consumer Federation of America, July 2004; Gary Larson and Jeffrey Chester, Song of the Open Road: Building a Broadband Network for the 21st Century, Center for Media Education, Washington, DC, 1999. Both documents accessed at Center for Digital Democracy: http://www.democraticmedia.org/resources/articles/openroad1.html (accessed August 10, 2006).

64. Adam Cohen, Why the Democratic Ethic of the World Wide Web May Be About to End, editorial, *The New York Times*, May 28, 2006.

65. Marguerite Reardon, FCC Changes DSL Classification, CNET News.com, http://news.com.com/FCC+changes+DSL+classification/2100-1034_3-5820713.html (accessed January 10, 2007).

66. Chester, The End of the Internet.

67. Cooper, The Public Interest in Open Communications Networks; Larson and Chester, Song of the Open Road.

68. For example, Tim Wu conducted a survey of network designs and usage restrictions in subscriber agreements and "acceptable use" policies of the ten largest cable operators and six major DSL operators. "On the whole," he found that these policies "favored the applications of the late 1990s (primarily the World Wide Web and other client-server applications), and disfavored more recent applications and usage, like home networking, peer-to-peer applications, and home telecommuting." Wu, 159.

69. Chester, The End of the Internet.

70. Chris Stern, The Coming Tug of War Over the Internet, *Washington Post*, Sunday, January 22, 2006.

71. Telephone interview with Tim Karr, July 25, 2006.

72. Public Relations Society of America, Pitching Blogs: Latest Type of Online Media Vehicle May Provide Valuable PR Opportunities, http://www.prsa.org/_Publications/magazines/0802news1.asp (accessed August 25, 2006).

73. http://www.savetheinternet.com (accessed August 12, 2006).

74. Interview with Karr.

75. http://www.savetheinternet.com (accessed August 12, 2006).

76. Tom Abate, Network Neutrality Advocates Hail AT&T's Concessions, *San Francisco Chronicle*, January 7, 2007.

77. Joseph Menn, *All the Rave: The Rise and Fall of Shawn Fanning's Napster* (New York: Crown Business, 2003); Trevor Merriden, *Irresistible Forces: The Business Legacy of Napster & the Growth of the Underground Internet* (Oxford, U.K.: Capstone, 2001).

78. Amanda Lenhart and Mary Madden, *Teen Content Creators and Consumers* (Washington, DC: Pew Internet & American Life Project, November 2, 2005), iii, http://www.pewinternet.org/PPF/r/166/report_display.asp (accessed July 25, 2006).

79. Robin D. Gross, DMCA Takes Full Effect – Millions of Americans Become Criminals, *EFFector Online Newsletter*, a publication of the Electronic Frontier Foundation, December 13, 2000, http://www.eff.org/effector/HTML/effect13.11.html (accessed June 11, 2005).

80. Lawrence Lessig, *Free Culture: How Big Media Uses Technology and the Law to Lock Down Culture and Control Creativity* (New York: Penguin, 2004), 141–43.

81. Bloggers' FAQ – Intellectual Property, Electronic Frontier Foundation, http://www.eff.org/bloggers/lg/faq-ip.php (accessed August 12, 2006).

82. Creative Commons, http://creativecommons.org/ (accessed August 12, 2006).

83. For example, one policy that has been the subject of intense battle in Washington, but is little understood outside the beltway, is the "broadcast flag," a digital marker that would make it technically impossible for consumers to copy content. The Federal Communications Commission ruling that would have mandated the incorporation of such devices into new digital broadcasting technologies was overturned by a court case brought by consumer groups, including Consumer Federation of America, Consumers Union, and Public Knowledge. For background on this issue, see Public Knowledge Web site at: http://www.publicknowledge.org/ (accessed January 10, 2007).

84. Holmes Wilson, Tiffiniy Cheng, and Nicholas Reville, interview, November 18, 2004.

85. Downhill Battle, iTunes Is Bogus, http://www.downhillbattle.org/itunes/index.html (accessed January 10, 2007).

86. Sam Howard-Spink, Grey Tuesday, Online Cultural Activism and the Mash-Up of Music and Politics, http://www.firstmonday.org/issues/issue9_10/howard/index.html (accessed January 10, 2007); Defiant Downloads Rise From Underground, *The New York Times*, February 25, 2004, E3.

87. Open Source Movement, Wikipedia, http://en.wikipedia.org/wiki/Open_source_movement (accessed August 12, 2006).

88. http://participatoryculture.org (accessed August 12, 2006).

89. The Administration's Agenda for Action, http://www.ibiblio.org/nii/NII-Agenda-for-Action.html (accessed August 10, 2006).

90. E-Rate, Federal Communications Commission, http://www.fcc.gov/learnnet (accessed December 15, 2006).

91. Greg Toppo, Schools Achieving a Dream; Near-universal Net Access, *USA Today*, June 9, 2004, 6D.

92. Judy Salpeter, Inside the Digital Divide, *Technology and Learning* 26, no. 8 (March 2006): 22.

93. Federal Communications Commission, Universal Service, http://www.fcc.gov/wcb/tapd/universal_ service (accessed November 12, 2006).

94. According to the Pew study, 70 percent of whites were online, compared to 57 percent of African Americans. The report also noted that almost all teenagers in households with income levels greater than $75,000 per year were online, most of them with high-speed connections. Lenhart, Madden, and Hitlin, *Teens and Technology*, http://www.pewinternet.org/PPF/r/162/report_display.asp (accessed August 12, 2006).

95. As Andy Carvin, who until recently ran the Educational Development Corporation's Digital Divide Network, explained, "According to 'A Nation Online,' the last major federal study on the subject published in 2004, Caucasian and Asian-American households were more likely to be online than African American households, which in turn were more likely to be wired than Latin households. And while overall Web use rose for each demographic group – about 60 percent of U.S. households were online, up from less than 20 percent in 1997 – the hierarchy of access has remained essentially the same for the last decade. Of the Income divide, the report revealed that more than 80 percent of households earning more than $70,000 per year are online, compared to barely 30 percent of households earning less than $15,000 a year." Andy Carvin, The Gap, *School Library Journal* 52, no. 3 (March 2006): 70.

96. John B. Horrigan, *Home Broadband Adoption 2006* (Washington, DC: Pew Internet & American Life Project, May 28, 2006), http://www.pewinternet.org/report_display.asp?r=184 (accessed August 10, 2006).

97. Robert W. McChesney and John Podesta, Let There Be Wi-Fi, *The Washington Monthly* 38, no. 1– 2 (January/February, 2006): 14, http://www.washingtonmonthly.com/features/2006/0601.podesta.html (accessed August 12, 2006).

98. Harold Feld, Gregory Rose, Mark Cooper, and Ben Scott, Connecting the Public: The Truth About Municipal Broadband, April 2005, http://www.freepress.net/docs/mb_white_paper.pdf (accessed August 12, 2006).

99. According to the American Public Power Association, the fourteen states that "have enacted laws that are anti-competitive barriers to [municipal] entry" into the broadband marketplace are Arkansas, Florida, Missouri, Minnesota, Nebraska, Nevada, Pennsylvania, South Carolina, Tennessee, Texas, Utah, Virginia, Washington, and Wisconsin. American Public Power Association, Private Providers Battle Cities and Towns, n.d. [2005], www.appanet.org/files/PDFs/TelecomFlyer.pdf. See also Baller Herbst Law Group, Proposed State Barriers to Public Entry, http://www.baller.com/pdfs/Baller_Proposed_State_Barriers.pdf (accessed August 12, 2006).

100. McChesney and Podesta.

101. Vikki Cravens, Dharma Dailey, and Antwuan Wallace, Can We Build a Wireless Communications Infrastructure That Values Everyone's Right to Communicate? Prometheus Radio Project, http://www.noemalab.org/sections/ideas/ideas_articles/cravens_wifi.html (accessed January 10, 2006).

102. As Heins explained in her book *Not in Front of the Children:* The "send" and "transmit" provisions of the law were dubious enough—applying, so it seemed, not only to one-on-one e-mail but to group

messages or online discussions among hundreds of people, if even one minor is present. But the provision criminalizing "display in a manner available" to minors was the truly loose cannon in the CDA. It applied to all of cyberspace—Web sites, archives and libraries, discussion groups, and mail exploders or listservs (emails sent to multiple recipients). And it did not require an identifiable young reader, merely the possibility of one. Marjorie Heins, *Not in Front of the Children: "Indecency," Censorship and the Innocence of Youth* (New York: Hill and Wang, 2001), 158–59.

103. See Heins, 157–79; See also chapter 3, A V-Chip for the Internet, in Montgomery, *Generation Digital*, 35–66.

104. William Triplett, Broadcast Indecency: Should Sexually Provocative Material Be More Restricted? *CQ Researcher*, April 16, 2004, 323–30.

105. Center for Democracy and Technology, The Court Challenge to the Child Online Protection Act, http://www.cdt.org/speech/copa/litigation.php (accessed March 24, 2006).

106. http://www.ala.org/ala/oif/ifissues/issuesrelatedlinks/cppacopacipa.htm#CIPA (accessed August 1, 2006).

107. Jim Puzzanghera, Bill Seeks to Block Access to MySpace in Schools; Legislation Is Prompted by Reports of Pedophiles Trolling Popular 'Social Networking' Sites, *The Los Angeles Times*, May 12, 2006, A26.

108. http://www.technorati.com/search/%22Deleting%20Online%20Predators%20Act%22 (accessed August 10, 2006).

109. Discussion: MySpace and Deleting Online Predators Act, http://www.danah.org/papers/MySpaceDOPA.html (accessed August 10, 2006).

110. The Commission on Online Child Protection, created with the passage of the Child Online Protection Act of 1998, studied a wide range of protective technologies and methods, including filtering and blocking services, labeling and rating systems, and the possibility of online "green spaces" containing only child-appropriate materials. COPA Commission, Final Report of the COPA Commission, Presented to Congress, October 20, 2000, http://www.copacommission.org/report (accessed December 3, 2006).

111. See Center for Information & Research on Civic Learning & Engagement at the University of Maryland, http://www.civicyouth.org (accessed August 10, 2006). See also University of Washington's Center for Communication & Civic Engagement, http://depts.washington.edu/ccce/Home.htm (accessed August 10, 2006).

Not Your Father's Internet: The Generation Gap in Online Politics

Michael Xenos

University of Wisconsin, Madison, Department of Communication Arts

Kirsten Foot

University of Washington, Seattle, Department of Communication

Introduction

Young people have traditionally been at the forefront of new information technology use, remaining at the top of Internet usage statistics and distinguishing themselves as early adopters of features such as instant messaging, peer-to-peer file sharing, and social networking tools.[1] As noted in the introduction to this volume, today's younger citizens are among the first to have come of age surrounded by digital technologies. They not only demonstrate fluency with new ways of communicating and connecting through them but are also helping to define the contours of their adoption. Despite a surge in voter turnout among eighteen- to twenty-four-year-olds in the 2004 presidential election, however, this age group has also typically been understood as trendsetters in the area of declining social capital, positioned at the forefront of falling rates of civic engagement and political participation.[2] With respect to voting in particular, researchers have long noted the general decline in youth voter turnout over the past few decades, interrupted only sporadically by spikes such as that seen in 2004.[3]

With an eye toward the dramatic growth in political communication and activity online in the past decade, many have hoped that developments in the political uses of new media might have the potential to help fuel a return of the young hypermedia generation to healthier patterns of electoral participation. In this way, we might imagine Howard Rheingold's Shibuya Crossing (2002) morphing into a raucous, youthful partisan convention.[4] On the surface, the events of the 2004 U.S. elections would seem to have buoyed such a convenient assessment of the intersections between trends in new media, politics and youth participation. During the 2004 primary process, citizens waged an online effort to "draft Wesley Clark" as a candidate, and the Howard Dean campaign took Web campaigning to new levels with the creative integration of tools such as Meetup.com and blogging. Although neither of these campaigns went beyond the primaries, the trend of increasing technological sophistication in the campaigns certainly did, as both major party presidential candidates fielded sophisticated campaign Web sites that supplemented traditional campaign Web site fare, such as candidate biographies and issues statements, with newer features like blogs, greater use of multimedia, and other interactive techniques.[5]

For their part, the wider electorate followed the candidates into cyberspace in 2004, in many ways led by young voters. Looking at the electorate as a whole, an estimated 75 million Americans, representing 37 percent of the adult population and more than half of American Internet users, went online to get information about the 2004 campaigns and engage in the political process; a substantial number, some 20 million, were estimated to have used the Internet to monitor campaign developments *daily* up to the close of the election.[6] In marked departure from their stereotypical indifference to politics, younger Americans were a surprisingly vibrant part of these broader statistics, showing marked increases in reading news of the election, talking about it with others, and thinking about the election and how the outcome might affect them.[7] An estimated 28 percent of eighteen- to twenty-nine-year-olds accessed *most* of their information about the 2004 election from the Internet, up from 22 percent in 2000, and more than those in any other age group.[8]

Most notably, turnout for young voters in the Internet-intensive 2004 election was the highest in more than a decade. Naturally, much of this increase can be explained by factors unrelated to new media, like the partisan tendencies of youth as a group and their particular interest in the Iraq war as a policy issue in 2004.[9] However, given the optimistic hopes associated with new media and the reliance of young people on the Internet for political information, it is tempting to view these developments as fueled in part by online politics. But a closer and more systematic look reveals a yawning generation gap between the Web production practices of traditional political actors (especially political candidates and their campaigns) and the preferences and expectations that today's young people bring to political cyberspace. As long as this gap remains unexplored, we believe optimism about the potential of online politics to reverse historic declines in youth participation in the electoral arena may be premature.

The generational disconnect in online politics is evident in the features typically used (and not used) by candidates campaigning online, and in the relative absence of direct (or even indirect) appeals to young voters on most candidate Web sites. To be sure, some of the roots of this gap lie in the exigencies of electoral competition in the United States, specifically the relatively small and historically shrinking part of the electorate represented by younger voters. However, we suggest that differences between campaigns' and young voters' perspectives on interactivity, control, and the value of coproduction may be significantly compromising the full potential of the Internet as a positive force for reinvigoration of youth political participation, thus exacerbating the problem.

In this chapter, we attempt to identify and help understand the basic structure of the chasm between typical uses of the Internet by political candidates and leaders, and the expectations of a younger cohort that is increasingly turning to the Internet for political information. To do so we draw on a variety of research data, ranging from feature analyses of campaign Web sites, to survey data and interviews with campaign site producers, as well as detailed focus group discussions with young citizens about their experiences with and expectations of campaign Web sites.

We begin by discussing a number of relevant patterns in the uses of digital media by young people, and their attitudes toward new communication technologies. By supplementing publicly available data from representative national samples with more finely grained responses from student focus groups conducted during the 2000 presidential election, we highlight important aspects of the modus operandi of young people's uses of the Internet for general, as well as political, purposes. Drawing from these data, we then derive a set of baseline expectations about Web production and Web use against which the potential for campaigns to capture and sustain the interest of young voters via the Internet may be assessed.

After establishing a basic understanding of youth preferences with respect to political uses of the Web, we turn to a counterpart examination of the contemporary practices of the primary players in the world of electoral politics online. In doing so, we focus on U.S. House, Senate, and gubernatorial candidates. Although presidential candidates typically get the bulk of attention from Internet observers and commentators, it is candidates for these lesser offices that make up the lion's share of online electoral campaigns, so we focus our attention on their efforts to campaign online. Here, we assess the feature characteristics of campaigns' Web production practices, drawing on prior analyses we conducted with other scholars of a very large sample of U.S. campaign Web sites.[10] With these data, we explore a distinction between different ways of approaching online campaigning we have demonstrated elsewhere, within the specific context of digital media, politics, and American youth. Specifically, we distinguish between Web production practices we identify as *adapting traditional campaigning to the Web* and those we identify as *Web campaigning*, which uniquely tap the interactive and networking potentials of digital media.[11] Consistent with other research in this area,[12] our data document the tendency of candidates to rely heavily on the former set of practices, remaining out of step with the expectations of a younger set of site visitors. Moving beyond basic features and design elements, we also discuss results from additional content analyses of campaign Web sites conducted during the 2002 and 2004 election cycles, which document the surprising paucity (given the relative dominance of younger citizens online) of direct or indirect appeals to youth on these sites.[13] Finally, we review research on similar campaign Web sites from the 2004 elections and discuss some of the patterns that emerged in online campaigning for the 2006 elections, which show the enduring nature of the disconnect between how candidates and young people appear to be engaging the political Web.

Having identified the basic structure of the generational gap between youth expectations about the presentation of materials and information on the Web and the actual products offered to young consumers of political information by those at the center of electoral politics online, we devote the remainder of the chapter to fundamental differences between younger citizens' and traditional political actors' approaches to digital media. Specifically, we explore a variety of ways of thinking about one of the Web's signature affordances, interactivity, as it relates to online politics and American youth. While most Web surfers are familiar with the general concept of interactivity, scholars have engaged in a lively debate over its essential elements.[14] Setting aside the search for consensus on the true nature of interactivity, we instead draw on some of the different dimensions of interactivity identified in these debates to explain more systematically the generation gap in online politics. By applying these ideas to the differences identified in the first two sections of the chapter, we hope to point the way toward strategies that political candidates and other practitioners of online politics can use to more effectively reach out to would-be young voters online.

Youth Demand for the Political Web

In considering the ways that younger voters use the Internet for political purposes, it is important to consider both the extent and nature of youth preferences and tastes for online political information resources. It is also important to consider some relevant aspects of youth Web use that fall outside of electoral politics or even the broader conceptions of politics found in other chapters of this volume. How much interest do young people exhibit in finding political information online? What kind of information do they seek? When young citizens use the Internet for political or other uses, what do they like to do, and how? By considering all of these factors together, we can begin to paint a picture of the kinds of expectations and preferences that young people bring to the Web when seeking information about politics, whether from Rock the Vote, the League of Women Voters, a candidate seeking office, or from their online peer network.

It is commonplace to refer to the crisis of youth disengagement from politics, but it is clear that in both the online environment in general and the world of politics and public affairs on the Web in particular, the youth cohort is active and vibrant. By a variety of measures, the demand for political information on the Web among young people rivals or eclipses that of those in other age groups. By now, most are aware of the widespread adoption of Internet technology among teens and eighteen- to twenty-nine-year-olds. Similarly, most are also familiar with the fact that survey data routinely shows this age group to possess relatively low general interest in politics as traditionally conceived (and practiced by the "dutiful citizen" described by Bennett in this volume). However, the presence of teens and eighteen- to twenty-nine-year-olds in the online world of news and political information is formidable. As noted earlier, the eighteen- to twenty-nine-year-old age group was the most likely age cohort to seek political information online during the 2004 elections.[15] And, if we look at a slightly broader category of turning to the Web for general news, we see similar patterns. Indeed, survey data suggests that eighteen- to twenty-nine-year-olds are the most likely to seek news from sources like the Internet and late-night comedy programs and are the least likely to seek news from the traditional channels of network programming and daily newspapers.[16] Simply comparing teens to adults in a head-to-head matchup, we find that regular Internet users in both categories get news from online sources at about the same rate, with "[t]hree-quarters (76%) of online teens and 73% of online adults" getting at least some news from the Internet.[17] Given that youth possess a lower interest in news generally,[18] these figures further highlight the preference of youth for new media over traditional channels. Moreover, as Kathryn Montgomery and others have documented, there has also been an explosion of youth-oriented political portals in recent years, with familiar sites like Rock the Vote being joined in a burgeoning youth political Web sphere by dozens of other youth sites related to campaigns and elections, and hundreds more devoted to broader public and social concerns.[19]

Another way of approaching the question of youth demand for politics online is through their reactions to the efforts of candidates to engage them through new media. Perhaps related to the fact that they have long been the most intensive users of the Web, youth are certainly among the Web's most discerning and demanding users. This point was made clear to one of the authors through focus groups conducted during the 2000 presidential primary elections with groups of college students. Equipped with a laptop, high-speed Internet connection, and projector, each group collectively navigated its way through several campaign and nonpartisan civic sites while a moderator elicited feedback from the group on various aspects of the sites. Student participants consistently provided highly detailed commentary, noting all manner of visual and technical details, including the specific placement of various items (and what that communicated), as well as the frequency with which sites were perceived to have been updated.

One focus group centered on the first ever online fundraising event, the John McCain campaign's "Cyber Express Webcast" in February 2000 which was promoted as a "live and interactive" event.[20] Those who wished to participate in the Webcast had to register with the campaign ahead of time and contribute $100 each to receive the URL for the hour-long Webcast. One member of the focus group research team registered for the event, and the Webcast was projected onto a large screen so that all focus group members were able to view it.

Webcast participants were invited to e-mail questions to the candidate during the event, and streaming video featured John McCain fielding questions—presumably a selection of those that were being received by the campaign via e-mail. The Webcast consisted of four primary information streams. A live video feed featured John and Cindy McCain sitting at a table, with Cindy McCain reading the questions and her husband answering them. In a window below the video feed, a text box streamed questions submitted by audience members. A series of still photographs and graphics were displayed in another part of the window illustrating Senator McCain's comments or emphasizing his issue positions. In addition, occasional "poll" questions and tallied results were presented to the audience.

Without question, the event featured an innovative use of the Internet, and was the first of several live Internet-based presentations by candidates during the 2000 campaign season and beyond. McCain's campaign took a risk by putting their candidate in a novel situation fraught with potential technical disaster. However, the focus group students— mostly committed Republicans and one strong McCain supporter—were disappointed that the McCain campaign did not make fuller use of Internet technologies during the Webcast. In contrast to the event's billing as a live and interactive Webcast, these young voters described it in bleaker terms. They perceived McCain's event to lack both the intimacy of an in-person fundraiser and the intensity of a live debate.

For example, even though the group witnessed the Webcast via a high-speed connection, the video feed froze frequently and the audio stream was interrupted every few minutes. "It's like the difference between going to a live concert and listening to a CD," one young man commented partway through the Webcast, "a bad CD." By the end of the event he had further downgraded his evaluation, saying, "It's worse than a CD."

Naturally, some of the technical aspects of this example are artifacts of a time when streaming video was not as reliable as it is today. However, focus group participants were also quite skeptical of the event on a deeper level. Of particular concern was the "interactive" nature of the question-and-answer process. For example, all subscribers to the Webcast could e-mail an unlimited number of questions and comments to the McCain Web site, and all e-mails received a nearly immediate response from a McCain staff member. Some questions were screened out by the McCain staff and not made visible to other subscribers, including a message submitted by a researcher containing intentionally inflammatory language. In all, more than 250 questions and comments were posted to the Webcast. During the fifty-minute event, McCain responded to twelve. Collectively, the students in the focus group submitted over a dozen questions, ranging from ones they considered "easy" to those they knew would be challenging for the candidate to address. Although McCain could not possibly have responded to all questions, he did not address any of the questions submitted by the focus group participants, nor any of the similarly oriented questions submitted by other Webcast viewers, which were visible to all viewers as they streamed across the bottom of the screen. The disenchanted consensus of the group was that McCain was only taking "softball questions." At least one other Webcast subscriber (not a focus group participant) expressed the same sentiment in the same terms, as he or she wrote in an e-mail to the Webcast that was incorporated in the video stream at the bottom of the Webcast:

Senator, almost all of the questions you've been asked (so far) have been softball type opportunities for you to speak without getting down to specifics. Don't you think that your supporters that contributed to this event want to get more details on your positions?

While most of the McCain staff responses to the Webcast viewers' e-mails were brief but appropriate, a staff member seemed to have misread the comment above, responding on McCain's behalf:

Thank you so much—I am honored by your support! (From: Staff (McCain Staff—Craig (#2)))

The McCain campaign, perhaps in an attempt to add another form of interactivity to the Webcast, also posted a series of single-question "polls" featuring a multiple-choice question to which subscribers could respond. Within five minutes, a bar chart of the tallied responses from subscribers was incorporated in the Webcast stream. Questions included "How often do you visit the McCain 2000 Web site?" (44 percent responded two to three times per week); and "Should paying down the national debt be part of the Republican platform?" (96 percent responded affirmatively). However, the focus group participants' response to the online questions may cause online pollsters to shudder. They expressed great delight in clicking on the response options they thought were least likely to be chosen by other subscribers, and several confessed to a habit of trying to "mess up the results" of online polls elsewhere on the Web.

Overall, the young voters in this focus group expressed desires for more creative uses of Web-based technologies, and a more informal, playful presentation of candidates. Suggestions offered by the participants included the use of cartoons, animation, and parody in addition to the still photos of McCain in mostly serious, formal poses. One participant commented, "People expect funnier images on the Internet . . . they expect the Internet to be weird and offbeat." Other participants agreed and added suggestion such as "Let's see him on vacation," and "Yeah, with his shirt off, or at least out of a suit." The consensus of the group was that McCain had used the Webcast like an expanded yet retrogressive TV broadcast—incorporating e-mail and instant calculation features, but restricting visual content to "talking heads" and still photos. As one participant noted, "the Internet has a lot more potential than what [McCain's staff] is doing with it."

At the end of the Webcast, the group concluded that while they appreciated the McCain staffers' attempts to respond at least briefly to each e-mail, their one-line acknowledgements did not constitute an "interactive" Web event. "This is not meeting John McCain," one student said, to which another added, "If he doesn't answer our questions, it's not interactive." Comments such as these provide a detailed picture of the generational gap in expectations and perceptions of interactivity.

Surveying the landscape of contemporary survey research on youth Web use beyond the terrain of electoral politics, we can consider from yet another angle how "interactive" may have a very different meaning to young people than to professional political consultants. As discussed by others in this volume, today's youth are well represented in online activities with content production and modification components (e.g., see the chapters by Earl and Schussman, Howard, Levine, and Raynes-Goldie and Walker in this volume). Within the relevant survey data from recent years, a recurrent theme is the demand for interactive features that allow users to exchange information of all sorts (messages, images, files) and to generally take an active part in communicative and expressive processes. For example, while e-mail remains the "killer app" for older Internet users, teens of today display a clear preference for instant messaging (IM). Even more telling, younger users of IM are also significantly more likely than older users to do things like personalize their "away messages," rather than simply use the standard options provided by most IM client software.[21] Similar patterns are also evident in the use of each new, and typically more interactive, element of

Web communication. Commonly referred to as "Web 2.0," an emerging category of applications such as social networking sites, blogs, and other collaboratively authored documents is extremely popular among young people. The dialogical and coproductive nature of the type of interactivity manifested in these applications affords "communicative, creative, and social uses" of the Internet—and appeals to young people.[22] Indeed, in testimony to the House Committee on Energy and Commerce Subcommittee on Telecommunications and the Internet, Pew researcher Amanda Lenhart summarized the appeal of social networking sites to younger users as stemming largely from their ability to enable them to create and share content, and to communicate through a broad variety of channels such as messaging, blogs, and other posting mechanisms.[23] Clearly, coproductive interactivity is foundational to the way that young people, more than any other age group, engage with the Internet.

Looking at these developments within the context of sanguine hopes for the Internet as a convenient pathway for young people toward greater participation in electoral politics evokes mixed feelings of hope and caution. To begin with, there is clearly a significant demand among young people for political information online as well as for tools to engage in a wide variety of political actions. To be sure, offline indicators of youth interest in politics remain underwhelming, and older adults have been more likely than younger adults to vote and to contribute to an electoral campaign or interest group. However, data on the frequency of online political information seeking among young people suggest that their greater rates of technology adoption may counterbalance these trends. Moreover, research on the general characteristics of youth new media use reinforces the notion that young people turn to the Internet not to join a passive audience for politics, but rather to seek their own audiences and engage in active processes of creation and interaction, as Peter Levine points out in this volume. As noted earlier, a few researchers have documented the emergence and growth of a variety of youth-oriented political portal Web sites to meet this demand, with many offering highly interactive and occasionally edgy political content that appears to be directly in line with these preferences.[24] However, if the rising tide of political activity on the Web is to bring a significant number of young people into the electoral process, political candidates and other actors central to the online world of electoral politics need to offer content and features that also resonate with the information seeking and sharing modes of online youth. In the next section, we will review a variety of research on candidate Web practices that provides insights into the extent to which candidates have met this challenge in prior elections.

Political Candidates on the Web

In 1994, Diane Feinstein launched the first ever political Web site;[25] this is sometimes referred to as the "Kitty Hawk moment" for online political campaigning. In the election years since, the use of the Web by political candidates has risen steadily. In the 1996 campaigns, approximately one-third of political candidates featured a campaign Web site.[26] Just two years later, the proportion nearly doubled as 63 percent of candidates took their campaigns online.[27] By the 2002 elections the proportion reached 73 percent,[28] which recent research suggests may be a plateau for online candidate campaigning, with comparable 2004 percentages hovering around the high 60s to low-to-mid 70s.[29]

As a growing number of people who have produced their own Web pages know, however, a mere presence in cyberspace does not in any way guarantee traffic to one's Web site, or return visits from those who happen to stop by.[30] In this respect, the kinds of content and features offered on Web sites and how useful or attractive they are to visitors are important factors. In this section, we review findings from the most comprehensive efforts to date in tracking the content and features offered by political candidates through the Web, along with some more recent examples that provide a glimpse of contemporary developments. Although a few encouraging signs may be found in these data, the overarching picture is of a significant gap between the online sensibilities of young people and the ways in which the vast majority of candidates for office in the United States conduct the online portions of their campaigns.

From August through Election Day 2002, we worked with a team of researchers to draw samples of several hundred Web sites produced by candidates for U.S. House, Senate, and gubernatorial seats nationwide on a weekly basis for feature analysis (see Table 1). At the end of the data collection period, all of our observations were merged into a single database, providing a detailed picture of how those at the center of electoral politics were incorporating the Web into their campaign strategies.[31] More than just a listing of features and percentages, we believe these data provide important indicators of the shape, structure, and tendencies of the emerging world of online political campaigning. By looking comprehensively at campaigns' Web production practices (what candidates do, and do not do, with their campaign Web sites) we can examine their posture toward the Web, and by extension how they might appear to young people using the Web as an information source about campaigns and elections.

We have argued elsewhere that some features employed by campaign organizations on their sites reflect the Web production practice of adapting traditional campaigning to the Web environment.[32] Providing basic information about the candidate, including background information and issue statements, as well as managing interactions with potential supporters both within and outside the district, are characteristic of traditional campaigning,[33] whether conducted offline or online. We operationally defined this Web practice as consisting of fourteen specific features, easily recognizable as the online corollaries of traditional campaign tools, including candidate biographies, issue statements, contact and donation information, campaign news releases and calendars, information about voter registration, lists of endorsements, texts of speeches, information about contributors, and encouragement to write letters to local newspaper editors.

Features and structural elements that manifest more novel, Web-specific techniques evidence a practice we have termed *Web campaigning*. The practice of Web campaigning is indicated by the production of elements that may have prototypes in traditional campaigning, but are uniquely or especially catalyzed by the Web. Various scholars have attempted to identify characteristics of the Web that differentiate it from other media channels and environments, such as the ease with which multiple forms of media can be integrated and disseminated, the interpenetration of consumption and production processes, and the potentially unbounded network enabled by hyperlinks,[34] and we have integrated these characteristics into our concept of Web campaigning. Specifically, we conceptualized this Web practice as manifested on campaign Web sites via fifteen specific features, including linking to other Web sites, enabling users to make contributions via the Web, providing the capability to send links to the campaign site via e-mail, provision of toolkits to facilitate Web-based political actions, downloadable electronic campaign paraphernalia, provision of multimedia content, interactive polls, acceptance of visitor comments, onsite delivery of letters to local newspaper editors, interactive campaign calendars, online events, and the ability to personalize or individualize site content. Analysis of the overall prevalence of each practice showed that campaigns were far more likely to adapt traditional campaigning to the Web than to engage in Web campaigning.

Table 1
Campaigns' Web practices in the 2002 U.S. elections

Feature	Sites with Feature Number	Percent	N*
Adapting traditional campaigning to the Web			
Campaign Web site	1168	100	1168
Candidate biography	965	92	1045
Issue positions	936	90	1045
Campaign contact information	491	83	589
E-mail address	851	81	1045
Donation information	837	80	1044
Campaign news	427	73	589
Signup to volunteer	721	69	1044
Online donations	321	55	589
Sign up to receive e-mail	429	41	1044
Campaign calendar	352	34	1044
Voter registration information	321	31	1044
Endorsements	154	26	589
Information about sending letters to the editor	29	5	589
Web campaigning			
Links to external Web sites	634	76	831
Photos of campaign events	250	42	589
Campaign advertisements	109	19	589
Send links from site	87	10	865
Web toolkits	80	9	858
Audio or video materials	52	9	589
Electronic paraphernalia	79	9	865
Site search engine	68	8	858
Text of speeches	49	8	589
Pop-up windows	55	6	865
Online polls	41	5	865
Online letters to editors	25	3	865
Visitor comments	20	2	865
Interactive calendar	2	<1	589
Online events	3	<1	865

*N's vary due to variations in the frequency with which different features were coded throughout the election cycle.

Interpreting these data from the perspective of the young political information consumer, the blunt reality is that candidates do not appear to be doing a very good job of using the Web to reach out to those who are arguably the most likely to be receptive to political Web communication. On the upside, the data do suggest that candidates and their campaigns appreciate the efficiency of using the Web to get out basic information about themselves and their quests for office. Biographical information and statements about various political issues were found on 92 and 90 percent of sites in our analysis, respectively. Given that young people have demonstrated a considerable appetite for this kind of information online, this is a good sign. But if one considers interactive features more in line with the typical Web experiences and tastes of younger voters, campaign sites come off more as static information booths than as dynamic places to connect, create, and interact. Thus

Table 2
Summary of Web practices

Practice	Number of Features in Practice	Number of Features on Sites							
		Minimum	Maximum	25th Percentile	Median	75th Percentile	Mean	SD	N
Adapting traditional campaigning	14	1	13	7.0	9.0	11.0	8.8	2.43	589
Web campaigning	15	0	10	1.0	2.0	3.0	2.2	1.68	446

based on our analysis of close to twelve hundred different candidate Web sites from the 2002 elections, we believe it is fair to say that many if not most campaign Web sites are markedly skewed more toward the parents of today's younger voters than toward youths themselves.

As if this were not enough, additional research on a random subset of campaign sites from 2002 has shown that even in the simple act of providing information on their issue stances, candidates often made little effort to reach out to younger voters. In a study of the rhetorical characteristics of candidate issue statements, Bennett and Xenos (2004) examined the frequency with which candidate Web site issue statements featured either direct or indirect appeals to younger voters as a group, and also the frequency with which older voters were similarly targeted.[35] The study sought to identify portions of the issue statement pages that made age-specific appeals either through direct, textual references, or simply through the presence of images or photos featuring younger or older people. Despite the disparities between how likely younger versus older voters were (and are) to seek issue information online, the study found that while candidates were comfortable reaching out to younger voters (typically when discussing issues like education), they were more likely to reach out to the senior demographic through their online issue materials. Even more than the relative emphasis of candidates on certain types of features in campaign Web site design, this finding further reinforces the impression held by many young people that candidates and politicians simply aren't speaking to them, even when they are using the medium of choice for the younger generation.

Although we analyzed a smaller number of campaign sites in 2004 (one hundred) our findings were consistent with those from 2002, reflecting a relative preference among campaigns to use their Web sites for providing information rather than for more interactive practices such as involving site visitors with the campaign, connecting them with other political actors, and mobilizing supporters to become advocates.[36] In another recent study, Conners examined the Web sites of 139 major- and third-party candidates for the U.S. Senate in 2004,[37] focusing in particular on their use of tools such as Meetup.com (a site that uses the Web to organize offline meetings for groups of all kinds), blogs, and features facilitating campaign involvement, such as donation and volunteering. Consistent with our data from 2002 and 2004, this study also points to relatively infrequent use of the kinds of interactive features that young people have come to expect from online communication. Specifically, Conners found links to Meetup.com on only 16.3 percent of Senatorial campaign Web sites in 2004, and blogs on only 26.3 percent (2005).

To their credit, candidates appear to be moving slowly in the direction of greater interactivity in campaign Web development, but the overarching tendency is still toward a style of

Web communication that is significantly out of step with the tastes and preferences of most young people seeking political information online. For example, a recent informal survey of candidate Web sites from the most competitive 2006 Senate races suggests that while features such as blogs and podcasts were employed on about one of three campaign sites, they were still absent from the majority. Given that we have typically found candidates in the most hotly contested races to be those with the most sophisticated Web sites,[38] this suggests that U.S. electoral campaigns in general are still largely reluctant to engage in more interactive Web practices. Moreover, many of the blogs currently offered on campaign Web sites tend to feature mostly press-release–style entries, and do not always offer users the opportunity to comment on posts. Where commenting is enabled, it is typically restricted to those willing to provide not only their name and e-mail address, but also, in some cases, the visitor is required to provide even more information, such as additional contact information, along with demographic, and issue interest information. For example, at the time of this writing, Jim Talent's 2006 Senate campaign Web site allowed only those willing to sign up as volunteers for the campaign (and indicate what types of volunteer activities they are willing to perform) to comment on the site blog.[39]

Two Approaches to Interactivity on the Web

In the preceding sections, we have demonstrated how the Web production practices of contemporary campaigns diverge significantly from the tastes and expectations of younger Internet users. Based on the best available indicators of what young people are looking for in an electoral politics experience on the Web, and what campaign organizations are providing, a substantial gulf is evident between them. If this gap is left unaddressed, we believe future developments in online campaigning will fail to attract all but the most politically oriented young voters into greater involvement with the electoral system. In the long run, this means that the potential of new media to help reverse significant declines in youth political involvement may go unrealized. In the following sections, we provide a conceptual map to help interested parties prevent such a tragic, missed opportunity. As mentioned at the outset, the concept of interactivity is at the center of this map, and we believe it is the key to understanding not only *why* candidates and young voters may be missing each other online but also *how* this disconnection may be remedied. Unfortunately, owing to the complex nature of both Internet technology and political behavior, there is no easy solution to the problem, and so readers will not find a simple recipe for online youth political engagement in these pages. Rather, we hope to provide the conceptual foundation for such efforts, and to highlight examples as well as questions that appear especially ripe for further study and experimentation.

In many ways interactivity is the defining element of Web communication. Some even go as far as to say that interactivity and new media are synonymous.[40] As such, the concept of interactivity has received a significant amount of attention from empirical researchers in marketing and communication. These studies emphasize the possibility for greater levels of interactivity present in a Web site to lead to all kinds of positive outcomes, including greater cognitive engagement with site content, increases in the perceived favorability of site producers, and the persuasive impact of the communication. Several studies of interactivity and political communication through the Web have been conducted on samples of college students, a substantial portion of the youth voting demographic. For example, Sundar et al. conducted an experiment in which three versions of a fictitious political candidate

Web site were given to study participants (for each Web site, content was held constant, while interactivity was manipulated by creating deeper and more complex levels of clickable pages).[41] Consistent with the idea that young people are favorably predisposed toward interactive site content, interactivity was shown to have a demonstrable positive impact on college students' perceptions of the candidate, as well as agreement with his or her issue stances.[42] In a similar study, Warnick et al. demonstrated the positive effects on college students of two different types of interactivity found in campaign Web sites: "text-based interactivity" consisting of features such as first-person text and captioned photos, as well as "campaign-to-user interactivity" consisting of features that enable two-way exchanges of information and correspondence between the user and the campaign.[43] Moving beyond simple persuasive effects on site visitors, Tedesco has also demonstrated the impact of interactivity on college students' feelings of political efficacy, or the extent to which they felt confident in their abilities to perform traditional citizenship roles and to trust that the political system would be responsive to such behavior.[44] After an interactive experience with political Web content, students reported increased feelings of efficacy and trust in the political system. Clearly then, we know that in general terms the increasing prevalence and sophistication of online campaigning stands a good chance of providing an attractive avenue to political participation for many young adults.

But, as we have discussed in the preceding sections, campaigns tend to favor simple information distribution over interactivity in their Web production practices. Moreover, as the McCain example illustrates, even when candidates attempt to be "interactive" the results are not always clear-cut or positive. Existing bodies of empirical research as well as ongoing theoretical debates reveal a variety of different dimensions to this quintessential aspect of digital communication.[45] Scholars agree that there are several variants of interactivity, even if they do not agree on a schema for characterizing forms of interactivity. With respect to questions about how new media are being used in the arena of electoral politics and the extent to which such uses promote greater involvement among younger voters, however, the specifics and outcomes of these debates are not as immediately relevant as some of the key concepts we see represented in the world of online political campaigning. We contend that not all forms of interactivity are as convincing or appealing to young people as site producers would like.

Two concepts from contemporary discussions of interactivity are particularly helpful in understanding the disconnect between young voters and candidates online. The first of these is the notion of interactivity as transaction between the site producer and site visitor. Although Web-based transaction can take a variety of forms, one important form is media customization. For example, you might visit a Web site and in the course of doing so provide some basic information about yourself. In response to that information, the Web site provides you with content tailored to the information you provided, offering you information on products you may be interested in or the weather conditions outside your home. By reacting to information you provide (consciously or not) this form of interactivity helps to create a custom communication experience, and like other forms is associated with positive attitudinal outcomes.[46]

A second concept from scholarly discussions of interactivity that is especially useful in the context of youth, new media, and civic engagement is that of shared control between the producer and the collectivity of site visitors. When interactivity is approached in this way, the content and experience of Web communication is coproduced by both users and Web site creators. This form of interactivity can at times stand in direct tension with transaction.

At a technical level, visitor or user control simply refers to the fact that, when surfing the Internet, you have a varying degree of control over what content is accessed, how it is accessed, and so forth. While there are only a few different ways of reading the newspaper, there are an almost unlimited number of ways you can explore the Web site of the *New York Times*, and by posting a comment to a discussion board on the *Times* Web site, you can even exert a small but noticeable level of control over site content. When a comment you post is responded to by other site visitors, the result is a collaboration between the *Times* and its readership in the production of the site. By applying these two concepts of interactivity to problems of youth political engagement and online campaigning, we can begin to get greater purchase on the generation gap in online politics.

Within the realm of online campaigning, our research and that of others suggests that to the extent that campaign organizations are likely to further pursue interactivity, they will do so through a carefully managed form of exchange that is manifest in transactional techniques of Web campaigning.[47] In practical terms, a transactional approach to interactivity is a preference for features that return strategic goods for the campaign while involving a relatively small investment of resources. As strategic organizations with a concrete goal (electoral victory), campaigns have structural imperatives to carefully manage and utilize all resources at their disposal, and resources that may be exchanged through the Internet are certainly no exception.

Typically, transactional techniques are achieved by creating online structures on campaign sites that facilitate the collection of personal information and contributions from site visitors.[48] For instance, one of the primary ways campaigns provide interactivity to site visitors is through online structures that collect and manage e-mail addresses, a relatively straightforward conduit for two-way exchange.[49] Viewed through the lens of the technique of transaction, site visitors' e-mail addresses are more than just a way to interact. Rather, they can also be understood as a resource that can be harvested and managed via the campaign site when appropriate online structures are produced and configured strategically. Beyond collecting and managing e-mail addresses, some campaign organizations have extended their transactional capacity to build ongoing and highly personalized relationships with site visitors. These campaigns have the capability to combine data provided intentionally and consciously by the site visitor with additional data about the site visitor that he or she may or may not be aware of. The visitor's experiences on the Web site, for example, including the frequency of page views, may be combined with data about the site visitor obtained from outside sources, such as party registration, turnout history, contribution record, and even purchasing patterns (from credit card company databases). These "constituent relationship management" (or CRM) systems attempt to extend to the political realm the powerful marketing tools commonly found in the business community, with the goal of providing relevant information to individually identified site visitors, and serving important strategic goals, principally fundraising, and efficient, effective persuasion.[50]

Keeping in mind the strategic imperative of campaign organizations, it is thus unsurprising that forms of interactivity other than those that serve a clear transactional purpose are less attractive. For example, online events such as the McCain Cyber Express Webcast, or even less complicated features such as interactive message boards, provide little in the way of tangible resources for campaigns, in comparison to their costs in terms of technical and staff resources. Indeed, this cost–benefit rationale is precisely what Stromer-Galley explored in her early study of the low frequency with which campaign Web sites engage in what she termed "human-interactive features."[51] Based on interviews with campaign staff members and an analysis of candidate Web sites in the 1996 and 1998 elections, she concluded that, for campaign organizations, interactive features like "direct e-mail exchanges and Web boards were not conducive to the objective of winning an election," and represented a style of Web campaigning that visibly "drains resources from more pressing campaign needs."[52] In addition, features that enable coproductive forms of interactivity, such as message boards, multiauthored blogs, and chats, allow users to produce content directly on a campaign site.[53] Such features can also pose tangible threats to the ability of campaigns to control their message. As a campaign professional interviewed in Howard's study of new media campaigning put it, "Anybody involved in a campaign. . . is always concerned about control. Chat is difficult to control."[54] Thus we see that by looking at interactivity in campaign Web practices through the lens of transaction, some forms of interactivity (those that enable fundraising and sophisticated targeting of persuasive messages) are more appealing than others (those that are relatively more costly in resources and compromise efforts to control campaign messages).

In direct contrast to the transactional approach to interactivity as a two-way exchange (preferably one that favors the campaign organization) is the notion of interactivity as user-control, which is more consistent with the preferences of younger Internet users. In general, youth tend to be suspicious of transactional relationships with campaign organizations and favor the more coproductive elements of Internet communication. For example, in a particularly telling portion of one of the focus groups discussed earlier in which college students participated in guided discussions of a variety of political Web sites during the 2000 campaigns, participants provided some interesting reflections on one of the principal ways in which transactional interactivity is instantiated on campaign Web sites, the personalization of site content.

I really don't like giving them all that information. I can see all the mail that will come in a few days. . . Even though I'm going to vote for Gore, I wouldn't want to get a bunch of mail. I wouldn't want them to have all that information that they don't need. I don't understand why they need my address, nor should they need my phone number for the Web page.

Another participant added the following comment:

I don't like the idea of personalizing a political site because if I personalize it for me, how can I tell what they are telling someone else? I like the idea of the same content and that I'm seeing what everyone else is seeing; otherwise, they could be changing their story for someone else.

Precisely because they are among the Web's most savvy and discerning users, younger voters are keenly aware of the transactional nature of many popular forms of campaign interactivity. Although Howard expresses a concern that most Internet users are unaware of some of the ways in which they are involved in transactional interactivity, these comments, along with the greater technical sophistication of younger Internet users suggests that they are not only aware but likely to be turned off by more transactional techniques of Web campaigning.

Unsurprisingly, some of the most popular forms of interactivity among young people are those that are coproductive—that is, they bring the user into the process of producing and manipulating the content of the site. This is an important element of interactivity as user-control, and represents what is arguably the most favored aspect of the medium for the younger generation. As mentioned earlier, the concept of user-control has a relatively straightforward technical meaning; by clicking, typing, accessing, and surfing a site the user provides input that generates noticeable changes in output. But at a deeper level, control is also about power. This notion of a shift in power is most strikingly seen in the kinds of interactive activities popular among younger Internet users—when these users engage in the "communicative, creative, and social uses" of the Internet,[55] they are taking advantage of the vastly greater level of control afforded by Web 2.0 applications, which enable them to create their own content, and share it with others in an ongoing and multifaceted exchange. At the same time, campaign organizations also have strategic imperatives to resist these forms of coproductive interactivity, on the very same grounds that they shift power, and control, away from the campaign itself.

Conclusion: Bridging the Generation Gap in Online Politics

It is hoped that through the foregoing discussion we have highlighted the need to be cautious about assuming that simply adding new media to old electoral politics will entice new and younger voters to greater participation. At the surface, we have documented the vast differences between the ways in which younger Internet users are accustomed to engaging with new communications technology, and the ways in which the principal actors in the arena of electoral politics, candidates, have been expanding their campaign operations into cyberspace. At a deeper level, we hope we have introduced concepts that can help candidates, and the broader public, to understand the nature of these differences. In our view, understanding the generation gap in online politics as a clash between differing notions of interactivity clearly identifies the ways in which these differences must be negotiated, if the true potential of the Internet as a medium capable of facilitating significant changes in political participation among American youth is to be realized. Simply put, if greater numbers of young voters are to be attracted to the system of electoral politics through the Web, candidates and their campaigns will need to learn how to balance the competing logics of transactional and coproductive interactivity. A balance, rather than a wholesale embrace, of coproduction is suggested because in the present system it is unrealistic to expect candidates to ignore the structural aspects of the electoral system that force campaigns to behave strategically. It is also reasonable to expect that while it may not be their favored form of interactivity, young voters accept some elements of transactional activity as part of political life.

This conclusion points toward two practical ways in which Web production practices might begin to bridge the generation gap in online politics: inclusive and transparent forms of transactional interactivity, and creative ways of splitting the difference between transactional and coproductive Web practices. Earlier, we pointed out that candidates in the 2002 election cycle were more likely to use their Web campaigns to target senior rather then junior citizens. One obvious way in which to make transactional, targeted forms of online campaigning more attractive to younger voters is simply to address them more often. As one of the students in the focus groups from the 2000 campaign study remarked in reference to a campaign site menu of pages for specific groups (e.g., women, firefighters, Latinos), "There's nothing wrong with being specific if you include everyone, but if you don't include someone then you are going to turn them away." In addition, it is especially important for campaigns deploying transactional Web campaigning techniques to supply transparent statements about how information is being collected and used by the campaign in its efforts to achieve electoral victory. There is a general need for more campaign sites to post these kinds of statements about their privacy policies, but the sophistication of younger Internet users suggests that it is of particular importance if younger voters are not to be put off by candidate Web sites in significant numbers. To their credit, an increasing number of campaigns are already moving in this direction, offering specific pages and materials targeted to young voters and providing clear statements about the privacy policies of the campaign. However, we believe further effort in these areas is needed if more young citizens are to be drawn into electoral politics through online campaigns.

With respect to creatively splitting the difference between transactional and coproductive forms of interactivity, there are also some fortunate (although all too rare) examples that help to illustrate the point. Perhaps the most famous example is that of the Howard Dean campaign's innovative and remarkable deployment of new media during the 2004 democratic presidential primary. In their study of the Dean campaign, Iozzi and Bennett document the ways in which many of its techniques represented a pioneering qualitative shift in American campaigning away from the traditional "War Room" style (which places a premium on message control) and toward a more fluid and dynamic "networked" style of campaigning.[56] In doing so, the campaign was able to realize tangible benefits from coproductive interactivity in return for modest compromises in message control. Less extreme (and less risky from the perspective of traditional campaigns) examples of creative compromise between competing forms of interactivity may be found in some of the Web campaigns for the 2006 elections. For example, on Rick Santorum's 2006 Senate campaign Web site, a "Running with Rick" campaign blog was offered, complete with comment functions.[57] Perhaps as a way of counterbalancing the costs of this coproductive element (in campaign staff and possible risks), however, when a user clicked on the "comment" button beneath each blog entry, they were directed to a registration page for the site, which asked for pieces of personal information, along with whether one identified with one of twenty different "coalitions," which included "youth" and "young professional" alongside more traditional groupings such as "seniors" and "women."[58] Another example from 2006 was the Bob Menendez for Senate campaign site, which in addition to the official campaign blog featured "diaries" or other Web logs created by individuals.[59] Similarly to the Santorum site, the Menendez site required would-be campaign bloggers to register with the site (i.e., provide the campaign with a useful informational resource). But once registered, the user was offered their own venue for creating and sharing content with others.[60]

To be sure, these examples are certainly not flawless from the perspective of the average young Internet user who may be curious about the campaigns. Moreover, the extent to which the coproductive elements in the immediately preceding examples were filtered and managed by the campaigns is unclear, potentially creating only more sophisticated, Web 2.0 versions of the McCain Cyber Express Webcast. Indeed, if opportunities for coproduction are only displayed for effect, and youthful voices and nonsoftball questions are systematically avoided, then there is a distinct possibility that such efforts will be for naught. To paraphrase one of the youth focus group participants quoted earlier, such efforts may come off as no better than poor-quality MP3 files, or worse, broken or virus-ridden MP3 files. However, on a more positive note, if young voters' voices are represented in experiments such as these, and the coproduction opportunities offered are genuine, then our research suggests that younger citizens curious about the campaigns will be more likely to linger on the sites, send their links to friends in their social networks, and begin to engage with a system that their demographic group has been disengaged from for a considerable period. To be sure, more research and experimentation in this vein are needed in order to find the optimal mix of features required to satisfy both the strategic demands of campaigns and the social good of simulating greater numbers of young people to participate in the electoral system. But we believe it is essentially through the negotiation of these competing forms of interactivity that political practice on the Web must pass if the generation gap in online politics is to be effectively bridged.

Notes

1. Jared Bernstein, Born Digital, Not Yesterday: Next-generation Web User Seeks Interactivity, *Econtent* 29, no. 4 (2006), last accessed June 15, 2007, at http://www.econtexting.com/Articles/articlereader.aspx?ArticleID-15480; J. Cole and M. Suman, *The UCLA Internet Report: Surveying the Digital Future Year Three* (Los Angeles, CA: UCLA Center for Communication Policy, 2003), last accessed June 15, 2007, at http://www.forbes.com/fdc/mediaresourcecenter/UCLA03.pdf.

2. Robert Putnam, *Bowling Alone: The Collapse and Revival of American Community* (New York: Simon and Schuster, 2000).

3. Mark H. Lopez, Emily Kirby, and Jared Sagoff, The Youth Vote 2004, Center for Information and Research on Civic Learning and Engagement, 2005, last accessed June 15, 2007, at http://www.civicyouth.org/PopUps/FactSheets/FS_Youth_Voting_72-04.pdf.

4. Howard Rheingold, *Smart Mobs: The Next Social Revolution* (Cambridge, MA: Perseus, 2002).

5. Andrew P. Williams, Kaye D. Trammell, Monica Postelnicu, Kristen D. Landreville, and Justin D. Martin, Blogging and Hyperlinking: Use of the Web to Enhance Viability During 2004 U.S. campaigns, *Journalism Studies* 6, no. 2 (2005): 177–86.

6. Lee Rainie, Michael Cornfield, and John Horrigan, *The Internet and Campaign 2004* (Washington, DC: Pew Internet and American Life Project, 2005), last accessed June 15, 2007, at http://www.pewinternet.org/pdfs/PIP_2004_Campaign.pdf.

7. Molly W. Andolina and Kristen Jenkins, Don't Write Off the Kids Just Yet... Hopeful Prospects for Youth in the 2004 Election (paper presented at the Pre-APSA Conference on Political Communication. Chicago, IL, September 1, 2004).

8. The comparative figures for those in other age groups reporting to have gotten most of their election news from the Internet in 2004 are as follows: All, 17%; 30–49, 21%; 50–64, 11%; 65+, 4% (Andrew Kohut and Scott Keeter, *Debates More Important to Young Voters, Young People More Engaged, More Uncertain* [Washington, DC: Pew Research Center for the People and the Press, 2004], http://people-press.org/commentary/pdf/99.pdf), last accessed June 15, 2007.

9. Thomas E. Patterson, Young Voters and the 2004 Election (2004), http://www.ksg.harvard.edu/presspol/vanishvoter/Releases/Vanishing_Voter_Final_Report_2004_Election.pdf, last accessed June 15, 2007.

10. Kirsten Foot and Steven Schneider, *Web Campaigning* (Cambridge, MA: MIT Press, 2006).

11. Kirsten Foot, Steven Schneider, Michael Xenos, and Meghan Dougherty, Candidates' Web Practices in the 2002 House, Senate, and Gubernatorial Elections, *Journal of Political Marketing*, in press.

12. Jennifer Stromer-Galley, On-line Interaction and Why Candidates Avoid It, *Journal of Communication* 50, no. 4 (2000): 111–32.

13. Mike Xenos and Lance Bennett, Young Voters and the Web of Politics: The Promise and Problems of Youth-oriented Political Content on the Web, in *Young Citizens in the Digital Age: Young People, Citizenship, and ICTs*, ed. B. D. Loader (New York: Routledge, in press).

14. See Sally J. McMillan, and Jang-Sungong Young Hwang, Measures of Perceived Interactivity: An Exploration of the Role of Direction of Communication, User Control, and Time in Shaping Perceptions of

Interactivity, *Journal of Advertising* 31, no. 3 (2002): 29–42; Dyung-Kwan Sohn and B. Lee, Dimensions of Interactivity: Differential Effects of Social and Psychological Factors, *Journal of Computer Mediated Communication* 10, no. 3 (2005): article 6; and Shyan S. Sundar, Theorizing Interactivity's Effects, *Information Society* 20, no. 5 (2004): 385–89, for helpful reviews.

15. Rainie, Cornfield, and Horrigan.

16. Rainie, Cornfield, and Horrigan.

17. Amanda Lenhart, Mary Madden, and Paul Hitlin, *Teens and Technology* (Washington, DC: Pew Internet and American Life Project, 2005), last accessed June 15, 2007, at http://pewinternet.org/PDF/r/162/report_display.asp.

18. See Bennett, also Levine, this volume.

19. See Montgomery, this volume; Xenos and Bennett.

20. http://mccain2000.com/, last accessed February 29, 2000.

21. Lenhart, Madden, and Hitlin.

22. Susannah Fox, *Generations Online* (Washington, DC: Pew Internet and American Life Project, 2006), last accessed June 15, 2007, at http://pewinternet.org/pdfs/PIP_Generations-Memo.pdf.

23. Amanda Lenhart, 2006. Testimony to the House Committee on Energy and Commerce: Subcommittee on Telecommunications and the Internet Hearing on H.R. 5319, The Deleting On-line Predators Act of 2006, U.S. House of Representatives, July 11, 2006, http://energycommerce.house.gov/108/Hearings/07112006hearing1974/Lenhart.pdf, retrieved November 14, 2006.

24. See Montgomery, this volume; Xenos and Bennett.

25. Philip Howard, *New Media Campaigns and the Managed Citizen* (New York: Cambridge University Press, 2006).

26. Elaine C. Kamarck, Campaigning on the Internet in the Elections of 1998, in *Democracy.com?: Governance in a Networked World*, ed. Elaine C. Kamarck and Joseph S. Nye (Hollis, NH: Hollis Publishing, 1999), 99–123.

27. David D'Alessio, Adoption of the World Wide Web by American Political Candidates, 1996–1998, *Journal of Broadcasting & Electronic Media* 44, no. 4 (2000): 556–68.

28. Kirsten A. Foot, Michael Xenos, and Steven Schneider, Online Campaigning in the 2002 U.S. Elections (paper presented at the American Political Science Association, Philadelphia, PA, 2003).

29. Joan Conners, Meetup, Blogs, and Online Involvement: U.S. Senate Campaign Websites of 2004 (paper presented at the American Political Science Association Conference, 2005); Howard.

30. In particular, see Levine, this volume.

31. For a detailed description of the data collection and methods employed, see Foot and Schneider.

32. Foot and Schneider.

33. Daniel M. Shea, *Campaign Craft: The Strategies, Tactics, and Art of Political Campaign Management* (Westport, CT: Praeger, 1996); Paul S. Herrnson, *Congressional Elections: Campaigning at Home and in Washington*, 4th ed. (Washington, DC: Congressional Quarterly Press, 2003).

34. Tim Berners-Lee, *Weaving the Web: The Original Design and Ultimate Destiny of the World Wide Web, by Its Inventor* (New York: Harper Collins, 2000); Robert Burnett and P. David Marshall, *Web Theory: An Introduction* (New York: Routledge, 2003).

35. Lance Bennett and Mike Xenos, Young Voters and the Web of Politics: Pathways to Participation in the Youth Engagement and Electoral Campaign Web Spheres, Center for Information and Research on Civic Learning and Engagement, Working Paper 42, 2004, http://www.civicyouth.org/PopUps/WorkingPapers/WP20BennettExecSumm.pdf, last accessed June 15, 2007.

36. See Foot and Schneider.

37. Conners, Meetup, Blogs, and Online Involvement.

38. Michael A. Xenos and Kirsten A. Foot, Politics as Usual, or Politics Unusual? Position Taking and Dialogue on Campaign Websites in the 2002 U.S. Elections, *Journal of Communication* 55, no. 1 (2005): 169–85.

39. http://www.talentforsenate.com/blog/postcomments.aspx?id=54 and http://www.talentforsenate.com/volunteer/, last accessed August 10, 2006.

40. Erik P. Bucy, Interactivity in Society: Locating an Elusive Concept, *Information Society* 20, no. 5 (2004): 373–83; McMillan and Hwang.

41. S. Shyam Sundar, Srinam Kalyanaraman, and Justin Brown, Explicating Web Site Interactivity: Impression Formation Effects in Political Campaign Sites, *Communication Research* 30, no. 1 (2003): 30–59.

42. Sundar, Kalyanaraman, and Brown.

43. Barbara Warnick, Michael Xenos, Danielle Endres, and John Gastil, Effects of Campaign-to-User and Text-based Interactivity in Political Candidate Campaign Web Sites, *Journal of Computer-mediated Communication* 10, no. 3 (2005).

44. John C. Tedesco, Web Interactivity and Young Adult Political Efficacy, in *The Internet Election: Perspectives on the Web in Campaign 2004*, ed. Andrew P. Williams and John C. Tedesco (New York: Rowman & Littlefield, 2006), 187–202.

45. Bucy; McMillan and Hwang; Sheizaf Rafaeli, Interactivity: From New Media to Communication, in *Advancing Communication Science: Merging Mass and Interpersonal Processes, Sage Annual Review of Communication Research 16*, ed. Robert P. Hawkins, John M. Wiemann, and Suzanne Pingree (Newbury Park, CA: Sage, 1988), 110–34, http://sheizaf.rafaeli.net (retrieved March 5, 2004); Sohn and Lee.

46. Sriram Kalyanaraman and S. Shyam Sundar, The Psychological Appeal of Personalized Content in Web Portals: Does Customization Affect Attitudes and Behavior? *Journal of Communication* 56, no. 1 (2006): 110–32.

47. Foot and Schneider.

48. Foot and Schneider.

49. E.g., http://www.candice-miller.com/, last accessed September 1, 2002.

50. Howard; Jouch Seiger, Privacy, Security and Trust on the Political Web. Institute for Politics, Democracy and the Internet, March 2003 [cited June 28, 2005], http://www.ipdi.org/UploadedFiles/privacy_security_and_trust_survey_final.pdf.

51. Stromer-Galley.

52. Stromer-Galley, 123.

53. E.g., http://bonnieb2000.com/soundoff.html, last accessed Febuary 2, 2001.

54. Howard, 35.

55. Mary Madden and Susannah Fox, Riding the Waves of "Web 2.0" (Backgrounder Pew Internet and American Life Project, 2006), from http://www.pewinternet.org/pdfs/PIP_Web_2.0.pdf (retrieved November 10, 2006).

56. David Iozzi and Lance Bennett, *Crossing the Campaign Divide: Dean Changes the Election Game* (Center for Communication and Civic Engagement, University of Washington, 2004), 3; A Chapter for E-Voter 2003, ed. K. Jagoda (E-Voter Institute) from http://depts.washington.edu/ccce/assets/documents/iozzi_bennet_crossing.pdf (retrieved November 15, 2006).

57. http://www.ricksantorum.com/Blog/BlogPost.aspx?BlogPostID=2479, last accessed August 10, 2006.

58. https://www.ricksantorum.com/Secure/SignUp.aspx?BlogPostID=2479, last accessed August 10, 2006.

59. http://blog.menendez2006.com/, http://blog.menendez2006.com/section/Diary, last accessed August 10, 2006.

60. http://blog.menendez2006.com/start_a_diary, http://blog.menendez2006.com/newuser, last accessed August 10, 2006.

Contesting Cultural Control: Youth Culture and Online Petitioning

Jennifer Earl

University of California, Santa Barbara, Department of Sociology

Alan Schussman

University of Arizona, Department of Sociology

To: Sony BMG

This petition is to request that the Backstreet Boys come to Asia for a tour. They haven't been on a tour in Asia (besides China & Japan) in almost 9 years.

The Backstreet Boys have numerous fans in Asia, who have been supporting them throughout their haitus [sic] & now, their new album & singles.

We are sick of reading about the boys touring Japan only. Yes, we know they toured China too, but that was only late last year. It's not as if Japan represents the whole of Asia!

Please let the Backstreet Boys tour Asia. At least a concert . . . please?

Petition number 211

A lot of kids don't get home from school in time to watch [programs on the Disney Channel]. I would like to start a Web site that would allow viewers to download episodes of the Disney Classics and of the newer Disney Channel shows at an earlier time. . . . However, I may have to get copyright permission to let viewers download tv shows from my Web site legally. You know what might increase the chances of me getting copyright permission? A lot of people signing this petition. The more signatures I have (especially if I have several hundred or several thousand signatures) the more apt the officials might be to give me copyright permission to let me let viewers download episodes from my Web site.

Petition number 79

Introduction

The above petition examples are illustrative of an online trend: using traditional social movement tactics, such as petitions, on the Internet to support, contest, or otherwise comment on cultural products and celebrities. Other petitions range from those seeking to address perceived problems in massively multiplayer online games such as World of Warcraft to petitions advocating for the open-source release of popular software to still other petitions that call on bands to share their concert recordings with fans. What this broad range of petitions has in common is a central focus on concerns that are important to youth culture and popular culture more broadly.

We would like to extend our deep thanks, and a public acknowledgment, to the operators of PetitionOnline, particularly Kevin Matthews and Mike Wheeler, who provided us with raw data for use in this chapter. We would also like to thank Lance Bennett and the other volume contributors for their lively exchanges and comments on this chapter.

However, many adults and nonenthusiasts approach these petitions with skepticism: are these petitions serious, and can they be thought of as politically oriented, or even civically oriented, in any way? In this chapter, we argue that, far from being exotic or marginal, such petitions are increasingly common online. Furthermore, we contend that this kind of petition is a predictable outgrowth of the convergence between "movement societies" and the affordances of digital technologies. As discussed in more detail below, movement society theorists assert that in many Western democracies, social movement schemas and practices (i.e., ways of understanding and acting in the world) have become so institutionalized that they are now part and parcel of everyday life.[1] Instead of ruptures in the political process, social movement tactics such as petitioning make up the fabric of everyday citizen politics in movement societies. Affordances of the Internet include markedly dropping costs of producing material online—including petitions—and the ability to easily and cheaply modify many types of cultural products—from mashups (i.e., the overlaying of multiple albums or music tracks into a single hybrid work of music) to e-books. These trends may have important implications for how consumers (and young consumers in particular) understand their relationship with cultural producers, be they corporations, artists, or celebrities.

In fact, we argue that what may seem like clearly nonpolitical acts—petitioning about the Backstreet Boys on the Internet, for instance—are actually an indicator of deeper transformations surrounding cultural consumption and civic engagement. Specifically, we maintain that a notable share of what we argue to be civic engagement—especially on the part of youth or with regard to youth-oriented issues—involves cultural contestation that may or may not eventually involve the state, which is a significant departure from a conventional understanding of social movements as state-directed challenges.[2]

Furthermore, enabled by digital technology, consumers are engaging with the producers and owners of cultural products, staking a new kind of claim to those materials. As we will illustrate, online protest surrounding cultural products suggests a redefinition of long-standing relationships between consumers and producers in which consumers are becoming much more active and (literally) demanding more from producers. This redefinition is highly salient to young participants who are developing repertoires of contention that may shape later civic engagement.

This chapter will explore this emerging form of engagement by empirically tracing the outlines of one specific area in which cultural contestation is visible: the proliferation of online petitions contesting cultural concerns. After reviewing the literature that informs our approach, we provide an overview of culture-related online petition material to argue that (1) these petitions are not marginal sideshows; (2) these petitions tend to focus on products and industries associated with youth culture; and (3) many of the petitions represent consumer-based contestation. We also discuss potential implications of these processes for future research on online-enabled protest; we discuss how cultural contestation might be transformed into more state-oriented battles over cultural ownership and intellectual property; and we discuss approaches to civic engagement likely to be adopted increasingly by young people.

Civic Engagement in the Digital Age

Before trying to make sense of youth-culture petitions, it is useful to situate these petitions within the wider terrain of civic engagement. As noted elsewhere in this volume, attention to civic engagement often comes in the form of concern about and debate over rising or falling levels of social ties, community connectedness, and electoral participation. Most assessments of these trends rely on formal definitions of civic engagement that focus heavily on explicitly political visions of civic engagement (e.g., research examining the relationship between social networks, voting trends, and protest participation). In fact, there is often only a thin distinction between political engagement and civic engagement, given that the activities that comprise civic engagement are marked by their institutional relationship to government (e.g., voting), or their noninstitutional relationship to government (e.g., protest).[3] To the extent that civic engagement has been more broadly understood to include volunteering and community service of other types, the focus has been on community activity that seemed expressly related to a sense of a community as a body politic.

But, increasingly corporations and other private entities are having identifiable, powerful, and contested roles in the everyday lives of citizens. Instead of channeling discontent about these effects solely toward governments as regulators, many are protesting against corporations themselves in hopes of directly changing corporate policies or products.[4] We argue that in a society where nongovernmental bodies wield so much obvious influence—whether at the global geopolitical level or in daily lived experience—it is important to reconsider protest against these bodies as a meaningful way of becoming civically engaged.

Thus, far from adding to a sense of crisis over an alleged paucity of civic engagement by youth, we step back and try to draw attention to ways in which younger citizens are engaging with issues that they find important and relevant to their lives, however removed these activities may seem from classic visions of civic engagement. Specifically, we draw attention to the ways in which younger citizens are focusing on nontraditional concerns—particularly more cultural concerns—using traditional methods of civic engagement such as petitioning.

In taking this approach, we are arguing that before certifying a crisis of civic engagement, one must ask whether existing notions of what comprises civic engagement tend to ignore, devalue, or otherwise marginalize ways in which younger citizens are connecting with one another to collectively make a difference in their own worlds. Culturally oriented concerns tend to be devalued, as shown by the skeptical reaction of many to the example petitions that opened this chapter. This devaluation has also been observed by Coleman, whose research compares attitudes of political enthusiasts to fans of *Big Brother*.[5] As Coleman points out, a consequence of such skepticism is the narrowing of what is considered worthwhile engagement: "Official strictures about what constitutes respectable (and respect-worthy) political participation have the effect of narrowing the repertoire of political citizenship."[6] In suggesting that adults more seriously consider the ways in which youth may be redefining civic engagement, we join other authors from this volume, including Coleman and Raynes-Goldie and Walker. And, in our case, the informality and relatively un-"managed" style of the petitions may even be one reason this kind of engagement is appealing to youth, as suggested in Bers's and Xenos and Foot's arguments in this volume about the unappealing nature of highly managed media experiences to youth.

In addition, we argue that marginalizing and ignoring these activities causes us to risk missing a harbinger of potentially deep changes in the role of consumers. As we argue in more detail below, the relationship between consumers and producers is being remade in the digital age such that consumers are increasingly challenging the authority and judgment of producers. No longer content to passively wait for products to come to market, or to have products updated, fixed, or improved, consumers are increasingly challenging producers' longstanding autonomy. In a world where corporations—and the goods and services that they produce—matter so much to daily life, we argue that it is useful to expand notions of civic engagement to include cultural contestation that attempts to redefine the relationship between corporations and consumers of their products.

Specifically, we argue that the confluence of a movement society and contention over culture and cultural ownership is a new venue for making sense of civic engagement, one that suggests that civic engagement may not look like what we have tended to expect. It is not formal—facilitated through well-established community organizations, activist groups, or political parties—and it may not even be conscientiously understood as engagement, but instead as a seemingly natural aspect of using or watching or gaming. We argue that it is important to trace empirically this kind of cultural contestation—which we do by studying online petitions about entertainment-related issues—and to try to understand the context in which this activity is occurring, which is the subject of the next two sections of the chapter.

Movement Societies: Protest as Part of Everyday Life

Historically used as a way to notify the ruler of subjects' concerns, and eventually as an avenue for raising citizens' grievances with legislators, petitions have long served as a forum for airing problems and seeking redress.[7] For instance, according to an interesting history of petitioning by Zaeske, petitions were a major venue for pressing for abolition when legislators tried to ignore concerns about slavery. However, while social movement scholars are increasingly attending to the often central role of cultural contestation in social movement struggles—such as struggles over language, media, and collective identities[8]—petitions have not previously been vehicles for much of that protest.[9] Social movement research can, nonetheless, leverage our understanding of entertainment-related petitioning through consideration of movement society arguments.

As social movements and protest have become increasingly institutionalized forms of political participation in Western democracies, scholars have begun to discuss the growth of movement societies.[10] In movement societies, a large and diverse population of actors uses forms of discourse and political involvement whose heritage can be traced directly back to social movements.[11] Unprecedented levels of diffusion of social movement discourse and tactics are characteristic of such institutionalization and may become so substantial that the forms of social action pioneered by social movements begin to pervade civic engagement and seemingly apolitical areas of life. For instance, classic protest tactics—such as petitioning—may be adopted by groups that had only used other forms of political participation before (e.g., only engaged in campaigning and voting before) and/or for purposes that seem distant from the protest heritage of petitioning. Movement society proponents argue that protest schemas and practices are becoming embedded in everyday life in some Western democracies. When this happens, people begin to understand their problems through the kinds of collective lenses that have been integral to classic social movements, and may begin to apply classic social movement practices, such as protest, to resolve their troubles.

Given this shift toward movement societies, at least in many Western industrialized states, we expect that new kinds of grievances—including grievances about products and celebrities, and more broadly about what we are referring to as grievances about cultural control—will be expressed using protest tactics that are now well-institutionalized means of engaging in collective conflict. Recent research conducted by Earl and Kimport on a quasi-random sample of Web sites discussing petitions, boycotts, and letter-writing and e-mail campaigns confirm these expectations.[12]

Earl and Kimport found that about 10 percent of online protest actions were focused on "nonstandard" claims, including entertainment-related claims like the ones discussed here. They also found claims that featured new combinations of individual and collective interests and action. Specifically, they found online protest actions attempting to address individual grievances with collective action, collective grievances with individual action, and individual grievances with individual action.

However, since their data set only had a small number of protest actions on these types of nonstandard causes, Earl and Kimport were not able to thoroughly outline these developments. We add to their initial contribution by examining a sample of petitions that we expect to be wholly focused on entertainment-related claims, which will allow us to dig even more deeply into movement society dynamics.

Affordances of Internet Technologies

We also make two arguments about the affordances of Internet, and digital technologies more broadly: (1) the online production of protest activities—such as online petition hosting—has dramatically reduced the costs of organizing collective actions, which has accelerated the growth of movement societies; and (2) digital technologies afford capacities to easily and cheaply change, recombine, and otherwise entirely reshape cultural products, which we argue is leading to more extensive changes in the roles of consumers and producers.

Making It on the Cheap

Research on a variety of different types of protest, social movements, and collective action has demonstrated that lower organizing and production costs seem to be a general affordance of Internet technologies.[13] Relevant to this chapter, it is much less expensive to create an online petition than it is to create and run an offline petition drive. In an offline petition drive, one would have to create the petition, get it printed in sufficient quantities (which can be expensive), and then either recruit volunteers or hire paid signature gatherers to go out to large public spaces to collect signatures.

In contrast, with sites like PetitionOnline (discussed further below), which offers free online petition setup and hosting, online petitioning can be quite easy and inexpensive to start and manage. Even users with fairly remedial computer skills can open a Web browser and fill out a Web-based form to create a petition. They can then send links to the petition to a wide variety of potentially interested parties and let the back-end software manage the signatures as they come in.

Research also suggests that the lowest organizing and production costs for protest or other forms of collective action are achieved when a movement emerges online and then stays online, instead of emerging offline and migrating online. Earl and Schussman call these fully online movements "e-movements."[14] Illustratively, in Earl and Schussman's research on the strategic voting e-movement, the authors identified an online organizer who put a notice on his Web site saying he did not need any donations (some people had clearly offered to donate to him) because operating his Web site was so inexpensive. It is difficult to imagine Amnesty International posting a sign indicating that donations are not needed!

There is a wide array of potential consequences for this change in the cost structure of starting and maintaining protest actions online.[15] Particularly relevant, though, is Earl's argument that the low cost of producing protest actions online (see below) should accelerate movement society trends.[16] She argues that very low organizing costs allow people to organize around issues that have never before (or at least rarely) been the subject of protest organizing. Put differently, the cost restriction that may have prevented people from applying traditional social movement schemas and practices to some cultural issues can be removed by Internet technologies. Earl and Kimport's research bears out this claim, showing that the low-cost production of protest facilitated by the Internet has allowed a variety of inexpensive petition and letter-writing campaigns to develop around entertainment-related issues.[17]

We are interested in how this cost structure affects the way young people use the Internet to engage in issues that seem relevant and important to their everyday lives. If young people are growing up in movement societies, where scripts and practices from social movements have become part of everyday thinking, and where producing online protest actions has become extremely inexpensive, then we should expect that young people will begin to use online protest-organizing tools to mount protests about issues they care about. As the next section argues, one set of issues that is likely to be proximate to many teenagers' and young adults' lives involves the cultural products and personalities that make up "youth culture" or "popular culture" more broadly.

Using, Making, and Owning Culture

As noted above, digital technologies have helped transform audiences into producers. Where digital media are concerned, inexpensive digital cameras, inexpensive but powerful video-editing software, and video-sharing services like OurMedia and YouTube allow everyday people to become filmmakers and distributors. This latter aspect is particularly important because it allows users to easily and widely spread home movies, amateur films, video clips, and music videos. Previously, this would have required users to have large amounts of their own storage and bandwidth, but YouTube users simply need to upload their digital movie files and then share the Web location; the service handles the storage and bandwidth for distribution. As the tools to make and edit music, video, and images become more and more accessible, these activities will continue to proliferate, a point that is developed more fully in Rheingold's discussion of participatory media in this volume.

Not only have digital technologies made it easier for everyday, "garage" cultural production to occur but digital media also make it easy to modify existing digital products, exemplified by mashups. One of the most well-known mashups was the "Grey Album," made by combining samples from the Beatles' "White Album" with the vocals from rapper Jay-Z's "Black Album." The *Village Voice* named the album one of the top ten records of 2004, but more recognition came when the owners of the Beatles' catalog cracked down over copyright infringements. Activists used the opportunity to highlight what they saw as overly restrictive copyright policies. As Howard-Spink notes, mashups signify an important role for amateurs and consumers: consumer participation in a culture where "the struggle for power over meaning-making has been concentrated in fewer and fewer hands."[18]

Massively multiplayer online games similarly seem to typify this potential for transforming relationships between products and consumers. In online worlds such as Second Life or World of Warcraft, players accumulate wealth, build on their own digital property, and engage in longitudinal campaigns with in-game alter egos. But they have an ownership in the game world that is more than symbolic, sometimes paying real money for rare in-game artifacts or abilities. Some stake further claims to their digital domains by petitioning game producers for enhancements and bug fixes.

Scholars have begun to consider the implications of these phenomena. Benkler discusses how a networked information economy, in which cultural goods are primarily digitally produced and distributed, has a profound effect on contemporary culture.[19] He considers collaborative platforms (e.g., Wikipedia and massively multiplayer online games) and more nominally individual activities (e.g., posting photos to the photo-sharing site Flickr), arguing that these platforms facilitate the "appropriation of media content for the purpose of commentary, annotation, and innovation" that Jack Balkin calls "glomming on."[20] Consumers are now empowered to participate in a new kind of "folk culture" that stands in sharp contrast to the "highly choreographed cultural production system of the industrial information economy."[21] Benkler writes that this form of engagement with cultural products means an important transformation in our understanding of culture's role in society:[22]

This plasticity, and the practices of writing your own culture, then feed back into the transparency, both because the practice of making one's own music, movie, or essay makes one a more self-conscious user of the cultural artifacts of others, and because in retelling anew known stories, we again come to see what the originals were about and how they do, or do not, fit our own sense of how things are and how they ought to be. There is emerging a broad practice of learning by doing that makes the entire society more effective readers and writers of their own culture.[23]

Jenkins speaks similarly of these transformations, identifying the power found in "writing over [culture], modding it, amending it, expanding it, adding greater diversity of perspective, and then recirculating it."[24] But Jenkins goes further to argue that such developments, taking place as they are "in the affinity spaces that are emerging around popular culture,"[25] are particularly relevant and important to young people who need to learn how to participate in "the deliberations over what issues matter, what knowledge counts, and what ways of knowing command authority and respect."[26]

Existing information indeed suggests that young people may be a particularly important segment of the population for whom the relationship between consumption and culture is changing. As Rheingold discusses elsewhere in this volume, youth are far from passive when it comes to consumerism: young people in the United States are both highly wired (87 percent of teens between twelve and seventeen are online) and have a seeming naturalness with reappropriating and remaking cultural products that is attendant with coming of age surrounded by media and media technologies. Furthermore, data from the WebUse survey of college students suggests that a large fraction of young people are doing creative things online: close to 27 percent of surveyed students report making music, while almost 22 percent report writing fiction or poetry.[27] Much higher percentages of respondents report daily or weekly use of online services to download or listen to music (78 percent), download or watch videos (58 percent), or browse online photo albums (57 percent). The explosion in popularity (and attendant controversy) of the MySpace service, where the majority of users are between fourteen and twenty-four,[28] further suggests that online public spaces—where users post photos and comments and share music, for example—constitute especially important avenues for young people. Chapters by Montgomery and Raynes-Goldie and Walker in this volume also discuss the youth focus of MySpace (and the adult concern prompted by that focus).

If we are correct that consumership is changing at the same time that protest organizing costs are dropping and people are thinking of using protest practices to solve their problems, then we would expect to find cultural contestation through collective action, thereby also contributing weight to Scammel's broader argument that "consumer critique is fundamental to citizenship in the age of globalization."[29] Anecdotes such as fan-led campaigns to "Save Firefly" being instrumental in the production of the film *Serenity*, for example, suggest this is the case. Our chapter moves beyond anecdotes to a more systematic empirical examination. In what follows, we consider how the rise of a movement society makes these instances of collective action more than an aberration on the part of fans or fanatics, but rather a part of an increasingly standard repertoire of action, used by savvy consumers as a seemingly natural way to shape the worlds of culture in which they participate.

Data and Methods

In order to study how contestation around youth culture may be taking shape through online petitions, we examine a large, random sample of online petitions targeted around entertainment concerns. Specifically, our data are drawn from a 5 percent sample of the 12,848 petitions that were included in the entertainment category on PetitionOnline[30] in June 2006. PetitionOnline is a free online petition-hosting Web site where individuals can use the site's software and servers to create, host, and manage a petition on any subject. Over time, the site has housed tens of thousands of petitions and collected more than 33 million signatures.[31]

This site was selected for several reasons. First, it is one of the largest and most popular petition-hosting sites online, allowing access to a wide variety of petitions on a large number of topics. Second, prior research suggests that so-called warehouse sites[32] like PetitionOnline, which house online protest actions for others, are important centers for organizing on nonstandard issues.[33] Thus, data from this site will allow us to paint a vivid and deep portrait of online petitioning on nonstandard subjects.

The site allows access to an overall list of active petitions, a searchable list of active petitions, a list of the top twenty-five petitions (in terms of signatures) from the previous day, and lists of petitions by category. Categories include "Politics & Government—International," "Politics & Government—USA," "Politics & Government—State," "Politics & Government—Local," "Environment," "Religion," "Technology & Business," and "Entertainment & Media."

We focus here on petitions categorized as "Entertainment & Media" petitions in an effort to showcase and make sense of the outcropping of youth-culture petitions that can be found on the Internet. It is important to note that our data do not allow us to directly establish the age of either petition authors or petition signers as we collect data on the petitions themselves, not their authors or signers (on whom data was not available). However, we strongly argue it is reasonable to assume that many, if not most, of the youth-culture petitioning we observed was undertaken by youth. Our argument is based on several grounds: (1) data we reviewed here suggests that youth are far more likely to be the consumers of the products and celebrities discussed in the petitions we study and have been statistically more common producers of similar online content; (2) consumer distribution makes it more likely that youth, versus other age groups, will engage in contestation over the products found in the entertainment and media sections of sites such as PetitionOnline (e.g., later we discuss the difference between petitions on video games versus Microsoft Office products); and (3) a reasonable reading of the actual text of many petitions also strongly suggests younger authors (i.e., the look and the feel of the petitions is suggestive of youth authoring).

In order to gather data on these youth-culture, and likely youth-authored, petitions, we collected data from PetitionOnline in June 2006. At that time, there were 12,848 petitions on the list of active petitions[34] available when Web site visitors clicked on the "Entertainment

& Media" link. We randomly sampled from this list at a 5 percent rate, yielding 642 sampled petitions. We then used freely available mirroring software to download the content of each petition from PetitionOnline.

We were also provided raw data, based on data that appeared publicly on PetitionOnline, by the operators of PetitionOnline. These data covered all petitions housed within the Entertainment category, and we extracted from that larger set the data on the 642 petitions we had sampled and mirrored. Data provided by PetitionOnline included whether a "community support" constituency (i.e., a set of people expected to support the petition) was indicated by the petition creator, preferred characteristics for potential signers that were listed by petition creators, whether or not the names of signers were displayed on PetitionOnline, what country and/or U.S. state (if any) the petition focused on, the listed target(s) of the petition, and the total number of signers as of the date the data was provided in July 2006.

These data were imported into a statistical package and variables were content coded to create categorical values out of the free text data, as depicted in tables and figures in the Findings section.[35] All results below exclude the seventy-eight petitions from our sample that were not in English and were therefore not coded, meaning that results shown below are based on a maximum of 564 petitions (the number of petitions is sometimes lower because of missing data or nonresponses on the petition startup form).

Furthermore, the actual petition text, which was mirrored from PetitionOnline, was manually content coded to determine what kinds of claims were made in the petition text, what types of industries and products were targeted in the text of petitions (separate from the target listed in the data provided by PetitionOnline), and how the petition labeled potential signers (e.g., "fans of WWE"). In all cases, data were coded by one of the two authors and postcoding checks for invalid values were completed. Using these data, we are able to paint a vivid portrait of online petitioning around youth-culture issues, as the next section demonstrates.

Describing Youth-Culture Online Petitioning

Data from PetitionOnline demonstrate four clear empirical points. First, they challenge the assumption that entertainment-related petitioning is a marginal activity in terms of prevalence, participation, reach, or impact. Where prevalence is concerned, the overall volume of entertainment-related petitions is itself impressive: on the day in June 2006 on which we sampled petitions, there were an astounding 12,848 petitions shown in the Entertainment & Media category. Only petitions signed within the last thirty days and with ten or more signatures are displayed in the category sections on PetitionOnline, so the 12,848 figure actually understates the total number of active entertainment-related petitions housed on the site. Data provided by PetitionOnline that include petitions with fewer than ten signatures indicate that there were 21,251 entertainment petitions in July of 2006. It is difficult to cast such a large volume of online petitions as a truly marginal activity.

Another way to consider prevalence is in relation to the number of petitions hosted by PetitionOnline in other categories. As mentioned above, PetitionOnline allows petitions to be assigned to one of eight categorical groupings. In November 2006 we returned to PetitionOnline and recounted the active Entertainment & Media petitions. In the months between June, when we sampled petitions from the site, and November, the Entertainment & Media category continued to grow: there were 14,395 active Entertainment & Media petitions in November. This was by far the largest of the eight categories at that time. In order

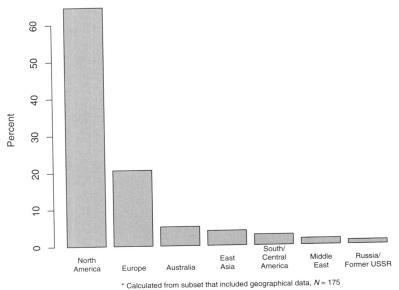

Percent

North America   Europe   Australia   East Asia   South/Central America   Middle East   Russia/Former USSR

* Calculated from subset that included geographical data, N = 175

Figure 1
Geography of petitions*.

of size, from next largest to smallest, the other categories were: "Politics & Government—International" with 3,470 active petitions; "Politics & Government—Local" with 2,687 active petitions; "Technology & Business" with 2,478 petitions; "Politics & Government—USA" with 2,208 active petitions; "Environment" with 1,379 active petitions; "Politics & Government—State" with 1,336 active petitions; and "Religion" with 662 active petitions. Given that the Entertainment & Media category hosts more than four times as many active petitions as the next largest category on PetitionOnline, there is evidence of strong interest in cultural concerns.

Participation is also impressive. Of the 642 petitions we randomly sampled in June, the mean number of participants was 965, the median was 143 participants, and the maximum was 81,260 signers. The bottom 25 percent of petitions in our sample still had up to thirty-seven signers, and the top 25 percent had 528 signers or more. Thus, in terms of sheer participation, it is difficult to cast these petitions as marginal.[36]

We also coded data on any geographic focus of the petitions, as indicated by petition creators when they registered with PetitionOnline. Although the majority of petition creators indicated no geographic focus, those that did have a geographic focus confirm that petitions nearly blanket the globe. As Figure 1 indicates, the majority of petitions in which authors indicated a geographic location were located in North America or Europe. Nonetheless, entertainment-related petitions focusing on Central and South America, the Middle East, Eastern Europe, East Asia, and Australia were also found in our sample. This suggests that, although entertainment-related petitions on PetitionOnline were largely American or European, the sample of petitions still had global reach and thus cannot be seen as extremely geographically confined, and hence marginal, activity.

This sense of a global reach is also supported by data we collected on second languages used in petitions. While we only coded petitions that were written in English, some petitions were written in both English and a second language. Data on those additional languages show that petitions were translated into Spanish, German, Portuguese, French, and even Maori.[37]

Although we lack systematic data on the outcomes of these petitions, we do have access to some anecdotal reports, as published on the PetitionOnline Web site, that document corporate reactions to these petitions. For instance, in one reaction recently featured on the Web site, a WebTV vice president wrote to express his concern for the customer complaints aired in the online petition that garnered fewer than a thousand signatures.[38] The official provided a detailed account of the ways in which WebTV was trying to resolve the set of customer complaints from the petition, including setting up special customer response teams and an ombudsperson e-mail address, among other responses. In other cases, "revival" movements attempted to bring particular programs back on air. While it can be hard to determine what role the petitions we studied play in corporate decisions to bring programs back, the goals of these groups are sometimes clearly achieved. For instance, a petition signed by just 592 fans of a canceled program was submitted, and shortly after the submission of the petition, the program was brought back.[39] Thus, there is some evidence that even smaller petitions still may affect their corporate targets.

Youth-Cultural Focus

Furthermore, data on the content of petitions convincingly demonstrate that these petitions tend to focus on products and industries associated with youth culture. Figure 2 shows what industries were discussed in petitions. Television tops the charts with 27.8 percent of our sampled petitions. Music (20.2 percent) and video games (17.2 percent) followed. When one looks at specific products discussed, as shown in Figure 3, television and TV shows (22.3 percent), singers and bands, or music generally, (21.3 percent), and video games (16.7 percent) are also major foci of attention.[40] For example, petitions frequently sought to bring bands—ranging from Evanescence to Asian boy band sensations—in concert to specific cities or countries, or encouraged game publishers to make sequels to popular video games. One such music petition, addressed to record company Sony BMG, read:

After hearing the news that YG Entertainment will be having a worldwide tour in celebration of their 10th Year Anniversary, I would like to gather those living in the states of Australia to sign a petition for YG Entertainment to bring their tour to this country. (Petition number 158)

Another petition was addressed to video game publisher Ubisoft:

Beyond Good & Evil—one of the greatest games in modern history and one of the few games that actually needs a sequel. It's a shame that the game didn't sell better, but with your help there may be a chance for us to get some attention and convince Ubisoft that they would be making a huge mistake not releasing a sequel. Sign up now to show your support and tell all your Jade-loving friends about this petition. (Petition number 201)

When one compares specific categories—like the prevalence of petitions on nongame software versus that of video games—the youth focus of these petitions becomes even clearer. Put bluntly, the petitions we analyzed were not predominately about whether Microsoft Access or PowerPoint should be updated (a decidedly non–youth-oriented set of concerns), but were instead about whether Halo was challenging enough. In fact, petitions about Microsoft Office products did exist on PetitionOnline but tended to be housed in the "Technology & Business" category. Instead, the petitions we examined called for such things as the publisher of World of Warcraft to fix "ridiculous downtime, unstable, laggy uptime and sub-par customer service."[41] Petitioners, who cast themselves as loyal fans, asserted that they face so

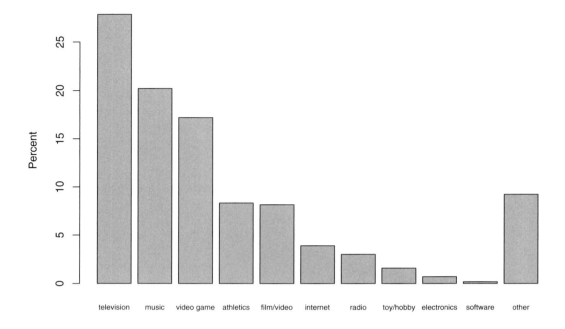

* Calculated from subset of English petitions with industry information, N = 564

Figure 2
Industry of product*.

much "pain and frustration" from the problems with the game. They saw their concerns as not only important for their own gaming experience, but important enough to make known to the game's producers.

Table 1 shows a breakdown of the explicit targets of petitions. Data were coded from information petition creators provided when they started a petition. Results provide powerful additional support for the youth-culture focus of these petitions, as shown by the substantial percentage of petitions that targeted entertainment-related companies, industry groups, or company representatives for such firms. Not surprisingly, given results from the prior section, companies that produce film, TV, video, and video games were primary targets. For instance, one petition implored:

As fans of college baseball and college universities, we politely ask EA Sports to either make a patch including more NCAA baseball conferences for MVP NCAA Baseball 06 or to include them all in NCAA Baseball 07. (Petition number 383)

The content of petitions on other market segments, such as athletics, also suggested a strong youth-focus. For instance, several of the "sports/athletics" petitions were focused on wrestling. One such petition read:

To: World Wrestling Entertainment Inc.

The fans of sports entertainment, are banding together and are pleaing [sic] with the powers to be at World Wrestling Entertainment, to induct Eddie Guerrero as a member of the 2006 Hall of Fame in Chicago during Wrestle Mania 22. (Petition number 552)

Table 1

Targets of petitions*

Target	Percent
Cultural producers and companies:	
Film/TV/video	28.014
Video and computer game	18.085
Music/radio	13.652
Company representative	13.298
Sports/athletics	6.028
Celebrity	4.078
Other producers	6.028
Private individuals and/or groups	10.816
Governmental target	3.546
Other, not elsewhere specified	2.305

*$N = 564$; table does not sum to 100% because petitions may have more than one target.

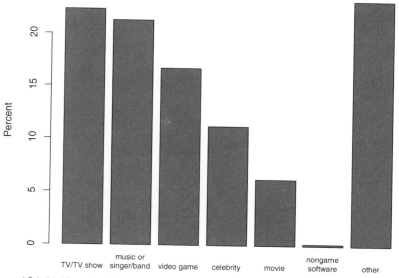

* Calculated from subset of English petitions with product information, $N = 564$. Note that 63.4% of products coded in the "other" category had a codeable industry form (See Fig. 2).

Figure 3

Product type*.

Active Consumers

Not to be lost among the findings shown in Table 1 is a major trend: the vast majority of targets in entertainment-related petitions were corporations (or their representatives), artists and celebrities, and other individuals and private groups. Government, however, was almost absent—quite conspicuously so—with fewer than 4 percent of petitions including a government target at all. Of course, this does not mean that only 4 percent of all online petitions target the government, but among petitions in the Entertainment & Media category, government was seldom seen as an appropriate target.[42]

Table 2
Claims made on petitions*

Claim	Percent
Advocacy:	
Revive	17.021
Oppose	11.702
Save	7.801
Support	6.738
Promote	3.546
Change:	
Add or expand	21.099
Change or modify	13.652
Update	6.383
Fix or repair	4.078
Port	2.482
Policy-related claim	2.482
Customer-related claim (e.g., service)	1.241
Other, not elsewhere specified	11.879

*$N = 564$; table does not sum to 100% because petitions may have more than one claim.

Table 2 provides data on the specific concerns, or claims made, in these petitions. Legal issues such as copyright or intellectual property, or law and government policy more generally, were rarely of concern: only about 2.5 percent of petitions focused on these issues. Instead, Table 2 shows that petitions tended to make claims in support of or opposition to products and celebrities, request changes to products, or voice concern about pricing and/or customer service. For instance, 17 percent of petitions were "revival oriented." These petitions usually sought to bring television programs such as *American Dreams* back to broadcast or tried to persuade record companies to release recordings of live concert performances.

Similar to this type of claim were claims about "saving" products, meaning that a product had not yet been cancelled but was at risk. About 8 percent of petitions we coded made such claims, which often sought to keep canceled TV shows such as *Conviction* on the air. Petitions in this category were by no means limited to television, however; they sought to save radio stations, video games, or music venues.[43]

In stark contrast to supportive petitions, roughly 12 percent expressed opposition to particular products or celebrities. Sports-related petitions in this category were not uncommon: one petition argued that the owner of the Baltimore Orioles had hurt the team and should no longer control the franchise. Another sought to have English soccer star David James dropped from the roster after too many "clangers."[44]

Between these two poles were generally supportive petitions that sought to support celebrities and products in some way (6.7 percent) and petitions that wanted greater promotion for products or celebrities (3.5 percent). One of these petitions sought to persuade MTV to broadcast more programming about the Backstreet Boys[45] while another expressed support for Ashlee Simpson after the singer had an embarrassing live performance on Saturday Night Live.[46]

Twenty-one percent of petitions requested an addition or an expansion to a product. Petitions sought to see the Rock and Roll Hall of Fame expanded, to bring Pearl Jam in concert to Columbia or No Doubt to play a show in Brazil, and to add a video screen to a

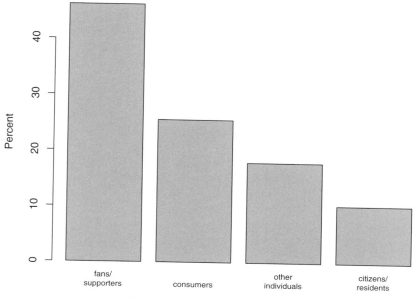

* Calculated from petitions with formal participant label, $N = 249$

Figure 4
Participants named in signup form*.

municipal concert venue. About 14 percent of petitions featured claims that did not postulate a specific problem with a product but nonetheless wanted a modification that did not clearly involve other coded types of change. One petition, for example, advocated casting Lucy Lawless in the role of Wonder Woman in an upcoming film; another sought to move the site of a large college football game; and another petition attempted to persuade Harry Potter filmmakers to include a favorite character. Similar in spirit to these two categories, another 2.5 percent requested that products (in this case, exclusively video games) be "ported" to different systems.[47]

Another 4 percent of petitions wanted changes that would fix what consumers saw as a defect in the original product. Games were prominent in this category, with petitions complaining about the ability to cheat in Halo 2 or errors in Warcraft III that prevented the game from running correctly. Slightly over 6 percent of petitions requested updates to products. Sequels were a common request here, with petitions that asked for a third *Bill and Ted* film, a sequel to the video game Skies of Arcadia, or a sequel to the film *Last Dragon*.

As is evident from the examples and their frequencies, the vast majority of these petitions attempted to compel producers to alter their practices or products. But is there any evidence that these petitioners understood these activities as part of their role as consumers? Data shown in Figures 4 and 5 provide some leverage over these questions, showing that the answer seems to be yes.

Figure 4 is based on data that petition creators provided when they created a petition. Specifically, in the petition startup form, creators are asked if there are particular "eligible signatories" for their petition. Unfortunately, over half of petitions did not have a specific

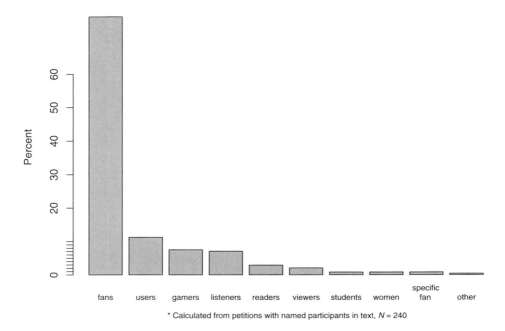

* Calculated from petitions with named participants in text, *N* = 240

Figure 5
Signers named in petition text*.

set of eligible signatories according to the signup form, and are thus not included in Figure 4. However, of data that were entered in the signup form, fans/supporters (46.2 percent) and consumers (25.5 percent) were among the most frequent categories.

Figure 5 is based on coding of the petition text itself, which often indicated some audience for the petition and/or characteristics of likely petition supporters. These data provide an interesting counterpart to the optional field in the signup form, confirming that petitions were overwhelming expected to be signed by "fans." Where an identity could be determined, 77 percent of petitions were designed for fans,[48] as in these examples: "We have been loyal fans to ECW since the beginning"[49] and "We, the loyal fans of the Dodgers and respecters of tradition, are appalled at the treatment of long time announcer Ross Porter."[50]

Beyond this general category of fan was a more specialized one in which signers or petition authors identified themselves as members of a very specific, named fan group: "Kopites"[51] are fans of Liverpool soccer; "Pottermaniacs"[52] are particularly enthusiastic Harry Potter fans. This category of fan was a small proportion of the total set of petitions (2.9 percent), but they are noteworthy for the highly specialized, personalized nature of the self-identification.

Other popular potential signers were identified as viewers or watchers (7.5 percent; one such petition identifies its signers as "Space-oriented viewers worldwide"[53] and another identifies signers as "Old Nickelodeon watchers"[54]). A number of petitions (7.1 percent) identified signers as gamers. Others were designated as users (2.1 percent): "This petition is designed to express the heartly [*sic*] disappointment and frustration of users using Valve™ Steam Platform for online gaming."[55] Smaller numbers (.83 percent) of petitions identified petition signers as listeners or readers, writing, for example, "We, the listeners of Hot 97 (WQHT) and family/friends/fans of Aaliyah Haughton, were outraged when morning show host Star made fun of the death of Aaliyah on August 27th 2001."[56]

Together, these data on petitions and desired signers support our claim that these petitions represent a reformulation of the consumer role. Far from passive consumers of prior decades, these consumers expect—and demand—particular things from producers. As such, these consumers are defying expectations that they are passive, instead challenging the authority of cultural producers to decide which products to produce and how they should be produced. These data also suggest a sense of something akin to collective identity, where consumers understand themselves not as part of a body politic but a cultural public that shares common interests, common desires, and common cause with other fans, or Xenites, or Pottermaniacs. We further see this as fitting well with Jenkins's suggestion that consumers' self-identification with fan communities "does not simply affirm their brand affiliation, but also empowers these groups to assert their own demands on the company."[57] To the extent that the petition writers identify themselves as fans, or as having specialized product-related identities, they are creating communities through which they can and expect to make claims about the products they consume.

Active Communities

To the extent that our data show some nascent sense of collective identity, or at least some shared perspective among consumers, does it also imply any collective organization behind these petitions and/or in support of these petitions? We have two pieces of evidence with which to address this question. First, the petition startup form asked petition authors to name any specific group or community what would likely support the petition, such as "members of the Sierra Club."[58]

We categorized the communities named and found that 178 of 564 petitions (or about 32 percent) did name some informal or formal group, including seventy-six petitions (13.5 percent of all petitions) that indicated some named fan community, forty-one (7.3 percent of all petitions) that indicated some organization or group that was not fan-based, thirty (5.3 percent of all petitions) that indicated the membership of some formal organization, and thirty-one petitions (5.5 percent of all petitions) that indicated a looser version of community where supporters shared common characteristics but did not come together in groups. While not a majority of petitions, it is notable that nearly a third of the petitions we coded were expected to be supported by a specific community.

Second, the petition startup form also asked petition creators to indicate whether expected supporters and/or support communities had a Web presence. About two-thirds of the petitions that were expected to be supported by communities had a Web presence (112 petitions out of 178). Another thirty-four petitions had a Web presence for supporters who were not labeled as a community (and hence not coded as part of the 178 community-supported petitions). These data suggest that the communities that underlie these petitions may be constituted or maintained online, potentially deepening the digital impact on civic engagement (and on the definition of *civic*) examined in this chapter.

Discussion and Conclusion

The prominent role of cultural industries in the day-to-day lives of consumers seems undeniable. We have argued that contestation centered on the goods produced by those industries is a meaningful form of civic engagement—perhaps even one that signals a significant shift in the relationship between consumers and producers. We have also argued that this engagement may be particularly important for youth. Petitioners are not passive consumers, content with whatever producers offer. They are active users who both take meaning from and assign it to cultural material. By asking for fixes, sequels, and improvements, users are making a different kind of claim to ownership, claims made even more pronounced when consumers reshape and redistribute those goods.[59]

Our findings have implications beyond the institutionalization of movement tactics and new relationships between consumers and products. One important implication concerns legal issues and digital property, a concern that has been raised by numerous scholars. DiMaggio et al., for example, identify some of the areas in which both political engagement and culture are subject to change as digital technology proliferates.[60] They highlight one of the issues that has been most enduring in the study of intersecting politics and culture online, suggesting that widespread "ideals of openness" online are likely to conflict with the needs of commercial actors in the digital marketplace to protect their investments via copy protection and copyright policies. Healy notes that policies about how cultural goods are shared and distributed will affect the extent to which consumers of those products will be passive or active users; that is, the protections that guarantee markets for cultural producers are likely to impinge on the ability of consumers to modify or redistribute digital products.[61] To the extent that policies favor producers, those producers might, as Balkin writes, "push consumers back into their pre-Internet roles as relatively passive recipients of mass media content."[62]

Lessig recognizes that this openness is not guaranteed, noting that the tradition of a "free culture" of fair use, or of reappropriating music, images, and text to make new creative or cultural works, is transformed into a "permissions culture" by restrictive policies or copy protection technologies.[63] It is clear that the mold of future digital products is yet to be cast, and, while consumers seem to be asserting new kinds of relationships with culture, the further development of law and policy will greatly affect the realization of those relationships. We take the fact that petitioners are collectively pursuing changes to cultural goods as an important opening for a potentially larger engagement between consumers (and youth as a critical subset of consumers), producers, and the state over these issues.

There are reasons to believe that the kinds of engagements we discuss here could in fact lead to more standard forms of political and civic engagement later. As Rheingold discusses in his chapter in this volume, research on online engagement suggests that some kinds of online interaction can lead to more explicitly political online engagement.[64] Rheingold also suggests two criteria for activities (or broader projects) that are more likely to turn Internet use into online political engagement: (1) whether the activity involves connection to others and (2) whether young people learn to express themselves. We think the cause-oriented engagements we studied here provide that connection to a community of other interested persons and that petition writing and signing can be a forum for learning how to express oneself in a collective context. Furthermore, we think it is important to note that young people are learning these things while they work on issues they care about—as opposed to issues that adults believe they should care about—and using tools that they appropriated—as opposed to tools that were assigned to them. The authenticity of these actions, then, might also be independently important to the experience of young people involved in cultural contestation.

Beyond the potential to spur political activity over time, the implications of our study for research are also significant. For instance, scholars need to consider how it is that participants come to take part in online petitions, or online protests more generally. Some well-known models for recruiting participation seem to be a good fit for explaining this kind of engagement: being asked to participate, for example, is a factor that seems important to offline political and protest engagement[65] and is also likely to fit an online model of forwarded e-mail, blog entries soliciting comment, and petitions that encourage signers to add their e-mail address to the list. Other models of participation, however, such as those rooted in organizational membership[66] may find less support online. It also seems likely that additional factors, unanticipated by prior models of participation, are at work; future research should explore this in more detail.

Much of the research ahead is also specifically focused on youth. For instance, in addition to the importance of cultural products to youth culture, are there other reasons why young people seem so interested in Internet petitioning on entertainment-related topics? One likely possibility is that people are often more likely to participate in protest, or politics more generally, when they think that their efforts may "matter." There are numerous anecdotes, some relayed above, of even small online petitions (a few hundred signers or less) resulting in changes to corporate policies or products. This fits with existing expectations on the part of scholars that a personal sense of efficacy may be an important factor that prompts people to engage in collective action. That sense of efficacy may be something young people are gaining from their cultural contestation that they do not get from interactions with government. For instance, research by Coleman suggests that in more formal political arenas, cultural consumers—such as *Big Brother* enthusiasts—often feel as though their opinions and actions won't matter.[67] If this efficacy is a motivator for participation, then online petitioning will translate into broader political engagement only where youth feel like their voices will matter. Consequently, it remains to be seen whether an early sense of efficacy in cultural contestation will translate into explicitly state-oriented activity in the future.

Another question for future research involves whether the kind of petitioning we analyzed here will continue. We suspect that it will and that we have actually only begun the chart the long course of Internet petitions involved in cultural contestation. Even if young people or adults begin to translate the concerns we discussed here into more explicitly political concerns over intellectual property, as we discussed just above, we suspect that this will be an extension, not a replacement, of ongoing petitioning. Of course, only time, and future research, will determine whether our best guess is correct.

Methodological Appendix

This appendix covers technical details of the manual content coding completed by the authors.

Data From PetitionOnline

Where data provided by PetitionOnline is concerned, the coding scheme was as follows:

1   "Support groups" was coded from data entered by petition authors in the COMMUNITY_SUPPORT field of the petition setup form. This field indicated which individuals or groups, if any, were likely to support the petition according to the petition author. Coding categories included fans (e.g., "fans of WWE" and "Xenites," who

are fans of Xena), individuals who shared specified characteristics other than being fans (e.g., "people who have taste"), groups or formal organizations (e.g., the Example Guild), and members of a group or formal organization but not the actual group (e.g., members of Example Guild).

2   "Web Presence of Support Group" was coded "1" if the individuals or groups coded in Support Group had a Web site or other identifiable Internet presence and "0" if they did not.

3   "Continent" was coded based on the country (if any) that was listed by the petition creator in the geographic fields in the petition setup form. Categories included North America, South or Central America, Europe, Africa (which had an observed frequency of 0), the Middle East, the former Soviet bloc or Russia, East Asia (including Japan but excluding former Soviet block countries), and Australia.

4   "Governmental Target" was coded based on the target listed by the petition creator in the petition setup form. Categories included governmental entities, quasi-governmental entities, private entities, and "other."

5   "Specific Target" was coded based on the target listed by the petition creator in the petition setup form. Categories included individuals based on a shared characteristics except for youth and/or students (e.g., fans, women); youth and/or students; celebrities (including musical bands); religious organizations; individual managers or employees of a company or other organization; a film, video, or television company or industry group; a music or talk radio company or industry group; a computer-related company or industry group (including video game producers and Internet Web sites); a publishing and print media company or industry group; a sports/athletics company or industry group (including wrestling and NASCAR); a toy company or industry group; an explicitly multimedia company (e.g., Sony); an entertainment company or industry group not elsewhere classified; a non–entertainment-related business not elsewhere classified; a private club or organization; the executive branch and/or an executive figure; a government agency (e.g., attorney general, IRS, FDA); a legislative branch of the government and/or a legislative figure; a judicial branch of the government and/or a judicial figure; a foreign government or their embassy; a tribal government; law enforcement and/or corrections; government bodies not elsewhere classified; and a category for "Other, not elsewhere classified."

6   "Total Signatures" was simply the count of signatures provided by PetitionOnline; it did not require any coding by the authors.

Data Coded From the Text of Mirrored Petitions

Additional data were coded from the text of petitions themselves, as detailed below:

1   "English" was coded "1" when petitions were written in English (including those written in English and a second language), and "0" otherwise. Non-English petitions were not coded further.

2   "Second Language" is the name of the second, non-English language that appeared in the petition, if any.

3   "Claims:" As many as four claims were coded for each petition. The claim is coded to represent the action sought by the petitioner. Claims codes included the support or revival

of a product or celebrity; seeking to save a product from being discontinued or canceled; calls for publicity for a product; expressions of support, concern, or care for a product or celebrity; requests to fix or repair a product that is asserted to be broken; requests to update an existing product, such as through the creation of a new album or a sequel; expansion of an existing product, such as by broadcasting to a wider area or distributing in an additional format; changes to a product otherwise unspecified; requests to "port" a product such as a game to another platform or hardware system; claims regarding intellectual property such as patent or digital rights management issues; claims regarding copyright as a specific issue; issues regarding prices of products or services; claims relating to customer service; claims pertaining to law or policy specifically; and a final category for other claims not represented by this list. In the case of claims not specified in by the earlier categories, text was entered to more fully describe the petition's claim.

4   "Product/Celebrity" is a categorical variable coded to represent the type of product on which the petitions are seeking some action. It contains the following categories: specific celebrity or group of celebrities (Eddie Guerrero or the Rat Pack); specific movie or set of films; specific television show or shows; specific singer, band, song, or music source (such as a radio station); specific video or online game(s); specific nongame software; and a category for other types of products.

5   "Product name" is a text field containing the actual name of whatever product is the focus of the petition.

6   "Industry" is coded to represent the umbrella industry that produces the focal product, and is coded with the following categories: radio, television, film and video, games, music, software, athletics, and a final category for industries not otherwise specified. When this last category was indicated, an additional text field was completed to describe the industry.

7   "Date" was coded any time the petition indicated a specific end date, and included fields for standard date elements (year, month, day) plus season (winter, spring, summer, fall).

8   "Signers" were coded up to four times for each petition to represent the types of people identified as the petitioners. Signer categories include fans, users, gamers, watchers, listeners, readers, students, men, women, and specific types of named fans such as "Pottermaniacs." A final category was included to allow text for types of signers not otherwise classified, such as "loyal followers," "family members," or "friends."

Notes

1. See David S. Meyer and Sydney Tarrow, A Movement Society: Contentious Politics for the New Century, in *The Social Movement Society: Contentious Politics for the New Century*, ed. David S. Meyer and Sydney Tarrow (Lanham, MD: Rowman & Littlefield, 1998), 1–28, for a longer discussion of this point.

2. Doug McAdam, Sydney Tarrow, and Charles Tilly, *Dynamics of Contention* (Cambridge, UK: Cambridge University Press, 2001).

3. Recent research has suggested that a large share of historical protest did not target the state, but instead targeted other powerful actors (Nella Van Dyke, Sarah A. Soule, and Verta A. Taylor, The Targets of Social Movements: Beyond a Focus on the State, *Research in Social Movements, Conflicts and Change 25*

[2004]: 27–51). This work shows that the centrality of government to classic forms of civic engagement such as protest has been more of an assumption on the part of scholars and policy makers than it was an empirical reality.

4. See Van Dyke, Soule, and Taylor for historical figures on offline protest in the United States, and Jennifer Earl and Katrina Kimport, The Targets of Online Protest: State and Private Targets of Four Online Protest Tactics (unpublished manuscript, 2006), for data on online protest in the United States.

5. Stephen Coleman, *How the Other Half Votes:* Big Brother *Viewers and the 2005 General Election* (London: Hansard Society, 2006).

6. Coleman, p. 12, is contributing to a broader debate about how to define politics, activism, and community both online as well as offline. Online, boundaries between institutional and extra- or anti-institutional activity are becoming less distinct and the costs of engaging in those activities are shrinking. Offline, the tactics of social movements are increasingly appropriated for new ends in a movement society. As both trends continue, scholars are increasingly confronting the question of how to define challenges to power.

7. Susan Zaeske, *Signatures of Citizenship* (Chapel Hill: University of North Carolina Press, 2003).

8. See Leila J. Rupp and Verta Taylor, *Drag Queens at the 801 Cabaret* (Chicago: University of Chicago Press, 2003), for an interesting discussion on this point.

9. W. Lance Bennett, Branded Political Communication: Lifestyle Politics, Logo Campaigns, and the Rise of Global Citizenship, in *Politics, Products, and Markets: Exploring Political Consumerism Past and Present*, ed. Michele Micheletti, Andreas Follesdal, and Dietlind Stolle (New Brunswick, NJ: Transaction Books, 2004), 101–26, provides some discussion that is complementary to this idea, exploring the way that activists engage in contestation over the public images of companies whose behavior they seek to change. While the domain of culture and consumer goods is common between our work and Bennett's, we differ in that the activists Bennett identifies are much more explicitly political in both their goals and tactics.

10. Meyer and Tarrow.

11. See Sarah A. Soule and Jennifer Earl, A Movement Society Evaluated: Collective Protest in the United States, 1960–1986, *Mobilization* 10 (2005): 345–64, for a review of this literature.

12. Jennifer Earl and Katrina Kimport, Movement Societies and Digital Protest: Non-traditional Uses of Four Protest Tactics Online (paper presented at the Annual Meetings of the American Sociological Association, Montreal, Canada, 2006).

13. See research by Jennifer Earl, Pursuing Social Change Online: The Use of Four Protest Tactics on the Internet, *Social Science Computer Review* 24 (2006): 362–77; Jennifer Earl, Step-Child Forms of Activism? Online Production and Participation in Protest Actions (unpublished manuscript, 2006); Jennifer Earl and Alan Schussman, The New Site of Activism: On-Line Organizations, Movement Entrepreneurs, and the Changing Location of Social Movement Decision-Making, *Research in Social Movements, Conflicts and Change* 24 (2003): 155–87; Jennifer Earl and Alan Schussman, Cease and Desist: Repression, Strategic Voting and the 2000 Presidential Election, *Mobilization* 9 (2004): 181–202; Alan Schussman and Jennifer Earl, From Barricades to Firewalls? Strategic Voting and Social Movement Leadership in the Internet Age, *Sociological Inquiry* 74 (2004): 439–63; Bruce Bimber, Andrew J. Flanagin, and Cynthia Stohl, Reconceptualizing Collective Action in the Contemporary Media Environment, *Communication Theory* 15 (2005): 365–88; and Andrew J. Flanagin, Cynthia Stohl, and Bruce Bimber, Modeling the Structure of Collective Action, *Communication Monographs* 73 (2005): 29–54.

14. Earl and Schussman, The New Site of Activism.

15. See Earl, Step-Child Forms of Activism? for a host of implications.

16. Earl, Step-Child Forms of Activism?

17. Earl and Kimport, Movement Societies and Digital Protest.

18. S. Howard-Spink, Grey Tuesday, Online Cultural Activism and the Mash-up of Music and Politics, *First Monday* 9 (2004). Retrieved October 1, 2006. http://firstmonday.org/issues/issue9_10/howard/.

19. Yochai Benkler, *The Wealth of Networks: How Social Production Transforms Markets and Freedom* (New Haven: Yale University Press, 2006).

20. Jack M. Balkin, Digital Speech and Democratic Culture: A Theory of Freedom of Expression for the Information Society, *NYU Law Review* 79 (2004): 10.

21. Benkler, 299.

22. In some ways, this kind of production mirrors that of "pro-ams" (i.e., professional-amateurs) in systems of "user-driven innovation," where it has been understood for some time that the skilled users and consumers of products can have an important role in subsequent development (Charles Leadbeater and Paul Miller, *The Pro-Am Revolution* [London: Demos, 2004]); Eric von Hippel, Open Source Shows the Way: Innovation By and For Users—No Manufacturer Required! *Sloan Management Review* 42 (2001): 82–86; Howard-Spink). But the significant difference is the scale of activity in an economy where malleable cultural goods are ubiquitous.

23. Benkler, 299.

24. Henry Jenkins, *Convergence Culture: Where Old and New Media Collide* (New York: NYU Press, 2006), 257.

25. Jenkins, 259.

26. Jenkins, 258–59.

27. Eszter Hargittai, Just a Pretty Face(book)? What College Students Actually Do Online (2006), http://results.webuse.org/uic06/ (accessed June 1, 2006).

28. danah boyd, Identity Production in a Networked Culture: Why Youth Heart MySpace (2006). Retrieved June 1, 2006. http://www.danah.org/papers/AAAS2006.html.

29. Margaret Scammell, The Internet and Civic Engagement: The Age of the Citizen-Consumer, *Political Communication* 17 (2000): 351–55.

30. http://www.petitiononline.com (accessed June 2006).

31. http://www.petitiononline.com (accessed July 2006).

32. Earl, Pursuing Social Change Online.

33. Earl and Kimport, Movement Societies and Digital Protest.

34. As discussed more later, active petitions are defined by PetitionOnline as petitions with more than ten signatures that have been signed within the last thirty days. Petitions that do not have at least ten signatures, or that have not been signed in the last month, are still hosted by PetitionOnline, but are not displayed in the category views.

35. See the methodological appendix for details on coding.

36. Admittedly, for a petition to appear within the category we sampled from it must have had at least ten signatures (see earlier), which does bias participation estimates upward. But, if participation was very low, then most of the petitions we did observe would have had just over ten signers, which was not the case.

37. Although we did not systematically identify the languages for all seventy-eight non-English petitions, it is clear that some of these were written in Chinese and Italian, among other languages.

38. See http://www.petitiononline.com/BAMMO49/petition.html (accessed August 2006).

39. See http://www.petitiononline.com/qzmania/ (accessed August 2006).

40. Regarding "other" categories for industry and product types, 8.5 percent of all petitions could not be coded with at least one industry or product category. We suggest that given the highly particularistic nature of claims facilitated by a movement society, this level of unclassified products is acceptable.

41. Petition number 56.

42. In fact, Earl and Kimport, The Targets of Online Protest, sampled online petitions and found that over 50 percent of online petitions targeted the government across various samples and populations.

43. We also coded petitions related to video games that were cancelled before they went to market (i.e., cancelled while in production) as making a "save" claim. Although the games had not reached market, we coded these as such because game developers regularly "hype" in-development products by releasing previews in order to build a consumer base. These events could not be readily coded as "revivals" since the products were not fully released.

44. Petition number 262.

45. Petition number 212.

46. Petition number 257.

47. Software is usually tied to a single gaming machine or computer system. Porting is the process of converting software built for one platform so that it will work on another system.

48. This percentage excludes the petitions where an identity category could not be coded, and so uses 240, instead of 564, as the denominator for the percentage.

49. Petition number 23.

50. Petition number 96.

51. Petition number 352.

52. Petition number 173.

53. Petition number 137.

54. Petition number 407.

55. Petition number 492.

56. Petition number 495.

57. Jenkins, 80.

58. See http://www.petitiononline.com/create_petition.html (accessed July 2006).

59. Some might alternatively consider the role of online petitions to be a source of information about cultural goods, rather than a genuine display of contention. However, our detailed reading of the petitions does not support this alternative reading. Authors generally phrased their concerns as a set of demands or desires, not as simply informative. As well, the choice of a petitioning Web site is highly suggestive of an at least somewhat adversarial posture.

60. Paul DiMaggio, Eszter Hargittai, W. Russell Neuman, and John P. Robinson, The Social Implications of the Internet, Annual Review of Sociology 27 (2001): 307–36.

61. Kieran Healy, Survey Article: Digital Technology and Cultural Goods, *The Journal of Political Philosophy* 10 (2002): 478–500.

62. Balkin, 21.

63. Lawrence Lessig, *Free Culture: How Big Media Uses Technology and the Law to Lock Down Culture and Control Creativity* (New York: Penguin Press, 2004).

64. See his discussion of Livingstone, Bober, and Helsper's 2005 research from the UKCGO project, for example.

65. See Bert Klandermans, *The Social Psychology of Protest* (Cambridge, MA: Blackwell, 1997); Alan Schussman and Sarah A. Soule, Process and Protest: Accounting for Individual Protest Participation, *Social Forces* 84 (2005): 1081–106; and Sidney Verba, Kay L. Schlozman, and Henry E. Brady, *Voice and Equality: Civic Voluntarism in American Politics* (Cambridge, MA: Harvard University Press, 1995).

66. Doug McAdam, Recruitment to High Risk Activism: The Case of Freedom Summer, *American Journal of Sociology* 92 (1986): 64–90; Doug McAdam and Ronnelle Paulsen, Specifying the Relationship Between Social Ties and Activism, *American Journal of Sociology* 92 (1993): 54–90.

67. Stephen Coleman, A Tale of Two Houses: The House of Commons, the *Big Brother* House and the People at Home, *Parliamentary Affairs* 56 (2003): 733–58.

Using Participatory Media and Public Voice to Encourage Civic Engagement

Howard Rheingold

Stanford University, Communication Department

As increasing numbers of young people seek to master the use of media tools to express themselves, explore their identities, and connect with peers—to be active creators as well as consumers of culture—educators have an opportunity to encourage young media makers to exercise active citizenship.[1] Might teachers enlist these young people's enthusiasm for using digital media in the service of civic engagement? I propose one way to do this: help students communicate in their public voices about issues they care about.

The eager adoption of Web publishing, digital video production and online video distribution, social networking services, instant messaging, multiplayer role-playing games, online communities, virtual worlds, and other Internet-based media by millions of young people around the world demonstrates the strength of their desire—unprompted by adults—to learn digital production and communication skills. According to a 2005 survey by the Pew Internet and American Life Project, "The number of teenagers using the internet has grown 24% in the past four years and 87% of those between the ages of 12 and 17 are online."[2] This interest by American (and Brazilian, British, Chinese, Indian, Japanese, Persian, etc.) youth in media production practices might well be a function of adolescents' needs to explore their identities and experiment with social interaction—and can be seen as a healthy active response to the hypermediated environment they've grown up in.[3]

Whatever else might be said of teenage bloggers, dorm-room video producers, or the millions who maintain pages on social network services like MySpace and Facebook, it cannot be said that they are passive media consumers. They seek, adopt, appropriate, and invent ways to participate in cultural production.[4] Another recent Pew study found that more than 50 percent of today's teenagers have created as well as consumed digital media.[5] This chapter focuses on those avid young digital media makers in the knowledge that addressing the needs of those who are not able to participate in cultural production, the other half of the digital divide, remains an important task. Although significant barriers remain in regard to less-privileged youth, this chapter addresses the educational needs and opportunities of the large minority of young people around the world, of many nationalities and socioeconomic levels, who are avid digital media creators.

Some recent data indicates that American youth are interested in civic engagement as well as in playing with media. A research team commissioned by MTV interviewed more than twelve hundred young people, conducted expert interviews and ethnographies, and took a national poll of a representative sample ages 12–24, between December 2005 and April 2006.[6] Although the research found, "With 70% believing in the importance of helping the community, 68% already doing something to support a cause on a monthly basis and 82%

describing themselves at least 'somewhat involved,' it does seem that the majority of young people are convinced that supporting a social cause is something they should do. However, there is a strong disparity between interest and involvement, an 'activation gap,' and there is significant room for growth."

Michael Xenos and Kirsten Foot, in their chapter for this volume, warn, in regard to youth involvement with traditional election campaigns: "Based on the best available indicators and techniques for understanding both what young people are looking for in an electoral politics experience on the Web, and what campaign organizations are providing, a substantial gulf is evident between them. If this gap is left unaddressed, we believe future developments in online campaigning will fail to attract all but the most politically oriented young voters into greater involvement with the electoral system. In the long run, this means that the potential of new media to help reverse significant declines in youth political involvement may go unrealized." Other authors in this volume—Bennett, Bers, Coleman, Earl and Schussman, Montgomery, Raynes-Goldie and Walker—echo this opinion in different ways.

Jennifer Earl and Alan Schussman in particular note, "If young people are growing up in movement societies, where scripts and practices from social movements have become part of everyday thinking, and producing online protest actions (which embodies these pervasive social movement schemas) has become extremely inexpensive, particularly to those who have moderate computing skills, then we should expect that young people will begin to use online protest-organizing tools to mount protests about issues they care about." Indeed, Kathryn Montgomery notes in her chapter in this volume that young people have used online social networks to engage one of the most contentious techno-political issues today, with more than seventeen thousand of them signing up as "friends of network neutrality" on MySpace.

The MTV-sponsored study group suggested, among other measures, that educators "integrate pro-social goals into activities that young people already enjoy doing." Yet another pair of US researchers, Skelton and Valentine (2003), looked at youth political activism and argued that "when young people's action is looked for, rather than focusing on what they are not doing, it becomes clear that even groups of young people traditionally assumed not to be active social agents are in fact demonstrating forms of political participation and action"[7] Earl and Schussman in this volume assert, "One must ask whether existing notions of what comprises civic engagement tend to ignore, devalue, and otherwise marginalize ways in which younger citizens are connecting with one another to collectively make a difference in their own worlds."

A U.K. research group that surveyed over a thousand young people, age eighteen and up, was less sanguine about the value of online media practices, concluding that "the broad decline in youth participation might be better redressed through offline initiatives, strengthening the opportunities structures of young people's lives and the 'communities of practice' available to them, rather than building Web sites which, though they will engage a few, will struggle to reach the majority or, more important, to connect that majority to those with power over their lives in a manner that young people themselves judge effective and consequential." Livingstone, Couldry, and Markham, the authors of the U.K. study, added, "Rather than blaming young people for their apathy, the finger might instead be pointed at the online and offline structures of opportunity that facilitate, shape and develop young people's participation. Focus groups with young people suggest a generation bored with politics, critical of the online offer, instead interested in celebrity and conforming to peer norms. Young people protest that 'having your say' does not seem to mean 'being listened to,' and so they feel justified in recognising little responsibility to participate."[8]

These trends suggest the importance of social scaffolding for any interventions involving self-expression—other peers in the class and the teacher must act as the first "public" that reads/views/listens and responds. For example, Peter Levine's chapter in this volume focuses on the problem of "finding appropriate audiences for students' work." Preliminary effort to recruit respondents willing to provide feedback from interest groups, peer communities, community organizations, the press, and especially political leaders and civil servants are essential to proper preparation. It isn't "voice" if nobody seems to be listening. Finding the first publics who can respond to bloggers is as important as introducing people to blogs as vehicles of potential public influence. In the blogosphere, speaking your mind is necessary to be hearable, but doesn't guarantee that you will be heard.

Participatory Media in the Curriculum—and in Society

What if teachers could help students discover what they really care about, then show them how to use digital media to learn more and to persuade others? Constructivist theories of education that exhort teachers to guide active learning through hands-on experimentation are not new ideas, and neither is the notion that digital media can be used to encourage this kind of learning.[9] Marina Bers in this volume offers a constructivist approach to using virtual worlds as an avenue to civic engagement for young people. What is new is a population of "digital natives" who have learned how to learn new kinds of software before they started high school, who carry mobile phones, media players, game devices, and laptop computers and know how to use them, and for whom the Internet is not a transformative new technology but a feature of their lives that has always been there, like water and electricity.[10] This population is both self-guided and in need of guidance: although a willingness to learn new media by point-and-click exploration might come naturally to today's student cohort, there's nothing innate about knowing how to apply their skills to the processes of democracy. Internet media are not offered here as the solution to young people's disengagement from political life, but as a possibly powerful tool to be deployed toward helping them engage.

It is not easy for many teachers to adopt this perspective and put it into action in the classroom—the political and economic necessity of teaching to the test leaves little room to fit these kinds of skills lessons into mandated and standardized curriculum. "Accountability" and innovation are often locked into a zero-sum game. Lack of resources, training, and technical support offer significant additional obstacles.

In *Confronting The Challenges of Participatory Culture: Media Education for the 21st Century*, Jenkins et al. see an entirely new kind of culture emerging from the use of participatory media, characterizing the shift as one that should not be reduced to the enabling technology, but "rather represents a shift in the way our culture operates.":

This context places new emphasis on the need for schools and afterschool programs to devote attention to fostering what we are calling the new media literacies – a set of cultural competencies and social skills which young people need as they confront the new media landscape. Participatory culture shifts the focus of literacy training from individual expression onto community involvement: the new literacies are almost all social skills which have to do with collaboration and networking. These skills build on the foundation of traditional literacy, research skills, technical skills, and critical analysis skills which should have been part of the school curriculum all along.[11]

If print culture shaped the environment in which the Enlightenment blossomed and set the scene for the Industrial Revolution, participatory media might similarly shape the cognitive and social environments in which twenty-first-century life will take place (a shift in the way our culture operates). For this reason, participatory media literacy is not another subject to be shoehorned into the curriculum as job training for knowledge workers. Jenkins et al. put it this way:

Much of the resistance to embracing media literacy training comes from the sense that the school day is bursting at its seams, that we cannot cram in any new tasks without the instructional system breaking down altogether. For that reason, we do not want to see media literacy treated as an add-on subject. Rather, we should see it as a paradigm shift, one which, like multiculturalism or globalization, reshapes how we teach every existing subject. Media change is impacting every aspect of our contemporary experience and as a consequence, every school discipline needs to take responsibility for helping students to master the skills and knowledge they need to function in a hypermediated environment.[12]

Arguing for the place of participatory media literacy in the curriculum is not a peripheral debate, but is part of one of the defining conflicts of our time, a power struggle that involves political, economic, technological, as well as educational dimensions. Participatory media literacy is an active response to the as-yet-unsettled battles over political and economic power in the emerging mediasphere, and to the possibility that today's young people could have a say in shaping part of the world they will live in—or might be locked out of that possibility. The struggle for participatory media literacy in schools must be seen in the context of these broader societal conflicts.

Participatory media include (but aren't limited to) blogs, wikis, RSS, tagging and social bookmarking, music-photo-video sharing, mashups, podcasts, digital storytelling, virtual communities, social network services, virtual environments, and videoblogs. These distinctly different media share three common, interrelated characteristics:

- Many-to-many media now make it possible for every person connected to the network to broadcast as well as receive text, images, audio, video, software, data, discussions, transactions, computations, tags, or links to and from every other person. The asymmetry between broadcaster and audience that was dictated by the structure of predigital technologies has changed radically. This is a technical–structural characteristic.

- Participatory media are social media whose value and power derives from the active participation of many people. Value derives not just from the size of the audience, but from their power to link to each other, to form a public as well as a market. This is a psychological and social characteristic.

- Social networks, when amplified by information and communication networks, enable broader, faster, and lower cost coordination of activities.[13] This is an economic and political characteristic.

Like the early days of print, radio, and television, the present structure of the participatory media regime—the political, economic, social and cultural institutions that constrain and empower the way the new medium can be used, and which impose structures on flows of information and capital—is still unsettled. As legislative and regulatory battles, business competition, and social institutions vie to control the new regime, a potentially decisive and presently unknown variable is the degree and kind of public participation. Because the unique power of the new media regime is precisely its participatory potential, the number of people who participate in using it during its formative years, and the skill with which they attempt to take advantage of this potential, is particularly salient. The outcome of contemporary regulatory battles that are obscure to the majority of citizens will likely determine whether future participatory media will be enclosed economically, controlled centrally, and co-opted politically, or whether participatory media will enable broad cultural production and authentically democratic political influence. Kathryn Montgomery's chapter in this volume offers a detailed description of the battle over "network neutrality."

If literacy is an ability to encode as well as decode, with contextual knowledge of how communication can attain desired ends—then "voice," the part of the process where a young person's individuality comes into play, might help link self-expression with civic participation.

Public Voice: The Bridge between Media Production and Civic Engagement

Making connections between the literacies students pick up simply by being young in the twenty-first century and those best learned through reading and discussing texts is an appropriate role for teachers today. My fundamental assumption for beginning to teach participatory media skills myself, based on my own encounters with students in social cyberspaces and the advice of more experienced educators, is that "voice," the unique style of personal expression that distinguishes one's communications from those of others, can be called upon to help connect young people's energetic involvement in identity-formation with their potential engagement with society as citizens. Moving from a private to a public voice can help students turn their self-expression into a form of public participation.[14] Public voice is learnable, a matter of consciously engaging with an active public rather than broadcasting to a passive audience.

The public voice of individuals, aggregated and in dialogue with the voices of other individuals, is the fundamental particle of "public opinion." When public opinion has the power and freedom to influence policy and grows from the open, rational, critical debate among peers posited by Jurgen Habermas and others, it can be an essential instrument of democratic self-governance.[15] James Fishkin at Stanford, John Gastil at the University of Washington, Peter Levine at the University of Maryland (see Levine's chapter in this volume) and others have been investigating whether better deliberative practice can produce better publics.[16] Deliberation, however, is only part of public discourse. Investigation, advocacy, criticism, debate, persuasion, and politicking are all part of the process.

The political philosopher Jürgen Habermas defined the public sphere decades before the Internet became a vehicle for political expression:

By "public sphere," we mean first of all a domain of our social life in which such a thing as public opinion can be formed. Access to the public sphere is open in principle to all citizens. A portion of the public sphere is constituted in every conversation in which private persons come together to form a public. They are then acting neither as business or professional people conducting their private affairs, nor as legal consociates subject to the legal regulations of a state bureaucracy and obligated to obedience. Citizens act as a public when they deal with matters of general interest without being subject to coercion; thus with the guarantee that they may assemble and unite freely, and express and publicize their opinions freely.[17]

Habermas drew attention to the intimate connection between a web of free, informal personal communications and the foundations of democratic society. Because the public sphere depends on free communication and discussion of ideas, it changes when it scales—as soon as your political entity grows larger than the number of citizens you can fit into a modest town hall, this vital marketplace for political ideas can be influenced by changes in communications technology. Communication media, and the ways the state permits citizens to use them, are essential to the public sphere in a large society. Ask anybody living under an authoritarian government about the right to talk freely among friends and neighbors, to call a meeting to protest government policy, or to raise certain issues on a blog or in a BBS. Brute totalitarian seizure of communications technology or automation of censorship are not the only ways that political powers can neutralize the ability of citizens to talk freely. Habermas also feared that the public sphere in the mass media era has already been corrupted by paid fake discourse—from the public relations industry to campaign media strategies.[18]

Although civic engagement encompasses many dimensions, this chapter focuses on participation in the public sphere through direct experience with online publishing, discourse, debate, cocreation of culture, and collective action. By showing students how to use Web-based tools and channels to inform publics, advocate positions, contest claims, and organize action around issues that they truly care about, participatory media education can draw them into positive early experiences with citizenship that could influence their civic behavior throughout their lives. Formal theories of the public sphere could be introduced most productively after, and in the context of, direct experience of exercising a public voice.[19] Talking about public opinion making is a richer experience if you've tried to do it.

In one sense, public voice can be characterized not just as active, but as generative—a public is brought into being in a sense by the act of addressing some text in some medium to it. Michael Warner has argued that any particular public (as distinguished from "the public") comes into being only when it is addressed by a media text, rather than existing a priori —"it exists by virtue of being addressed."[20] By writing a blog post about an issue, a blogger brings together people whose only common interest is the issue addressed, bringing about "a relation among strangers" that would probably not otherwise exist. Creating a wiki about a local issue has the potential to precipitate a public that can inform itself, stage debates, even organize collective action.

I recognize that precipitating publics and organizing collective action are volatile practices that are often interpreted (and prohibited and punished) as "rebellious" by parents and schools. Stephen Coleman notes in his chapter in this volume that "[t]he policy of 'targeting' young people so that they can 'play their part' can be read either as a spur to youth activism or an attempt to manage it. Indeed, the very notion of youth e-citizenship seems to be caught between divergent strategies of management and autonomy.... The conflict between the two faces of e-citizenship is between a view of democracy as an established and reasonably just system, with which young people should be encouraged to engage, and democracy as a political as well as cultural aspiration, most likely to be realised through networks in which young people engage with one another." This tension between parental and teacher authority on one hand and the contentious, even rebellious, processes that are as fundamental to democracy as they are vexing to authority figures is an obvious site of potential conflict.

In particular, Coleman contrasts the adult view of training young people to be part of the existing political system—"good citizens"—and the view that democracy lives precisely within the unruly peer-to-peer relationships, networks, and norms that young people seek to develop for themselves. danah boyd, whose chapter, "Why Youth (Heart) Social Network Sites: The Role of Networked Publics in Teenage Social Life" appears in the *Identity* volume of the *MacArthur Series on Digital Media and Learning*, asserts the same case that Coleman argues. The value of the peer-to-peer network is not only essential, boyd argues, but necessarily prior to more orthodox forms of democratic discourse:[21] "In order to engage in political life, people have to have access to public life first. Youth need publics—networked or physical—before they can engage in any form of political life. Politics start first with the school, with your friends . . . then they grow to being about civics. Pushing the other way won't work. You need to start with the dramas that make sense to you."[22]

I propose that learning to use blogs, wikis, digital storytelling, podcasts, and video as media of self-expression within a context of "public voice" should be introduced and evaluated in school curricula, after-school programs, and informal learning communities if today's youth are to become effective citizens in the emerging era of networked publics.[23] In the twenty-first century, participatory media education and civic education are inextricable. For those educators who believe this assertion is worth testing in practice, this chapter and its references, including a public Web site for sharing experiences and knowledge, is offered by the author as a public resource.[24]

From the Blogosphere to the Public Sphere

A blog is a Web page that is updated frequently, with the most recent entry displayed at the top of the page. Given the simplicity of this definition of *blog*, a wild variety of diaries, news sources, reference repositories, collaboratories, filters, compendia, lab journals, classroom discussions, critical essays, rants, polemics, jokes, guides, advertising pitches, and social and political movements has resulted, with over seventy million blogs tracked worldwide by Technorati by 2006.[25] The term *blogosphere* to describe the interlinked web of blogs was invented as a joke in September 1999, according to Wikipedia.[26]

The political power of the blogosphere grew visible to the mainstream in 2003. Volunteer investigator-bloggers kept alive the story of Senate Majority Leader Trent Lott's racist public remarks and unearthed similar incidents in the past, eventually costing him his leadership position.[27] In September 2004, CBS newscaster Dan Rather claimed to have documents that showed presidential candidate George W. Bush to have whitewashed his absences from National Guard duty. Again, amateur fact-checkers organized online and turned up evidence that the documents cited by Rather were forgeries.[28]

Millions of people appear to be expressing their opinions online. Does that add up to a significant revitalization of the public sphere? The answer to that question is still contested. In the days of the pre-Web Internet, Fernback and Thompson argued against such a notion, warning of the danger that people would sit in front of their computers and mistake typing at each other for political action: "Indeed, it seems most likely that the virtual public sphere brought about by CMC will serve a cathartic role, allowing the public to feel involved rather than to advance actual participation."[29] A decade later, Yochai Benkler, in his 2006 book, *The Wealth of Networks*, commented:

We are witnessing a fundamental change in how individuals can interact with their democracy and experience their role as citizens. Ideal citizens need not be seen purely as trying to inform themselves about what others have found, so that they can vote intelligently. They need not be limited to reading the opinions of opinion makers and judging them in private conversations. They are no longer constrained to occupy the role of mere readers, viewers, and listeners. They can be, instead, participants in a conversation.[30]

Participants, like literate citizens, aren't automatically produced by computer ownership: access to the Internet and the capability of publishing a blog by a population is not sufficient to guarantee that blogging will have a significant positive impact on the political public sphere. The way in which that population *uses* the medium will matter. The literacies that this curriculum seeks to impart could be a crucially influential battle in this struggle over the political impact of blogging. Knowing how to take a tool into one's hand is no guarantee that anyone will do anything productive, but without such knowledge, productive use is less likely—and hegemonic control becomes more likely by those who do know exactly how to exercise the power of the new media.

It is not yet clear whether the blogosphere or any aggregation of online arguments constitute the ideal of constructive debate that public sphere theorists posit, but if Benkler's assessment is correct—that many-to-many media afford a window of opportunity for populations to exercise democratic power over would-be rulers—it seems possible that education could play a pivotal role by equipping today's digital natives with historical knowledge, personal experience, rhetorical skills, and a theoretical framework for understanding the connection between their power to publish online, their power to influence the circumstances of their own lives, and the health of democracy.

A Few Examples of Participative Media and Civic Engagement

An exhaustive or even fully representative cross-section of case histories is not possible within the scope of this chapter, but real examples of participative pedagogy should not be ignored either. Pointers to many more examples are available on the chapter's companion wiki.

Listening to what young people care about is the necessary first step in enlisting their enthusiasm. Youth-initiated applications of media to public issues is the first place I would begin my knowledge gathering. What are young people cooking up on their own accord? How are they appropriating media for public advocacy or contestation?

One illustrative example: While he was a Toronto high school student, Wojciech Gryc started a blog that attracted the attention of other high school students; together, they created an online webzine[31] that turned into an organization dedicated to youth, media, and civic engagement, "Five Minutes to Midnight."[32] In correspondence with the author, Gryc wrote that his organization "gets youth involved in human rights through media and journalism. We are based in Toronto, Canada, but use the Web to promote our work. We publish a Web magazine, run workshops on Web development, and have even travelled to Chad and Brazil to promote youth involvement through the use of open source software, development of media, and similar projects. The entire organization is run by youth 20 years of age or under (this includes the entire Board of Directors)."[33] Gryc and another young volunteer, Émanuèle Lapierre-Fortin, spent more than three weeks running workshops on open-source software in Chad for Rafigui.[34] "During that time, we made a video commercial for a picnic, taught the group how to work on their newspaper using GIMP, OpenOffice, InkScape, and got donations of laptops and a digital camera."[35]

The youth of the "Fantasy Congress Founding Fathers" is clear from the photograph of their Web site, and is reflected in their self-description:

The mission of Fantasy Congress™ is to involve individuals in the legislative process and the daily goings-on of Congress by means of computer simulation. Fantasy Congress™ is easy to use, making it simple for anyone to monitor the performance of his or her team, track the contributions of individual senators and representatives to the team, and follow latest news on their team members. Discussion boards make gameplay even more dynamic by enabling players to interact more directly with each other. By inspiring people to care about government as much as they care about sports, Fantasy Congress hopes to encourage government transparency and responsibility while educating the governed.

Fantasy Congress™ is more than just a totally sweet game. Drawing from the broadest and most up-to-date database of its kind, it ranks sitting members of Congress by legislative efficacy and other criteria.[36]

Fantasy Congress™ founders were four students at Claremont McKenna College. Founder Andrew Lee came up with the idea for the game when he asked whether the enthusiasm his classmates put into fantasy sports could be cast as a game that models the legislative process. He then enlisted three other students.

What have trained adult observers been able to report about youth media production practices and civic engagement? Direct observations of young people's actual media making and consuming practices is where anthropologist Mizuko Ito has been directing her attention. Ito is codirecting a study, funded by the MacArthur Foundation, titled "Kids' Informal Learning With Digital Media: An Ethnographic Collaboration," a joint effort between researchers at the University of California, Berkeley, School of Information and the University of Southern California Annenberg Center for Communication. "The goal of this three-year study is to observe how young people between the ages of 10 and 20 use digital technologies outside the classroom and then determine if these 'native' practices can be adapted for use in the classroom as a means to make the educational experience more engaging and effective."[37] Led by Peter Lyman, Mimi Ito, and Michael Carter, the Digital Youth project involves multi-institutional, interdisciplinary teams studying different aspects of youth media practices.[38]

Henry Jenkins at MIT also combines theory, empirical study, and pedagogical practice in "preparing students for jobs that don't yet exist."[39] Another project supported by the MacArthur Foundation's Digital Media and Learning program, the New Media Literacies project at MIT is "developing a theoretical framework and hands-on curriculum for K-12 students that integrates new media tools into broader educational, expressive and cultural frameworks. The NML team, led by Dr. Jenkins and based at MIT's Comparative Media Studies program, is currently exploring K-12 digital literacy, guided by two questions: What do young people need to know in order to become full, active, creative, critical, and ethically responsible participants in a media-rich environment?, and what steps do we need to take to make sure that these skills are available to all?"[40]

After first looking at what young people as individuals and small groups are inventing, I'd ask, "What are the most forward-looking communities of learners doing? Where are the pioneering students, teachers, and schools who have joined participatory media and civic engagement, and what are they doing?" An illustrative example, started in 1988, iEARN is "the world's largest non-profit global network that enables teachers and young people to use the Internet and other new technologies to collaborate on projects that both enhance learning and make a difference in the world.... All projects in iEARN are initiated and designed by teachers and students, and provide powerful examples of how new and emerging technologies can make a difference in teaching and learning."[41] Many of the iEARN projects link classrooms via online dialogue about civic issues, often involving Web publishing, digital photography and video production. The Global Learning Project, for example, deployed online dialogue and digital media while teaching about civil rights.[42]

Kathryn Montgomery cites in her chapter in this volume a number of examples, including The Community Information Corps, of St. Paul, Minnesota, which "enlists teens to do public art"; Tolerance.org, a project of the Southern Poverty Law Center that provides young people with an activist approach to fighting racism; Free the Planet! which "provides resources for activists, and help students win campaigns for environmental protection"; Out Proud for gay, lesbian, bisexual, transsexual youth; and WireTap, "Youth in pursuit of the dirty truth," a youth journalism effort by the progressive online magazine, Alternet. Montgomery also cites the extensive use of Internet media by MTV's "Rock the Vote" campaign. Also in this volume, Kate Raynes-Goldie and Luke Walker detail their experiences with TakingITGlobal, a global community of young activists, to register young voters.

Another collaboration of teachers and students uses video to give Harlem youth a world-wide forum to highlight issues that matter to them. HarlemLIVE blog, "Harlem's Youth Internet Publication" directly addresses civic issues of interest to Harlem youth and Harlem-LIVE video produces and publishes teen-created videos about civic and cultural issues.[43] HarlemLIVE "began in early 1996, at the beginning of the internet revolution, with just five students, one laptop, a digital camera, and an advisor."[44]

Note how student podcasters in a school in the U.K. don't make a strong distinction between "argue about issues that matter to us" and "share the music we write": "Podminions is the podcast of King's Norton Boys' School in Birmingham, U.K. Here we will tell stories of the local community, the things we do in and out of school, argue about the issues that matter to us and share with you the music we write."[45]

Yet another important avenue of inquiry is opened by asking what universities are doing to study, invent, or practice participatory media applications to civic engagement.

David Brake, doctoral student at the London School of Economics, is engaged, with professor Nick Couldry, in interviewing youth in the U.K. aged sixteen to nineteen "who have produced weblogs that are principally narratives about themselves, examining the influences and constraints on such storytelling. The research will focus primarily on the influence on their practice of these young people's relationship with their audiences (real and imagined), but will also consider the technological characteristics of the weblogging service that they use, the limits of their own digital and 'traditional' literacies and their understanding of emergent expectations of the genre of personal weblogging."[46]

In Australia, the Youth Internet Radio Network was established at Queensland University of Technology to engage young people in creative forms of cultural production through online networks. Using a combination of ethnography and action research, the researchers will then observe and analyze how young people participate in these networks, and how they are affected by this kind of interaction and participation. Youth Internet Radio Network has launched a Web site that functions as both a social network and a platform for the creation and distribution of creative content. Queensland researchers Notley and Tacchi wrote: "Mitra and Watts (2002) cite a central theme for communication scholars in the twenty-first century as the 'resuscitation of voice.' In redefining the Internet, they envision 'a discursive space produced by the creative work of people whose spatial locations are ambiguous and provisional.' They consider that new constructs of 'voice, agency, discourse and space' in 'cyberspace' may have 'liberating and empowering characteristics' (ibid: 486)."[47]

In addition to the MacArthur Foundation's Digital Media and Learning program, other foundation-supported efforts include a spinoff from Save The Children Foundation, Youth Noise, a webzine, social network, and online forum for young people concerned with creating social change.[48] The Web site, which claims 113,000 registered users from more than 170 countries, provides an interactive space through which young activists can connect to one another and express their views. See the chapter by Kate Raynes-Goldie and Luke Walker in this volume for more detailed discussion of Youth Noise. News 21 involves journalism students among five participating research universities under the Carnegie–Knight Initiative on the Future of Journalism Education.[49] News 21 student journalists from Berkeley produced broadcast-quality digital video from Kyrgyzstan in Central Asia, Djibouti in East Africa, South Korea, the Persian Gulf, and the South China Sea to "bring home the world of the American soldier serving abroad."[50]

These examples are meant to be illustrative, not exhaustive—to suggest how a broad range of motivations and institutions has begun to awaken to the civic potential in the media that both fascinate, manipulate, and potentially empower digital natives. The remainder of this chapter describes exercises for linking specific media with civic practices. A detailed, open-ended repository of resources, syllabi, and best practices is maintained at http://www.socialtext.net/medialiteracy/. This chapter and the wiki associated with it is an invitation and jump start for an ongoing community.

Blogging with a Public Voice

The following suggestions about ways participatory pedagogy might work in a classroom assume broadband access to the Internet by students who are comfortable using the Web and other digital tools, and have some time and permission to explore on their own. It is important to assess the knowledge and tech base of the students before starting; some basic instruction may be needed to bring all students up to the same skill level before embarking on the exercises suggested here. Providing instruction is far less effective without access. Individuals and small groups need time and freedom to experiment and explore alone and together, in addition to the exercises performed during class time. Students should be encouraged to teach one another whenever possible. A short portion of class time and online time could be devoted to peer-to-peer lore sharing.

The following section is phrased in the voice of a teacher directly instructing students on how to undertake exercise of a public voice through blogging. Although I go into some detail about blogging, by way of concrete illustration of the theory I've presented, the suggested exercises for other media will be presented here in abbreviated form; more detailed descriptions of these exercises are on the Participatory Media Literacy wiki[51]:

- Assuming that you have set up a blog and know how to create html links and basic formatting and publish a post, the next objective is to go beyond the mechanics of blogging to work with blogging rhetoric—and to connect that rhetoric with your role as a citizen in a democracy.

- First, you will make a post that serves a community of interest by directing attention to a worthwhile resource on the Web via an annotated link, including short, salient quotes, and explaining why your selected resource is worthy of attention from this community. Attracting a community of interest is not often an easy task.

- Then you will construct a blog post that links to two or more Web sites and explain the overarching idea that connects the sites you select—connective writing.

- Then you engage in online critical public discourse by analyzing the content of a site you link in a blog post, asking probing questions about the assumptions, assertions, and logic of the arguments in the site you link.

- Moving on to the exercise of a public voice, you will construct a post that takes a position on an issue, using links to other relevant Web sites to support your position.

Blogger as Intelligent Filter: The Annotated Link Post
Many bloggers serve as "intelligent filters" for their publics by selecting, contextualizing, and presenting links of particular interest for that public. In this context, a "public" differs from an "audience" because you, in your role as a blogger, have in mind when you write a

community of peers who not only read but actively respond to what you write, who might act upon your advice, and who might join you in discussion and collective action. The public you choose to address could be a public in the sense of a political public sphere that undergirds democracy—the communications you engage in with your fellow citizens, with whom you share responsibility for self-governance. The public doesn't have to be political, however. It could be an engaged community of interest—others who share your profession, avocation, or obsession. When fans begin writing fan fiction or remixing and sharing cultural content, they are acting as a public—a culture-producing public. When bloggers researched discrepancies in Dan Rather's story about George W. Bush's National Guard service, they were acting as a public. AIDS patients organized collective action that influenced research funding and the pharmaceutical industry—creating an effective public through their discussions about their mutual interest.

What interests you, the blogger? What issue or idea strongly, even passionately, draws your attention and provokes your opinion? Is there a community that shares your interest? Could you and the others constitute a public? Clearly defining and understanding your public is the necessary first step to developing a public voice—the voice you use when you keep that public, and your potential to act together, clearly in mind as you blog.

Your first exercise:

1   Define to your satisfaction and in your own terms a particular public. Use the resources available to you and your research skills to inform yourself about the focus of that public's interest (see the Participatory Media Literacy wiki to use blogs and RSS to research the subject). Compose a post addressed to that public, establishing the subject of shared interest you plan to blog about.

2   Keeping that public in mind, post a link in a blog post to any site on the Web—a blog post, a mainstream news item, a Wikipedia entry, an online community or marketplace, audio or video content—that has the potential to enhance that public's knowledge, incite that public to take action, and provoke that public to respond to you.

Blogging as Connected Writing

Will Richardson began using the term *connected writing* to refer to a specific kind of critical, disciplined blogging that he described in this way:

What I have been trying to celebrate, however, is what I see as an opportunity for a new type of writing that blogs allow, one that forces those who do it to read carefully and critically, one that demands clarity and cogency in its construction, one that is done for wide audience, and one that links to the sources of the ideas expressed.... I'm talking about something uniquely suited to blogs. I'm talking about this post, about our ability to connect ideas in ways that we could not do with paper, to distribute them in ways we could not do with the restrictiveness of html, and to engage in conversations and community in ways we could not do with newsgroups or other online communities before.[52]

Your second exercise:

1   Present to your public at least two links in the context of a post that makes clear their value to your public and explains the connection between the links.

2   Use search engines and blog indexes like Technorati to find other blogs that represent or address your public or segments of your public, submit your posts to other bloggers. See if you can get your friends to respond. "Priming the pump" of public response sometimes requires marketing and personal persuasion.

3   Elaborate a larger point, using the connection between the links you select to suggest a wider pattern. Explain the connection and suggest a meaning. You don't have to prove your point in this exercise—just use two links and the connection between them as the context for your own point, which should stand on its own. You can start with your opinion and use the links as support or illustration; or you can start with the links and approach your point inductively, by example.

Contributing to Critical Public Discourse: The Analytic Post

Loss of certainty about authority and credibility is one of the prices we pay for the freedom of democratized publishing. We can no longer trust the author to guarantee the veracity of work; today's media navigators must develop critical skills in order to find their way through the oceans of information, misinformation, and disinformation now available. The ability to analyze, investigate, and argue about what we read, see, and hear is an essential survival skill. Some bloggers can and do spread the most outrageously inaccurate and fallaciously argued information; it is up to the readers and, most significantly, other bloggers to actively question the questionable. Democratizing publishing creates a quality problem, the answer to which is—democratizing criticism. Critical thinking is not something that philosophers do, but a necessary skill in a mediasphere where anybody can publish and the veracity of what you read can never be assumed.

Your third exercise:

1   Link to a Web site—a blog post, online story from a mainstream media organization, any kind of Web site—and criticize it. If you can provide evidence that the facts presented in the criticized Web site are wrong, then do so, but your criticism doesn't have to be about factual inaccuracy. Debate the logic or possible bias of the author. Make a counterargument. Point out what the author leaves out. Voice your own opinion in response.

Exercising Your Public Voice: Making a Case for a Position

When you speak in a public voice—as a citizen appealing to other citizens as part of the serious business of self-governance—you are undertaking the cocreation of democracy. Your liberty probably depends on how well and how many citizens learn to use many-to-many media to exercise their public voice.

Your fourth exercise:

1   Pick a position about a public issue, any public issue, that you are passionate about: immigration; digital restrictions on music; steroid use by athletes; why the older generation misunderstands the younger generation's taste in music. Any issue you care about strongly enough to argue for or against.

2   Inform yourself. Search for information, and check the sources of authority of that information—what do others say about the author of the information, what sources does the author cite? Who has the freshest, most credible information about the issue you care about, and what are they saying? Track several sources through Web searches and blog feeds (see the Participatory Media Literacy wiki for instructions on RSS, blog feeds, and search feeds). Use your ability to gather and track information online as a means of knowing what you are talking about before you start saying anything in a public voice.

3   Make a case for something—a position, an action, a policy—related to this public issue. You don't have to prove your case, but you have to state it. You don't have to always present an original position, but you always need to go beyond simply quoting the positions of others. Again, you need to provide your public with the context you can see, but which is absent from the quote or link alone. Provide an answer to your public's question: "What does the author of this blog post want me to know, believe, think, or do? What point is the author making with this link?"

4   Use links to back up or add persuasiveness to your case. Use links to build your argument. Use factual sources, statements by others that corroborate your assertions, and instances that illustrate the point you want to make.

Contributing to Public Discourse: Commenting
Your fifth exercise:

1   Add a constructive comment to the blog posts of three other students in your class. Build on a point they make, offer evidence in support or in opposition to a position they take or claim they make, post a link to a resource that can illuminate or extend the post. If the blogger whose post you comment then posts a reply to your comment, see if you can extend the dialogue, invite others to participate and contribute.

2   Try to solicit comments in a post on your blog. Ask for opinion, examples, evidence. End your post in a question that invites comment.

3   For an advanced exercise, use a blog post or series of blog posts and invited comments to organize collective action—a meeting, a petition, a boycott, letters to the editor.

Using Wikis for Civic Engagement

A wiki is a Web site or digital document that anyone can edit, using simple markup language and hyperlinking to create visually consistent, interconnected pages of information. Most wikis are collaborative Web sites that can be edited by any user, though some require registration or a password. Wikis allow for collaborative communities that can share knowledge and ideas with minimal technical know-how, so that any user can be a writer, editor, and content creator and groups can harness collective intelligence to coauthor documents. In this case, "voice" is not an individual, but a collective expression, which involves structured debate and discussion about the form a group's wiki takes.

Wikis were invented about ten years ago by Ward Cunningham, who also created the name, appropriating the word *wiki*, which comes from a Hawaiian word for "quick." Wikis became the collaboration tool of choice for knowledge-building communities because they are simple and flexible to create and edit, because every version is saved and easily findable, because it is easy to learn the syntax of any wiki by inspecting it via the "edit this page" link that all wikis have, and because mistakes or damage can be repaired with a single click. A wiki is the essence of participatory media—a community, not an individual, is the author of many wiki documents. Such communities can work together to become knowledge communities and create public goods—Wikipedia (http://en.wikipedia.org/wiki/Main_Page), a volunteer-created encyclopedia that anybody can edit, is the most well-known example of such a community-created public good. This chapter touches on exercises that enlist the group communication and deliberation process inherent in wiki building for the purpose of civic decision making.

A Civic Engagement Exercise for High School Students

This issue-based self-government and problem-solving exercise requires students to write free-form on their user pages in a wiki, invite comment, and then discuss and refactor for use in actual public wiki pages. First, the class suggests and discusses, then the teacher selects a topic that appears to be engaging to them. The students then go into a wiki and, on their individual user pages, write what they think about it (this can be imported or refactored content from their blogs, or their other past work, if it is relevant and useable). Students are then asked to rationally and civilly discuss and debate the pros and cons of each other's individual work on these user pages, borrowing rules and social norms from existing wiki communities, when applicable. It is preferable that students actually choose themselves the rules that they will be governed by. The teacher encourages students to turn parts of their work into actual pages about the different facets of the subject, and to grow these pages. Each student is required to create at least two new pages from the note pages he or she has written in his or her initial work. Each student is also required to add a comment to at least two other nonuser pages, and instructed on how to refactor his or her comments and discussion into content on the page itself. All of the student wiki participants are then tasked with creating one or more joint resolution/proposals about how they think they should be governed regarding this issue. This wiki exercise could become an integral part of ongoing student involvement in all student issues (sports, fundraisers, activities, educational programs, etc.).

A civic engagement exercise for cocreating a meeting agenda in a wiki, cocreating meeting notes, and postmeeting codiscussion: Running a meeting is an everyday form of civic engagement—discussing and arguing with peers, making decisions, authoring group summaries is also what Congress does. The public sphere is not constituted only in high-minded discourse about public policy by powerful elites, but in a broad culture of civil discourse, in which meetings serve as socially structured discourse, often with a decision-making component. A wiki page can become a centralized forum in which to cocreate an agenda for any type of meeting. This exercise will teach students to build plans from the ground up as a group, to refine those plans, and to use wiki plan building to supplement and support face-to-face meeting and discussion. In this instance, the wiki serves as both an agenda cocreation tool and a group knowledge commons about meeting content, and an organically growing coauthored notebook to capture thoughts before, during, and after the meeting. Using a wiki to organize face-to-face meetings joins online collaboration skills of participatory media literacy with the offline requirements for a healthy public sphere—rational, critical debate about issues of mutual concern.

An example exercise: Students are given two weeks or more to cocreate and then vote on a meeting agenda and rules on a wiki page. Students then hold a face-to-face meeting based on this agenda; they are encouraged to post notes about the meeting to the wiki. Students should then continue asynchronous discussion online after the meeting for at least one week, within the wiki and on their blogs. Students should make wiki pages for concepts that emerge from this discussion. The skills learned through this exercise can be reapplied to many civic engagement uses. Almost any meeting could be potentially supplemented both by using a wiki for agenda and rule creation and discussion and by incorporating other forms of participatory media.

Citizen Journalism/Digital Storytelling

Although not all young people are interested, those who do express an interest in using participatory media to do journalism have unprecedented access to both the tools of production and the means of distribution: digital audio and video production via laptop computer today is equivalent to expensive professional equipment of only a few years ago, and while Internet publishing does not guarantee that a worldwide audience will pay attention, it does provide inexpensive access to it on a scale never before possible.

Several recent incidents have moved citizen digital journalism closer to the center of world attention: The first images of the disastrous Asian tsunami of 2005 were published on the Internet, many of them from camera phones.[53] The news photo of the year in 2005 was the shot of the London tube immediately after the terrorist bombing of July 7, sent directly from a cameraphone to the Internet.[54] The Korean citizen-journalism webzine, OhMyNews, now with more than 40,000 citizen reporters, is widely credited with having helped tip the Korean presidential election in favor of the underdog and eventual winner, now President Roh Moo-Hyun.[55] In terms of youth-led citizen journalism, a News 21 team at Northwestern University uncovered information about surveillance of students and other citizens.[56]

Citizen journalism, still in its infancy, is a general term that covers different kinds of activities:

1   *Reporting news* (e.g., cameraphone pictures from Asia tsunami and London attacks),

2   *Investigative blogging* (e.g., Trent Lott and Dan Rather incidents),

3   *Hyperlocal journalism* (e.g., reporting on local meetings and sporting events), and

4   *Digital storytelling* (e.g., narrated oral history and audio–video interviews edited with scanned still images).

Opportunities for eyewitnesses to introduce their stories, and especially their pictures, into mainstream media abound. The famous London bombing cameraphone picture was sent directly to a free Internet photo-sharing service, Flickr (http://www.flickr.com). OhMyNews accepts international reports and services such as NowPublic (http://www.nowpublic.com) enable citizen-reporters to sell their journalism. Since Kevin Sites started "backpack journalism" blogging from the war in Iraq, freelance war reporting has become a more likely option for daring independents (http://www.kevinsites.net/). Although it is unlikely that purely citizen-created journalism will replace mainstream journalism, it is already clear that a niche exists.

In the pre-Internet age of multimedia publishing, pioneer digital storytelling enthusiasts showed people how to digitize the old photos in their family albums, interview their relatives and digitize the interviews, then arrange the audiovisual elements into a narrative, often with a voiceover narration. While this technique can be applied to personal genealogy and history or pure entertainment, digital storytelling, when used to construct a narrative presentation of true historical events, personages, and geographical locations, is one way of introducing students to participatory media, to the communication basics of compelling narrative production, and to local civic affairs. Journalism doesn't have to be global. Hyperlocal journalism that delves more deeply into local events than mass media does can also serve as a springboard for civic engagement. See Peter Levine's chapter in this volume for more about local community involvement.

Susan Johnston at Tam Valley public school in Tamalpais Valley, California, sends elementary school students to record interviews with the people who own and work in neighborhood stores, as part of a local history of nearby Mill Valley.[57] Students take digital photographs, scan old photos from City Hall and the newspaper, then put them together as hotspots on a clickable map of Mill Valley. Digital storytelling about your immigrant grandparents, the woman in your community who worked as a maid and sent her children through college, about the hotly contested development of a local historical site, are all issues in which the fun of putting interviews, found images, photographs, and artwork together into an entertaining narrative can be combined with serious discussion of public issues.

Learning opportunities can be unlocked by questions that present themselves: In which part of the digital storytelling process does "public voice" enter into it? In what way do the decisions about questions to ask, who to interview, and how to edit the interviews represent a deliberate point of view, a kind of public voice on an issue, represented perhaps in words other than those of the author, but representing the perspective the author intends to present? Identifying and discussing the specific narration, captions, choice of subject matter, juxtaposition, and editing decisions that present the storyteller's point of view is a way of connecting media production practices with a public voice.

Podcasting: From Personal to Public Voice

Audio programs that are recorded and distributed digitally are known as "podcasts," because they allow listeners to subscribe online and automatically download each episode to their computers or portable MP3 players (named for the popular iPod from Apple). Podcasts are ordinary MP3 files, like most digital music files which are compressed so they don't take up too much space on listener's computer drives. You don't have to own an MP3 player to listen to podcasts—you can listen to them on your computer, by downloading them or by streaming the content directly from the podcast's Web site.

Podcasts are also easy to create and span the range from professionally recorded radio shows to homegrown audio blogs, music showcases, and social or political commentary. As such, they are a way for young journalists and advocates to produce and distribute radio programs inexpensively. The following exercises are intended to introduce a personal voice and provide pathways for shifting into a public voice via narrative and documentary audio production.

Before you start, look at what is already out there: http://www.bbc.co.uk/yourstories has a number of examples; the chapter's companion wiki lists other sources and detailed versions of the following suggested exercises.

First Exercise: Writing a Personal Story
Identify an interesting or poignant story from your own experience (not necessarily about yourself). Look for something character-based, with conflict and resolution. Narrate this story as a series of anecdotes, and the story under five minutes long. Pause and reflect on the significance of each part of the story—what's your larger point? It doesn't have to be profound. "People love their pets" and "First dates are awkward" are examples of such larger points. Try to tie the anecdotes together by highlighting the overall relevance of each portion, and making sure they point to a broader meaning or point. Make notes as you go, and write a transcript you can read from later. See the Participatory Media wiki for instructions on how

to record the transcript you've written by reading it aloud, then edit, add music, encode, and upload your podcast.

Second Exercise: Interviewing

Find a friend who's done something that interests you—maybe an art project or political activism or an adventure—and ask to interview them (on tape!). Come up with two or three main topics you want them to address about their project in your interview. Prepare yourself with some basic notes outlining the structure of the interview. During the interview, ask questions to get at the main points you want your interviewee to discuss. Probe to get the details. As you go, encourage them to be descriptive so your audience can visualize their story more clearly. As they narrate, raise broader questions to get them to reflect on the meaning of their work, and how it all ties together. Listen to your recording, log key moments, and then edit it down to half its unedited length. Encode and upload.

Third Exercise: Move to a Public Voice

Now that you have experience, repeat the first four exercises, but choose stories, characters, and issues that relate to some public or civic topic that you care about. Is there no place for young people to hang out in your town? Talk to young people, local police, local city council people. Would a skateboard park be a solution? Is there local opposition to a chain store moving in? Ask about issues that most interest you. Interview people on both sides. A local election coming up? Is there a candidate or a ballot measure that you care about? Look up the advocates for both sides and interview them, tell the story of the issue. Be neutral and journalistic, or advocate a position.

Publish your final production as a podcast. Find local bloggers, local news media, or national bloggers or news media who might find your podcast worthy of note in their publication, use the suggestion forms on their sites or send them e-mails describing your podcast in the context of their public, along with the URL.

Where to Go from Here

Media technologies and practices are moving too quickly for us to wait for empirical understanding of changed learning and teaching styles before engaging young people with the civic potential of participatory media: it is important for the future of the public sphere and the future of the young people who will constitute it that today's young people should be included—should demand inclusion—in the discussion of how they are to be educated as citizens. Stephen Coleman states this point eloquently in his chapter in this volume:

Technologies of e-citizenship turn cyberspace into a locus for the contestation of claims about citizenship. Because entry into the virtual public sphere is cheaper and less burdensome than making one's presence felt in the conventional public sphere, it is particularly attractive to young people whose experiences and aspirations might otherwise be marginalized or forgotten. The inclusion of these voices and traditions in the development of e-citizenship is of the utmost importance, if there is a genuine commitment to cultivate a democratic culture of participation.

Although I advocate an activist approach, I know that we need empirical study of the fundamental hypotheses underlying the approach I advocate—that active use of networked media, collaboration in social cyberspaces, and peer production of digital cultural products has changed the way young people learn and that their natural attraction to participatory media could be used to draw youth into civic engagement. Are these hypotheses borne out by observation? And what might they mean for the future of learning?

Jonathan Fanton, president of the MacArthur Foundation, succinctly stated the questions the Digital Media and Learning program is aimed at answering, which strike me as the proper frame for empirical studies of participatory media:

This is the first generation to grow up digital—coming of age in a world where computers, the internet, videogames, and cell phones are common, and where expressing themselves through these tools is the norm. Given how present these technologies are in their lives, do young people act, think and learn differently today? And what are the implications for education and for society?"[58]

Both research and practice will be required before the pedagogical strategy advocated in this chapter can be fully evaluated for eventual abandonment or wider adoption. The wiki that accompanies the chapter is a vehicle for accomplishing that evaluation and for increasing the value of resources found there. If you know about recent research that adds to what we know about the effectiveness of participatory media in increasing youthful civic engagement, share it on the wiki. If you have tried the exercises suggested here and find that they work well or not at all, share what you know on the wiki. If you know additional exercises, additional resources, additional pedagogical issues, share them on the wiki. Invest a small amount of value, harvest a much larger amount, the way Wikipedians do. That's how a cornucopia of the commons can work.

Notes

1. danah boyd, Identity Production in a Networked Culture: Why Youth ♥ MySpace (2006), http://www. danah.org/papers/AAAS2006.html, accessed November 13, 2006, archived at http://www.webcitation. org/5KPNVZWVg.

2. Amanda Lenhart, Mary Madden, and Paul Hitlin, *Teens and Technology: Youth Are Leading the Transition to a Fully Wired and Mobile Nation* (2006), Pew Internet & American Life Project, http://www.pewinternet. org/pdfs/PIP_Teens_Tech_July2005web.pdf (accessed November 2, 2006).

3. Any discussion of *youth* and *civic engagement* must necessarily generalize; however, the author wishes to acknowledge data that indicates significant racial, socioeconomic, and gender differences in opportunity and engagement. It appears that multiple "digital divides" have to be taken into account, as well. Moreover, the definition of *youth* is contentious, socially constructed, and changing. See Brandi L. Bell, Children, Youth, and Civic (dis)Engagement: Digital Technology and Citizenship (CRACIN working paper no. 5; Toronto: Canadian Research Alliance for Community Innovation and Networking Alliance, 2005); and Eszter Hargittai, Just a Pretty Face(book)? What College Students Actually Do Online, in *Beyond Broadcast* (2006), http://results.webuse.org/uic06/, for research on skill differences among college students. The author's intention is not to discount these issues, but to specifically address the needs of those young people who are indeed demonstrating enthusiasm for digital media. Perhaps the resources provided in this chapter and the supporting Web site can be adopted for use in multiple social environments. Questions of which issues young people care about, the social assumptions and skill sets that they bring to media practices, and equality of opportunity and access will differ from group to group, but perhaps the core skills of media production and distribution can be useful (or adapted to be more useful) in many contexts.

4. See also Marina Bers in this volume in regard to the connection between cultural production and civic engagement skills.

5. Amanda Lenhart and Mary Madden, *Teen Content Creators and Consumers* (2006), Pew Internet & American Life Project, http://www.pewinternet.org/pdfs/PIP_Teens_Content_Creation.pdf (accessed November 13, 2006).

6. MTV Networks, *Just Cause: Today's Activism*, http://www.mtv.com/thinkmtv/research/ (retrieved November 13, 2006) (at http://www.webcitation.org/5KPOQuDF5).

7. Tracey Skelton and Gill Valentine, Political Participation, Political Action and Political Identities: Young D/deaf People's Perspectives, *Space and Polity* 7, no. 2 (2003): 117–34.

8. Sonia Livingstone, Nick Couldry, and Tim Markham, Youthful Steps Towards Civic Participation: Does the Internet Help? in *Young Citizens in the Digital Age: Political Engagement, Young People and New Media*, ed. Barney Loader (London: Routledge, forthcoming).

9. Barney Dalgarno, Constructivist Computer Assisted Learning: Theory and Technique (paper presented at ASCILITE Conference, 1996), http://www.ascilite.org.au/conferences/adelaide96/papers/21.html (accessed November 6, 2006).

10. Marc Prensky, Digital Natives, Digital Immigrants, *On the Horizon* 9, no. 5 (2001), http://www.marcprensky.com/writing/Prensky%20-%20Digital%20Natives,%20Digital%20Immigrants%20-%20Part1.pdf (accessed November 6, 2006).

11. Henry Jenkins, Katie Clinton, Ravi Purushotma, Alice J. Robinson, and Margaret Weigel, Confronting the Challenges of Participatory Culture: Media Education for the 21st Century (2006), http://www.digitallearning.macfound.org/atf/cf/%7B7E45C7E0-A3E0-4B89-AC9C-E807E1B0AE4E%7D/JENKINS_WHITE_PAPER.PDF (accessed November 6, 2006).

12. Jenkins et al.

13. Manuel Castells, Why Networks Matter, in *Network Logic: Who Governs in an Interconnected World?* ed. Helen McCarthy, Paul Miller, and Phil Skidmore (London: Demos, 2004), 221–24, http://www.demos.co.uk/files/File/networklogic17castells.pdf (accessed November 6, 2006).

14. Phil Agre, Find Your Voice: Writing For a Webzine (paper presented at Webzine '99, San Francisco, 1999), http://polaris.gseis.ucla.edu/pagre/zine.html (accessed November 6, 2006, http://www.webcitation.org/5KPOpp2RB).

15. Douglas Kellner, Habermas, the Public Sphere, and Democracy: A Critical Intervention (1998), http://www.gseis.ucla.edu/faculty/kellner/papers/habermas.htm.

16. James Fishkin, The Nation in a Room: Turning Public Opinion Into Policy, *Boston Review of Books*, March/April 2006, http://bostonreview.net/BR31.2/fishkin.html; J. Gastil and P. Levine, eds., *The Deliberative Democracy Handbook: Strategies for Effective Civic Engagement in the Twenty-first Century* (San Francisco: Jossey-Bass, 2005) (accessed November 6, 2006, webcitation.org/5KPP8BMUI).

17. Jürgen Habermas, The Public Sphere: An Encyclopaedia Article, *New German Critique* 3 (1974): 49–55.

18. Habermas.

19. Pieter Boeder, Habermas Heritage: The Future of the Public Sphere in the Network Society, *First Monday* 10, no. 9 (2005), http://firstmonday.org/issues/issue10_9/boeder/ (accessed November 6, 2006, webcitation.org/5KPPBFF2).

20. Michael Warner, Publics and Counterpublics, *Public Culture* 14, no. 1 (2002): 49–90.

21. danah boyd, Why Youth (Heart) Social Network Sites: The Role of Networked Publics in Teenage Social Life, in *Youth, Digital Media, and Identity*, ed. D. Buckingham (forthcoming).

22. E-mail correspondence with author, October 31, 2006.

23. Jenkins et al.

24. Participatory Media Literacy, https://www.socialtext.net/medialiteracy/ (retrieved November 14, 2006).

25. Technorati, http://www.technorati.com (retrieved November 14, 2006).

26. Blogosphere, in *Wikipedia*, http://en.wikipedia.org/wiki/Blogosphere (retrieved November 14, 2006), archived at http://www.webcitation.org/5KPPLPhSS.

27. Noah Shachtman, Blogs Make the Headlines, *Wired News*, December 23, 2002, http://www.wired.com/news/culture/0,1284,56978,00.html (accessed November 6, 2006, webcitation.org/5KPPev0).

28. Dropping the Anchorman, *The Economist*, November 25, 2004, http://www.economist.com/people/displayStory.cfm?story_id=3428729 (retrieved November 6, 2006). Archived at http://www.webcitation.org/5KPPWjuzZ.

29. Jan Fernback and Brad Thompson, Virtual Communities: Abort, Retry, Failure? (1995). A version of this paper, "Computer-Mediated Communication and the American Collectivity: The Dimensions of Community within Cyberspace," was presented at the annual convention of the International Communication Association, Albuquerque, New Mexico, http://www.well.com/~hlr/texts/VCcivil.html (accessed November 6, 2006, webcitation.org/5KPPe06).

30. Yochai Benkler, *The Wealth of Networks* (New Haven: Yale University Press, 2006), http://www.benkler.org/wealth_of_networks/index.php?title=7._Political_Freedom_Part_2:_Emergence_of_the_Networked_Public_Sphere (accessed November 6, 2006, webcitation.org/5KPPZoRWq).

31. Five Minutes to Midnight Blog: A Youth Commentary on International Issues in Today's World . . . , http://fiveminutemidnight.blogspot.com/ (retrieved November 9, 2006).

32. Five Minutes to Midnight, http://www.fiveminutestomidnight.org/ (retrieved November 9, 2006).

33. E-mail correspondence with author, July 2006.

34. Rafigui, http://www.rafigui.net/ (retrieved November 9, 2006).

35. E-mail correspondence with author, July 2006. See also http://www.a13i.org/report.pdf for a report on Chad project.

36. Fantasy Congress, http://fantasycongress.org/fc/public/AboutUs.jsp (retrieved November 14, 2006).

37. USC Digital Connections: Digital Youth Project, http://eon.annenberg.edu/details/project.digital.youth.php (retrieved November 9, 2006).

38. Digital Youth Research: Kids' Informal Learning With Digital Media, http://digitalyouth.ischool.berkeley.edu/node/20 (retrieved November 9, 2006).

39. Comparative Media Studies, http://cms.mit.edu/ (accessed June 27, 2007).

40. Project NML, http://www.projectnml.org (retrieved November 9, 2006).

41. iEARN, http://www.iearn.org/index.html (retrieved November 9, 2006).

42. Civil Rights Teaching, http://www.civilrightsteaching.org/CRTglobal.htm (accessed June 27, 2007).

43. HarlemLIVE: Harlem's Youth Internet Publication, http://harlemlive.blogspot.com/ (retrieved November 9, 2006); HarlemLIVE Video, http://www.harlemlive.org/Video/Video/videomain.html (retrieved November 9, 2006).

44. HarlemLIVE, on *NewJour*, http://gort.ucsd.edu/newjour/h/msg02485.html (retrieved November 9, 2006). Archived at http://www.webcitation.org/5KPQ0bGmZ).

45. King's Norton Boys' School, http://www.kingsnortonboys.bham.sch.uk/ (retrieved November 9, 2006).

46. Weblogs as Self-Representation, Intermedia, http://www.intermedia.uio.no/projects/research-projects-1/mdiatize/weblogs (retrieved November 9, 2006).

47. Tanya Notley and Jo Tacchi, Online Youth Networks: Researching the Experiences of "Peripheral" Young People in Using New Media Tools for Creative Participation and Representation, *3CMedia. Journal of Community, Citizen's and Third Sector Media* 1, no. 1 (2005): 73–81, http://www.cbonline.org.au/3cmedia/ 3c_issue1/3ciss1_art7.pdf (accessed July 16, 2006); Amanda Mitra and Eric Watts, Theorizing Cyberspace: The Idea of Voice When Applied to the Internet Discourse, *New Media & Society* 4, no. 4 (2002): 479–98.

48. Youth Noise, http://www.youthnoise.com/ (retrieved November 13, 2006).

49. The Initiative on the Future of Journalism: News 21, http://newsinitiative.org/ (retrieved November 13, 2006).

50. News 21 Blogs, http://newsinitiative.org/news21/blogs.html (retrieved November 9, 2006).

51. Participatory Media Literacy, https://www.socialtext.net/medialiteracy (accessed June 27, 2007).

52. Connective Writing, Weblogg-ed blog. http://www.weblogg-ed.com/2005/11/06 (retrieved November 9, 2006), archived at http://www.webcitation.org/5KPRYIBob.

53. James Owen, London Bombing Pictures Mark New Role for Camera Phones, *National Geographic News*, July 11, 2005, http://news.nationalgeographic.com/news/2005/07/0711_050711_londoncell.htm (accessed November 6, 2006, webcitation.org/5KPRgQH).

54. Owen.

55. Christopher Schroeder, Is This the Future of Journalism? *Newsweek* (Web Exclusive), June 18, 2004, http://www.msnbc.msn.com/id/5240584/site/newsweek/ (accessed November 6, 2006, webcitation.org/5KPRpd104 and /5KPRhaM).

56. News 21 Blogs, http://newsinitiative.org/news21/blogs.html (retrieved November 13, 2006).

57. Interview with author, 2006.

58. MacArthur Investing $50 Million in Digital Learning (MacArthur Foundation press release for Digital Media and Learning, October 19, 2006), http://www.digitallearning.macfound.org/site/c.enJLKQNlFiG/b.2108775/apps/nl/content2.asp?content_id={68ADB304-A991-462E-BFEA-3B2C3EC7E22C}&notoc=1 (accessed June 27, 2007).

A Public Voice for Youth: The Audience Problem in Digital Media and Civic Education

Peter Levine

University of Maryland, CIRCLE (Center for Information & Research on Civic Learning & Engagement)

Students should have opportunities to create digital media in schools. This is a promising way to enhance their civic engagement, which comprises political activism, deliberation, problem solving, and participation in shaping a culture. All these forms of civic engagement require the effective use of a public voice, which should be taught as part of digital media education. To provide digital media courses that teach civic engagement will mean overcoming several challenges, including a lack of time, funding, and training. An additional problem is especially relevant to the question of public voice. Students must find appropriate *audiences* for their work in a crowded media environment dominated by commercial products. The chapter concludes with strategies for building audiences, the most difficult but promising of which is to turn adolescents' offline communities—especially high schools—into more genuine communities.

Why Do We Need Civic Engagement?

A good society cannot be governed by a few, even if the governors were skillful, ethical, and representative of the whole society. We always need broad civic engagement, for four important reasons.

First, evidence shows that institutions work better when many people participate. For example, Robert Putnam has shown that American "states where citizens meet, join, vote, and trust in unusual measure boast consistently higher educational performance than states where citizens are less engaged with civic and community life." Putnam finds that such engagement is "by far" a bigger correlate of educational outcomes than is spending on education, teachers' salaries, class size, or demographics.[1] Likewise, the most successful activist governments in the world—the Nordic social democracies—also have among the world's highest rates of voting, signing petitions, boycotting, joining protests, and reading the newspaper. On the other hand, strong governments with weak civil societies are, without exceptions, corrupt and tyrannical.[2] It seems likely that active citizens check corruption and mismanagement. They also reduce the burdens on public institutions, such as schools, by lending their own passions, ideas, and labor. Governments work better when people communicate among themselves about public problems. As Lewis A. Friedland writes, "Communities in which there are rich, cross-cutting networks of association and public discussion are more likely to formulate real problems, apply and test ... solutions, learn from them, and correct them if they are flawed: in short, to rule themselves, or work democratically."[3]

Second, social outcomes are more likely to be *just* when participation is equitable. People who vote and otherwise engage in politics and civil society tend to get a better deal, and that is a reason to encourage everyone to participate. For example, in one survey, all the respondents who had ever received a federal small-business loan said they always vote. They represented a relatively wealthy stratum of society that qualified for business assistance. In contrast, just over half of those who received welfare or public assistance claimed always to vote. These turnout estimates are probably inflated, but the gap of 44.4 percentage points between the two groups is consistent with other research.[4] A task force of the American Political Science Association recently found that people with education and money have far more than an equal share of influence on government.[5]

Third, some crucial public problems can only be addressed by people's direct public work, not by legislation.[6] Effective governments are capable of redistributing money and defining and punishing crimes. But many important problems call for persuasion, guidance, contestation, and other forms of "voice," accompanied by citizens' concrete action. For example, to change public attitudes toward gender roles or to encourage young people to value academic knowledge are goals that require persuasion and argumentation along with examples of personal behavior. Rarely can governments reduce prejudice, enhance the appreciation of nature, or deliver personalized care. Although governments express values through laws and institutions, their ability to persuade is severely limited. Besides, liberal states are not *permitted* to offer certain persuasive arguments (such as those that explicitly favor particular religious views or that invoke ethnic solidarity). Voluntary public work expresses values in ways that are sensitive to context and embodied in human behavior and relationships. Public work thus plays an essential role in defining and addressing social problems.

Public and Private Voice

All of these purposes of civic engagement are best served when people deliberate before they act, expressing opinions to some body of peers in an appropriate voice. Styles of communication differ profoundly by culture and context, but a public voice is always one that can persuade other people—beyond one's closest friends and family—to take action on shared issues. As Howard Rheingold notes in this volume, "Moving from a private voice to a public voice can help students [or anyone else] turn their self-expression into a form of public participation."

An example of a very private voice is an e-mail or a social networking site that is meant for close associates of the author. It may include personal references that would be obscure to a casual visitor; it is not intended to interest a community or to address their concerns. An example of a public voice is a political blog in which the author, much like a conventional newspaper columnist, expresses opinions on the issues of the day and hopes to draw a massive or influential audience. There are many mixed and intermediate forms as well—both offline and online.

Some contemporary political theorists define public communication in highly stringent and demanding ways. According to Amy Gutmann and Dennis Thompson (drawing on Jürgen Habermas and others), to speak publicly imposes a set of obligations.[7] When in the public sphere, one must advance arguments that any rational person can accept. That means that one may not express arbitrary opinions, assert purely selfish interests, or appeal to authorities—such as Scripture—that others reject. One may not shift positions when speaking to different audiences or give reasons that contradict one's conclusions. On this view, the public speaker is a kind of ethical and rational legislator, addressing an assembly of peers on matters of public concern.[8]

These definitions seem much too stringent for the practical purpose of this chapter, which is teaching young people to be reasonably effective in public domains. Indeed, as Stephen Coleman notes in this volume, idealized standards of public communication have two serious drawbacks. They impose norms that people are supposed to internalize and use for self-regulation, at some cost to their spontaneity, diversity, and freedom. And they teach a style of political engagement that would be naïve and ineffective "in any real political party, trade union, or local council." Hence my looser definition of a *public voice* as *any* style or tone that has a chance of persuading any other people (outside of one's intimate circle) about shared matters, issues, or problems.

This broad definition encompasses topics beyond conventional politics. For example, bad software is a shared concern, and one can write a blog to explain to others how to fix technical problems. Poor customer service can be a public issue if one chooses to address or organize one's fellow customers instead of complaining privately to the company. (See the chapter by Jennifer Earl and Alan Schussman on consumer petitions, which often adopt rhetorical styles drawn from conventional politics.) In these cases, one's voice is public even though the issues belong to the private sector.

We may disagree about which topics are legitimate for public discussion. For instance, disclosing one's own sexual history may be inappropriate—or it may be a means of challenging prejudices and limits. Despite these disagreements, however, it is pretty clear that standard instant-messaging chatter is (or ought to be) private. But most good blogs are public. And effective citizens need to understand the difference.

Culture, Media, and Democracy

The previous section on deliberation and public voice implies that to be civically engaged is to address matters of policy or politics. However, civic engagement is a broader concept that also comprises cultural production.

A democratic people not only controls its own government's budget, laws, and relations with foreign nations; it also shapes its own identity and self-image. Any self-governing community must be able to illustrate and memorialize its values and present its identity to outsiders and future generations of its own people. This is true at the level of a nation, but also in a small community such as the student body of a school. Thus, *civic engagement* includes the production of culture, at least insofar as cultural expression shapes norms and priorities.

Truly engaged citizens produce *heterogeneous* cultural products. Engaged people clump together in communities and associations, each of which inevitably takes on a distinct character. Many communities and associations choose to display their identities through music, statuary, graphic design, narrative history, and other forms of culture. But cultural identity is always contested; it provokes debates, parodies, and expressions of dissent as well as consensus. In other words, it requires the use of a public voice to defend or criticize forms of expression.

While heterogeneity is evidence of civic engagement, a homogeneous mass culture is a threat to democracy: when only a few people produce products that reach a mass market, they obtain great influence. Today, various groups of Americans criticize mass culture for being secular, materialistic, superficial, violent, sexist, and racist and for undermining local, traditional, and minority cultures. These critiques are not always mutually consistent and may not all be valid. But it seems clear that people feel powerless to change mass culture, and that feeling demonstrates the tension between mass culture and democracy.

Mass culture is, in part, a product of corporate capitalism. Capital increases the audiences for certain books, films, and songs. Sometimes corporate power is relatively weak: for instance, when there is competition among many producers (as in the Jacksonian era of small printers or in today's age of blogs) or when the government sponsors cultural production (as in Western Europe today). However, there remains an *intrinsic* tendency for liberal and democratic societies to develop mass cultures.

When people are free to choose which cultural products to consume, we often observe a "power law" distribution, in which a small handful of products are enormously more popular than the rest. It is not certain why this occurs, but it seems plausible that people want to know what other people are reading, hearing, or viewing; thus they gravitate to what is already popular, making it more so. That instinct is perhaps especially strong in a democracy, where people are taught to believe that average or majority opinion is a reliable guide to quality. Books are advertised as best sellers, movies as blockbusters, and songs as hits because democratic audiences trust popularity. In aristocratic cultures, on the other hand, elites have disproportionate consumer power and tend to view popularity as a mark of *poor* quality. Aristocrats want to have uncommon tastes. As Tocqueville wrote,

Among aristocratic nations every man is pretty nearly stationary in his own sphere, but men are astonishingly unlike each other; their passions, their notions, and their tastes are essentially different: nothing changes, but everything differs. In democracies, on the contrary, all men are alike and do things pretty nearly alike. It is true that they are subject to great and frequent vicissitudes, but as the same events of good or averse fortune are continually recurring, only the name of the actors is changed, the piece is always the same. The aspect of American society is animated because men and things are always changing, but it is monotonous because all these changes are alike.[9]

Tocqueville thought that mass culture posed a serious threat to liberty, but he proposed a solution. Strong voluntary associations would have the means and the incentive to produce differentiated alternatives to mass culture. Members of associations would want to communicate with one another about common concerns and collaborate in producing cultural products primarily for themselves. In that way, civic engagement—meaning especially group membership—would diversify the culture.

Cultural Production in the Era of Networks

The Internet does not make Tocqueville's argument irrelevant, but it creates new opportunities and challenges for the participatory cultural production that he valued. During the second half of the twentieth century, voluntary associations weakened, American communities became more alike, and corporate media dominated. More recently, however, the Internet and other new electronic media have allowed people to produce and disseminate their own ideas, which can be diverse and relevant to their communities (geographical or otherwise). Never has it been as cheap or quick to generate text, sound, or moving images for public access. This opportunity for creativity has great civic potential; it could turn people from spectators and consumers into innovators and creators.[10]

On the other hand, the same technology that allows millions of people to produce public materials also gives them easier and quicker access to the most popular digital products—whether music, video, or political news and statements. A few items gain global audiences.

They often feature talented celebrities who are backed by technical experts and corporate funding. Although some corporate products fail in the marketplace, they have the best odds of obtaining a large audience.

The easy availability of celebrity culture could reduce demand for ordinary people's creativity and make the world more homogeneous, thus frustrating local communities (and even whole nations) that want to govern their own cultures. The more that slick, professional products penetrate the international market, the less scope exists for ordinary people to create cultural products that others will value.

This shift is not the result of corporate investment alone. Not many of the successful blogs that arose between 2000 and 2002 had significant financial backing or famous writers; none used complex software that was out of the reach of ordinary users. Nevertheless, a handful of these blogs drew, and have retained, an enormous proportion of the total traffic. Instapundit, for example, became thousands of times more popular than average conservative blogs, and it is hard to believe that it was that much *better* than the average. An alternative explanation for its popularity involves path dependence: people want to know what the most popular sites are saying. Thus, what is already popular tends to become more so.[11] Path dependence plus corporate investment combine to produce a web in which a few disseminate ideas to the many—increasingly reminiscent of radio and television.

Some early enthusiasts for the Internet assumed (with the Supreme Court in *Reno v. ACLU*) that everyone with a computer could become a "pamphleteer," putting ideas into the public arena that would reach audiences simply in proportion to their relevance, value, or popularity. In that case, the popularity of Web sites would follow a bell curve, with more sites near the median than near the tails.

But Yochai Benkler rejects such "mid-1990s utopianism."[12] A few sites are enormously more popular than the median, and there is a long tail in which sites show little evidence of an audience at all. For example, the median blog currently tracked by Truth Laid Bear (a popular ranking service) has two incoming links, whereas the top blog has 4,696. Figure 1 shows the incoming links of top-ranked blogs, revealing a precipitous decline.

Early papers that discovered this power-law took a skeptical or critical line. The Internet was not a democracy or a meritocracy. Rather, people and search engines linked to sites that were already popular, thus making them more so. The rich got richer, regardless of merit. But Benkler summarizes findings that are more optimistic than a pure power law theory would imply. Mathematical models of the Web suggest that unknown sites do rise in popularity, and popular ones fall. There are many stories about innovations in tactics, techniques, or ideas that spread very rapidly. For instance, BoycottSBG—a response to the Sinclair Broadcasting Group's alleged Republican bias—obtained enormous participation within a week. As Benkler says, "It was providing a solution that resonated with the political beliefs of many people and was useful to them for their expression and mobilization."[13]

Benkler observes a "self-organizing principle" on the World Wide Web.[14] People with strong mutual affinities find one another and link their Web sites or leave comments on each other's pages. Within these affinity groups, some sites become more popular than others. But (a) there are many affinity groups, and (b) the popularity curve is not always steep within a group. "When the topically or organizationally related clusters become small enough—on the order of hundreds or even low thousands of Web pages—they no longer follow a pure power law distribution. Instead, they follow a distribution that still has a very long tail—these smaller clusters still have a few genuine 'superstars'—but the body of the distribution is substantially more moderate: beyond the few superstars, the shape of the link distribution looks a little more like a normal distribution."[15]

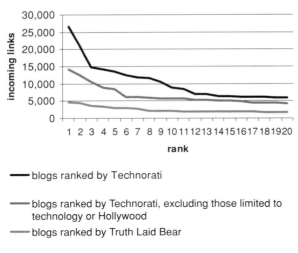

━━ blogs ranked by Technorati

━━ blogs ranked by Technorati, excluding those limited to technology or Hollywood

━━ blogs ranked by Truth Laid Bear

Figure 1
Incoming links to blogs by blog ranking.

Clusters of affinity groups then aggregate, often through sites that are or become superstars. We thus see a highly skewed distribution of popularity on the Internet as whole, yet the Web remains plural and open because of all the smaller groups. As Benkler says, "There is a big difference between a situation where no one is looking at any of the sites on the low end of the distribution, because everyone is looking only at the superstars, and a situation where dozens or hundreds of sites at the low end are looking at each other, as well as at the superstars."[16] On Benkler's model, "filtering for the network as a whole is done as a form of nested peer-review decisions, beginning with the speaker's closest information affinity group."[17] Lively dialogues begin "with communities of interest on smallish scales, practices of mutual pointing, and the fact that, with freedom to choose what to see and who to link to, with some codependence among the choices of individuals as to whom to link, highly connected points emerge even at small scales, and continue to be replicated with ever-larger visibility as the clusters grow."[18]

Benkler's portrait of the Internet permits cautious optimism about its value for Tocquevillian associational life. The Net does not give everyone an equal audience, let alone a large one, but it offers more opportunities for cultural creativity, cooperation, and effective public voice than the mass media system that prevailed twenty years ago.

Why Should We Be Especially Concerned about Youth Civic Engagement?

So far, this chapter has emphasized that many people should express their views on public issues and help create a heterogeneous democratic culture. I now turn to adolescents, whose civic participation is especially important.

Contrary to popular stereotypes about "slackers," today's youngest generation of Americans (the Millennials, who were born after 1985) are in some ways quite civically engaged. For example, according to separate surveys collected by Monitoring the Future and the Higher Education Research Institute, American youth have become increasingly likely to volunteer. According to the DDB Lifestyles Survey, there was a substantial gap between the volunteering rates of older people and youth in the 1970s, but that gap has vanished. Also, whereas the whole U.S. population has become distinctly less likely to participate in a community project since the 1970s, the rate among youth has been unchanged over that time.[19]

Young Americans are heavily represented in innovative online activities such as blogging and wikis. In 2004, The Pew Internet & American Life Project identified a group of Power Creators who each created online material in an average of two different ways: for instance, maintaining a personal site and also posting on other sites. This group had a median age of twenty-five. Since the youngest people surveyed were eighteen, the real median was certainly lower.[20] A year later, the project found that 17 percent of teenagers (defined as ages twelve to seventeen) had created their own blogs, compared to 7 percent of adults.[21]

In some other respects, however, youth are less engaged compared to past generations. For example, their news consumption and interest in public events fell deeply and consistently over the last thirty-five years. The big drop in news consumption occurred in the 1980s, before the Internet. Young Americans' voter turnout fell by one third in the three decades after 1972 (the first year in which eighteen- to twenty-one-year-olds were allowed to vote), while older people's turnout showed no decline.

Given the importance, noted above, of using a public voice, we should assess the degree to which young people express themselves publicly. Among the nineteen survey indicators of civic engagement that Scott Keeter et al. developed in 2003, five are activities that require individuals to express their own political or social opinions in public forums (persuading others about an election, participating in community problem solving, contacting an elected official, contacting a newspaper or magazine, and calling a talk show). Several other indicators measure participation in public discourse (e.g., taking part in a protest, displaying a campaign sign, button, or sticker).[22] For most of these indicators, youth were *not* heavily involved. People do not naturally or automatically acquire an effective public voice or the motivation to use it. They must be taught.

We might debate whether, overall, youth civic engagement has improved or declined in the United States and other countries: that would depend on how we weigh the various forms of engagement. Regardless, we should try to strengthen youth participation, for several reasons.

First, as John Dewey observed, young people are relatively "plastic."[23] Adolescents develop habits and attitudes relevant to civic life when they first encounter the world of news, issues, and events. During that initial period, their ideas are flexible and subject to influence. However, once they develop a political identity, it cannot be changed without much effort and discomfort. As Karl Mannheim noted in the 1920s, "Even if the rest of one's life consisted in one long process of negation and destruction of the natural world view acquired in youth, the determining influence of these early impressions would still be predominant."[24] Longitudinal data show remarkable persistence in adults' political behaviors and beliefs over the decades of their lives, whereas young people seem susceptible to change.[25] For example, careful studies have found that giving high school students opportunities to participate in extracurricular groups enhances their civic participation many decades later.[26]

Second, young people have special needs that can be met by encouraging them to participate in civic and political affairs. There is a strong correlation between adolescents' civic engagement and successful development. For instance, using three national longitudinal surveys, Nicholas Zill and colleagues found, "Compared to those who reported spending 1–4 hours per week in extracurricular activities, students who reported spending no time in school-sponsored activities were 57 percent more likely to have dropped out by the time they would have been seniors; 49 percent more likely to have used drugs; 37 percent more likely to have become teen parents; 35 percent more likely to have smoked cigarettes; and 27 percent more likely to have been arrested." These relationships remained statistically significant even after the researchers controlled for other measured characteristics of families, schools, and students (such as parents' education levels), and similar results have emerged from other studies.[27]

One explanation is that young people respond well to being given responsibilities and opportunities to serve their communities. In fact, there is some evidence that adults can address adolescent pathologies better by providing civic opportunities than by trying to detect, prevent, and mitigate problems. For instance, the Teen Outreach Program (TOP) significantly reduced teen pregnancy, school suspension, and school failure. TOP was successful even though it focused "very little attention on the three target problem behavior outcomes." In other words, the staff did not directly address pregnancy or school-related problems. Instead, youth in the program were enrolled in service projects and asked to discuss their work in classroom settings. An average of 45.8 hours of service reduced teen pregnancy through the *indirect* means of giving young women valuable civic work to do.[28] The TOP experiment provides evidence in support of the philosophy known as "positive youth development," which emphasizes adolescents' need to contribute their talents and energy.

Another argument begins with the observation that youth have a quasi-autonomous culture. Variation in that culture can have enormous impact on kids. For example, it makes a huge difference whether one participates in a gang or a chess club. But adults and adult institutions are not able to manipulate youth culture. Therefore, it is important for young people to develop their own civic skills. Then, for example, they will be able to do their own conflict mediation and violence prevention within their own peer groups. If young people are helped to develop civic motivations, they may create associations that have positive purposes and are attractive to peers.

Finally, American youth are particularly susceptible to being influenced by corporate-funded mass culture, which is aimed directly at them even though it reaches a global audience. For that very reason, they have special leverage over media corporations, especially if they act cooperatively. It is not an exaggeration to say that youth civic engagement in the United States could benefit democracy around the world if youth-led associations challenged mass culture.

Why Would We Expect Media Production to Boost Youth Civic Skills?

There are not yet enough rigorous evaluations of youth media programs, especially in school settings. We need studies that use control or comparison groups and that measure civic outcomes. However, convergent evidence from similar projects suggests that youth media could be highly effective for teaching public voice and might also boost academic skills.

Service learning means a combination of community service and academic work or classroom discussion; it is now present in half of American high schools.[29] A 1999 evaluation found that federally funded service learning had positive effects on students' civic attitudes, habits of volunteering, and success in school.[30] In a smaller study published in 2005, Shelley Billig and colleagues found that students who had been exposed to service learning gained more knowledge of civics and government and felt more confident about their own civic skills, compared to a matched group of students who had taken conventional social studies classes.[31]

Earthforce is a school-based program that involves students in environmental research and political action. Students choose their own issues and strategies. Earthforce was evaluated by Alan Melchior and Lawrence Neil Bailis in 2001–2002, using pre and post student questionnaires, teacher questionnaires, and focus groups (but no comparison groups or test-like assessments). There were many positive changes in self-reported skills, knowledge, and attitudes over the course of the program, and teachers were favorable.[32]

These and other studies support the view that active civic participation is an inspiring and effective approach to civic education that also enhances academic skills and engages youth in their schooling. They are tests of what Marina Bers calls "praxis-based" rather than "knowledge-based" civic education. Some of the examples (especially Earthforce) are what she calls constructionist rather than instructionist.

It is important to note, however, that the evaluations cited above were limited to programs that appeared to be well implemented. Many other programs that receive service-learning funds do not implement basic recommendations, such as offering students opportunities for reflection.[33] Even having screened out weaker programs, Billig and colleagues found a great range in impact. Their study underlines the importance of *quality*. Active learning can be counterproductive unless projects are well conceived and executed. And even the best programs can have mixed effects. For instance, youth participants in Earthforce gained skills but became *less* confident in their own civic efficacy over the course of the program. Their agreement with the following statements actually declined: "I believe I can personally make a difference in my school or community," "I believe that people working together can solve community problems," "It is important to listen to people on all sides of a community issue if we want to find a solution that will work," "I think it is more important to look for ways to help the environment for a long time than to do something that will just make a difference for a few days," and "I pay attention to local environmental issues when I hear about them." The evaluators conclude, "One possible explanation is that the decline reflects an increased understanding on the part of participants of how slow and difficult change can be, and that participants are both more realistic and in some cases discouraged by the challenges they face in addressing issues in their communities."

Similar results would likely be found if digital media production were evaluated using surveys and other quantitative measures. There would be a range of outcomes depending on the quality of the programs; and even some of the best would reduce students' efficacy by confronting them with obdurate social problems.

Youth Media Production in the School Context

Much of the exciting youth media work that one can find by searching on the Web is created in after-school and community-based programs that have support from foundations. These projects are crucial laboratories and will play a lasting role by allowing youth to undertake projects too controversial for schools. For example, *Raices* is an initiative of the Main Street Project that helps Latino youth in rural Midwestern communities to make digital media. Amalia Anderson, director of the initiative, told me that "our media work is grounded in a right to communicate, to challenge the camera as a tool of colonization, and to use our voices to speak truth to power as well as preserve and protect our culture, languages and identity."[34] That kind of mission would have to be submerged in a typical comprehensive public school.

However, most adolescents do not have opportunities for community-based engagement; and voluntary projects always draw self-selected youth. Therefore, school-based programs are essential if we want to reach a broad spectrum of students, including youth who don't find their way into after-school programs.

In their study of civic learning among Chicago public school students, Kahne and Sporte found small positive effects from community-based projects, but very large positive effects from service learning in the schools. This is striking, because most service-learning classes are often *not* very ambitious or engaging, whereas Chicago is a hotbed of excellent community-based youth work. But the youth who have the most to gain do not sign up for after-school programs, and they appear to benefit from service learning in their public schools. It is likely that they would also benefit from youth media courses.[35]

There is a substantial base on which to build digital media production classes that could reach all American students. In the Knight Foundation's Future of the First Amendment survey, 21 percent of randomly selected schools said that they had a "Student Internet or World-Wide Web publication with a news component that requires students to make judgments about what is newsworthy."[36] The question was framed so that it missed some other forms of digital media production of civic value. Thus more than one in five schools may have relevant programs in place today.

Nevertheless, many obstacles stand in the way of adequate opportunities in schools. Some problems, such as the lack of equipment and trained teachers, could be addressed with more public investment. Of course, providing adequate support is a challenge, given budget deficits, opposition to taxes, competing priorities, a history of underinvestment in many school districts, and a system of predominantly local educational funding that leaves poor communities with scarce resources for schooling. However, youth media production could be allocated a larger proportion of existing money and—just as important—of students' time.

Schools are increasingly influenced by research, because state legislation and the No Child Left Behind Act 2003 (NCLB) require them to achieve specified outcomes, and they are looking for tested ways to do so. By showing that youth media production improves academic skills or high school completion, researchers could persuade school districts to invest in equipment and professional development and to provide instructional time.

We have circumstantial evidence that would support this case. Many students drop out because the assigned work is boring and because they lack personal connections to teachers. For instance, in a 2006 study of recent dropouts, more than half said they had satisfactory grades before they left school (C or better), but half said that classes were boring. Furthermore, "only 56 percent said they could go to a staff person for school problems and just two-fifths (41 percent) had someone in school to talk to about personal problems."[37] There have been rigorous evaluations of programs—albeit not media production courses—that help students to work on community problems in collaboration with adults. For instance, an evaluation of the Quantum Opportunities Program (QOP) studied randomly selected students and a control group. For about $2,500 a year over four years, QOP was able to cut the dropout rate to 23 percent, compared to 50 percent for the control group. QOP's approach included academic programs that were individually paced for each student, mandatory community service, enrichment programs, and pay for each hour of participation.[38]

We also have anecdotes about media production classes that may have prevented individuals from dropping out. For example, in an evaluation of the Educational Video Center (EVC), one student said, "EVC helped me stay in school. Like last year, I was really going to drop out but . . . the teachers [at EVC] are like so cool I was able to go to them and talk to them and tell them what was going on in my life, tell them all my problems."[39] Participants also reported gains in skills and academic engagement.

I find such testimony promising, especially since it is consistent with fairly relevant experimental results (noted above) and the theory of positive youth development.[40] However, administrators who control scarce resources will not place large bets on youth media production on the basis of such evidence. They may suspect that (a) students who sign up for voluntary media programs already have positive attitudes and skills on entry, (b) students' self-reports of skills are unreliable, (c) participants are generous in their evaluations of programs, and (d) other opportunities for student engagement, such as service learning, have been better researched. To influence educational policy, I believe we need randomized field experiments that measure the impact of digital media creation on relatively hard measures, such as high school completion or valid and reliable measures of skills.

If such experiments showed positive results, then NCLB and the standards movement that it typifies would provide some leverage. But these laws also create a challenge by focusing on basic literacy and mathematics as measured by pencil-and-paper tests. That focus makes it harder to devote instructional time to media production; media skills are not directly tested, yet what is tested is taught. Nevertheless, NCLB and other current policies could accommodate youth media work if we could show that providing creative opportunities is an efficient way to keep kids engaged in school.

The Audience Problem

I do not pretend that the struggle for adequate resources will be easy. However, in the rest of this chapter, I will address a different issue that is more complex and less amenable to being solved with money alone: the audience problem.

As noted above, democracy requires broad and diverse cultural creativity. The new digital media—Web sites, e-mail, digital cameras, digital voice recorders and video cameras, and the like—offer opportunities for individuals and voluntary groups to create their own cultural products and to use a public voice, and many have done so. However, the technology is not enough; people must also *want* to create—and specifically to make products with public purposes—rather than use the Internet to get access to mass-produced culture.

One important motivator is the belief that one can reach other people: an audience. Not everyone wants to maximize the sheer number of people reached, although the popularity of Site Meter and other tools for counting visits suggests that some do care about numbers. But others may be more interested in finding a responsive audience that provides comments and feedback; or they may seek a politically relevant audience that can act in response to their media. (A politically relevant audience might comprise especially influential people, such as reporters and elected officials, or it might consist of fellow members of a community who could act collectively.)

In any case, we communicate in a public voice in order to address someone, and it matters *who* listens. It is discouraging to build something if no one comes. As Howard Rheingold says, "Teachers would do well to ask 'are [students] connecting with others?' as well as asking 'are they expressing themselves?' when evaluating the outcome of digital media project-based learning."[41]

Global Action Project (GAP) is an independent nonprofit that teaches media production to youth in several countries so that they can "use their media as a catalyst for dialogue and social change."[42] In response to my query, Megan McDermott, the GAP director, asked a group of participants whether and why an audience was important to them. According to her notes, they said that they needed people to watch their videos in order to affect the social issues that concerned them: "Because that's how we're going to make it work to open up the audience's eyes." Students also wanted honest feedback from an attentive group, "because it lets you know if your video is hot or not. . . . They give feedback and point out things you might miss in your own film. They give feedback that might be good and can make your video or film better."[43]

McDermott said that youth in GAP are encouraged to think about their audience from the beginning of their projects. At first, they want to reach everyone, but then they fine-tune their goals to be more realistic and to enhance their impact on their communities. They are less concerned, she said, with the number of viewers than with the kind of conversations that they provoke.

EVC is "dedicated to the creative and community-based use of video and multi-media as a means to develop the literacy, research, public speaking and work preparation skills of at-risk youth."[44] EVC's executive director Steven Goodman told me, "Students certainly enjoy knowing that their work will be seen by audiences. . . . I'm sure the students prefer larger audiences but respond more to the quality of audience response and engagement. . . . At EVC, a responsive audience is one which gives the students positive feedback, asks a lot of questions, and is engaged in the screening. The students do look for this kind of engagement and feel their work may not have been received well if it is lacking."[45]

The Community Arts Center Teen Media Program in Cambridge, MA, holds an annual festival to screen student videos. According to written questionnaires, students were pleased with the event but more satisfied with the turnout than the quality of the discussion. "The crowd on Friday was a highlight—'lots of people.'" "Some of the questions in the discussion were good, but some were stupid."[46]

Anderson of the Main Street Project concurred that numbers weren't as important as "having the right audience—not just an audience for the sake of people to watch. In my experience youth are most interested in making sure their work (stories) are first screened with family and friends and other people of color. Since their work is often personal, and because they have learned through the workshops the importance of people of color telling our own stories and speaking for ourselves . . . they are far more interested in thinking through where the community screenings will take place, and how sharing their stories can empower others, challenge isolation and lead to organizing campaigns." She added that they want audiences who have deep respect for their work and who can participate in creating change.

Creating Audiences for Youth Media Products

Given the media environment sketched above, I am concerned that we may set kids up for disappointment when we imply that the Internet will make them pamphleteers or broadcasters who can change the world by reaching relevant people. Even if some kids are highly successful, most will *not* draw a significant or appropriate or responsive audience. Most Web sites remain in the tail of the distribution. If you create a site that hardly anyone visits, you will get little feedback. Kids who build such sites may feel that they are failures, especially in a culture that prizes popularity. That is why efforts to draw friends and to advertise (or exaggerate) the size of one's network are so prominent on social networking sites such as MySpace.

The topics that young people know best are very local. For instance, when the Lower Eastside Girls Club in New York City began podcasting, they chose to create an audio segment on school uniforms. This was important to them, but not to many others. Even their most likely audience, their fellow students, seemed to shun their amateur work in favor of professional digital media. Other kids across the country are concerned about school uniforms, but they have no reason to listen to a podcast on that subject from New York City.

Students are unlikely to obtain a substantial audience through sheer talent or innovation. Some kids will, but the average won't. Furthermore, many adolescents do not belong to tight affinity groups, differentiated from the mass youth population. Benkler mentions "communities of interest on smallish scales" that conduct peer review and create audiences by linking to one another. But adolescents do not automatically have such communities. The typical U.S. high school is a massive and anonymous institution to which students feel no attachment. Kids have common concerns, but they tend to share them with millions of others. Mass media culture is profoundly homogenizing.

Four Strategies

In this final section, I explore four responses to the audience problem, each of which has some promise.

The first response is to create highly interactive, gamelike environments in which youth can express public views and do civic work. An example is Zora, as described by Bers in this volume. Student participants in Zora clearly have an audience—the other players. The question is whether schools can be encouraged to devote significant amounts of instructional time to such activities. They would have to be shown that playing Zora advances some of the objectives for which they are held accountable, such as reading test scores or retention in school.

The second response is to expand audiences by marketing youth products or by organizing face-to-face events. This appears to be a common strategy in the foundation-supported, community-based groups. Often, they organize screenings so that youth can get feedback. Goodman of EVC described premiere screenings at which 50–150 people convene face-to-face to watch student videos. He reported, "Our students almost always come away from their screenings feeling a sense of accomplishment, pride, success and recognition they never experience in school or elsewhere in their life. These are times when their parents, friends and teachers see their creative and intellectual potential; the audiences see what they are truly capable of, and the students are just overjoyed."

McDermott of GAP said that adult audiences often ask unhelpful questions, such as, "Why did you choose this topic?" or "Do you want to be a professional film-maker?" The youth in GAP have begun to circulate better questions in advance, such as, "What can we do about the problem that you have presented in your video?" or "What were the strongest and weakest parts of the documentary?" Apparently, adults appreciate such guidance.

Most of this discussion and feedback occurs in face-to-face settings. McDermott described a public screening of a youth-made video about gentrification that drew academic experts, activists, and some of the kids' parents and friends. The discussion was very rich and rewarding for the young filmmakers. Overall, McDermott thought that youth were both satisfied and dissatisfied with their audience—glad for the feedback they received, but not fully satisfied by their impact on their communities.

A strategy of recruiting face-to-face audiences makes good sense for community-based groups that also want to achieve social change by organizing residents. Their leaders have the skills and motivation to follow through once students have created media projects. If they were unable or unwilling to convene residents, their whole strategy of social change would make no sense.

However, I worry that this strategy will not work well in schools, particularly if media production becomes more common. In general, teachers are not trained or supported—or even allowed—to convene community meetings. Besides, if we could massively enlarge the number of youth who were involved in media production in schools, we would find it increasingly hard to find audiences for their work.

A third strategy is to enable students to create digital media products with relatively low investments of time and expertise. When J-Lab, the Center for Interactive Journalism, offered mini-grants for citizen journalism, scores of youth-oriented projects applied, asking for support to build ambitious online products such as GIS maps of gentrification or databases of video interviews. (I served on the selection committee in 2004 and 2005.) Youth who commit the time necessary for such projects will be sorely disappointed if no one uses their work. However, one can produce public media without that much investment. Whereas a custom-built Web site is a huge job, one can launch a site on MySpace or create a blog within DailyKos in a few minutes.

Luke Walker, education project manager of TakingITGlobal, writes: "The 'old' model of spending hours/days/weeks creating a website, securing server space, and sharing it for all (or no one) to see is both outdated and largely irrelevant for the average young person, although it's still happening far too often in the school context. As long as that is the production model that teachers are using in their classes, then yes, we are setting children up for failure and disappointment—particularly if we're stopping at the point of posting the content on the web (where many people's knowledge/expertise ends) and not teaching students to employ all the marketing tactics that make commercial/mainstream/high-profile websites successful. More and more, though, young people are moving away from traditional websites to creating a presence in social networking spaces like MySpace."[47]

Most (62 percent) adolescents who read blogs say that they only read blogs by people they already know.[48] That is evidence of Benkler's "communities of interest on smallish scales." There is no reason to believe that teen bloggers are disappointed if only friends visit their sites. After all, they can launch their blog in five minutes using a service like Blogger. The investment is commensurate to the payoff.

I see promise in these user-friendly formats. However, we need examples in which they advance educational or civic purposes. A made-from-scratch Web site or video requires many skills (technical, creative, and organizational) and is thus highly educational. It is not yet clear that MySpace can serve those functions. To be sure, students could create an elaborate product, such as a video or a map, and post it on a social networking site as a means of distribution. But would they be satisfied if only their friends visited?

Furthermore, can students learn to use a public voice and achieve civic purposes by interacting mostly with friends? Adolescent culture (at least in the United States) is strongly segregated, not only by race, ethnicity, and class, but also by identity type. In an influential study begun in 1985, Eccles and Barber asked students to identify themselves with one of the characters in a then-recent Hollywood movie, *The Breakfast Club*. All but 5 percent readily placed themselves in precisely one of the following categories: jock, princess, brain, criminal, or basket case. Moreover, each type of student spent most of his or her time with others of the same self-ascribed category.[49] Students' identities at tenth grade were strongly predictive of outcomes a decade later.[50] Thus, if we leave students to self-associate, given the norms in a modern American high school, they are likely to segregate into groups that reinforce social stratification and that cannot address broad or shared problems.

Optimists might predict that technologies built on network principles will overcome segregation and make it less important for youth to develop an effective public voice. Each participant can communicate privately with friends who have similar backgrounds, interests, and social circumstances, yet inclusive networks will emerge to shape public opinion and gain political influence. Possibly. But network structures are equally compatible with balkanization and can segregate those who have political interests from those who do not feel connected to the public sphere.[51] It is difficult to see how one social group can change the opinions of another without using their voice to reach a large and diverse audience.

Howard Rheingold, in his contribution to this volume, provides thoughtful guidance for educators—in schools, colleges, and after-school programs—who want to encourage youth to develop an effective public voice. He recognizes that young people begin with interests and concerns, but they do not naturally or automatically possess the motivations and skills necessary to influence public opinion and institutions. He proposed exercises that would develop their skills, making full and creative use of digital technologies.

I strongly endorse this guidance, but I worry that it may never directly benefit the vast majority of students. We know from a century's experience with student newspapers and school governments that they tend to draw an elite group of young people who begin with comparatively strong civic skills and motivations, as well as superior academic records and prospects. They enhance their own civic skills by exercising a public voice, but their work is largely ignored by most of their fellow students. According to survey data, an average high school newspaper benefits those who produce it but has no effects on the student body as a whole, because students are not sufficiently connected to the school community to care about its news.[52]

In short, there are limits to any strategy that gives kids online opportunities without changing their lifeworlds. Factors such as segregation and stratification are powerful determinants of how people use technology. I do not believe that youth media can be fully satisfactory until young people's communities become more democratic. That is a very tall order, but I suggest that technology does not provide an alternative to the hard task of reforming the offline communities and institutions in which young people come of age.

Locally produced media matter more to people who belong to a community or a public, in the sense that John Dewey meant: "Wherever there is conjoint activity whose consequences are appreciated as good by all singular persons who take part in it, and where the realization of the good is such as to effect an energetic desire and effort to sustain it in being just because it is a good shared by all, there is in so far a community. The clear consciousness of a communal life, in all its implications, constitutes the idea of democracy."[53]

One potential community to which most adolescents belong is their school. But the standard American high school is too big and unfocused to support conjoint activity or consciousness of a communal life. It has no common normative framework. As Harry Brighouse describes it,

It is a 2000-plus student institution, in which no individual knows every other individual; in which many children never have any teacher for more than one year of instruction; in which the prevailing values include pep rallies for sports and a slavishly conformist loyalty to school and neighbourhood.

These schools maintain a deafening silence about spiritual or anti-materialist values, take sides in the Cola wars, and accept as a given the prevalence of brand names and teen-marketing.[54]

Most secondary schools allow enormous internal segregation, or even encourage it by allowing students to choose diverse academic tracks. Furthermore, school buildings are isolated from the broader community—behind bars and metal detectors in the inner cities, or behind great lawns and parking lots in the suburbs. Students are asked to make very consequential choices about academic programs, extracurricular activities, and peer groups without much attention from adults, unless they receive good guidance at home. If there are forums intended for deliberation in the whole student body, such as school newspapers, student governments, cultural events, or Web sites, they attract only particular subcultures. There is no common agenda or interest that can draw everyone—no "public" in the Deweyan sense.

Dewey acknowledged that "in any social group whatever, even in a gang of thieves, we find some interest held in common, and we find a certain amount of interaction and cooperative intercourse with other groups. From these two traits we derive our standard. How numerous and varied are the interests which are consciously shared? How full and free is the interplay with other forms of association?"[55] These criteria are relevant to school culture. Do students feel that they have a great deal in common, beyond the bare obligation to enter the same building every day? And do the various associations within the school overlap with one another and connect with groups beyond the school walls?

If students do not have much in common and do not belong to overlapping groups, then celebrity culture will attract most of their interest. Youth will not be interested in products created by peers that address local issues. They will not even *know* most of their peers. It is not only people who are concerned about civic engagement and digital media who now believe that the standard American high school is poorly organized and must be turned into more of a community. The low rate of high school completion—only two-thirds in some studies—has caught the attention of powerful institutions. The Bill and Melinda T. Gates Foundation, the National Governors Association, and other national organizations are calling for smaller, themed institutions with more student participation in common work. Thomas Toch wrote a manifesto for the small schools movement in which he argued that most large high schools fail to "engender a strong sense of community." Instead, they "tend to be intensely impersonal places." The results include "alienation and apathy among students and teachers," a pervasive anonymity that "saps students' motivation to learn and teachers' motivation to teach."[56]

The mean student population of American schools rose about fivefold between 1940 and 1970, and high schools of two thousand or more became common.[57] But the tide is turning. "New York City is phasing out large high schools and planning for 200 new small schools over the next five years. Chicago is planning 100. Los Angeles is converting 130 middle and high school campuses to smaller units."[58] And so on across the country.

Early in the movement for high school reform (circa 2000), there was a lot of enthusiasm for simply reducing the average number of students per building. Evidence of impact was not especially compelling. The movement has shifted away from school size to other strategies. Without necessarily decreasing the student–teacher ratio, it is possible to make each teacher responsible for fewer students by assigning youth to clusters that stay together for several years and that continue with the same teaching staff. Schools can be connected more closely to external institutions such as universities, community colleges, museums, and major non-profits (also, more controversially, to churches). Schools can adopt curricular themes so that everyone in the building has some common interest or frame of reference. (Examples of schoolwide themes include the environment, the U.S. Constitution, Africa, and health care.) Giving each school a curricular focus means that students and their families will exercise more choice among schools but less choice within schools, which will become inclusive communities. A common theme can be deliberated and contested, provoking meaningful conversations in a public voice.

The movement for high school reform has momentum and exemplifies one way to address the audience problem. High schools happen to be physical, local venues. I think that geographical communities remain important, because many of our interactions with one another and with governments occur at the local level. If our immediate geographical settings fail to be communities—as is the case in most high schools—then we lose our ability to engage in some important ways. As Friedland concludes, "place, the environment of action, not technology, is the critical element in civic and democratic participation."[59] However, high school reform is an *example* of the broader claim that adolescents need communities and associations. Some valuable ties may be dispersed and virtual, not local and face-to-face.

Conclusion

Community-based, nonprofit youth media groups have developed an impressive body of experience and knowledge. The next step is to increase the scale of media work dramatically, which means offering more and better courses in schools. Given current policies, that will take rigorous experimental or quasi-experimental studies that show the impact of youth media work on outcomes that major institutions care about—not so much civic engagement as high school completion and preparation for college.

Meanwhile, as youth media work becomes more common in schools, it will be important to find responsive, engaged audiences for students' products. Deliberately marketing students' work and using new user-friendly formats (such as social-networking software) may help. But ultimately, schools will have to be restructured so that they function more like communities before youth media work is fully satisfying.

As a first step, it would be useful to study the ecology of youth media within different kinds of schools. Does a higher proportion of the student body seek youth-produced media in schools that are small and focused (as I hypothesize), or does school size make no difference? What are the effects of having a diverse or a homogeneous student population on media consumption? What are the apparent effects of academic tracking on students' interest in one another's work? Do digital media become means of connecting various peer groups and subcultures within schools, or do they reinforce divisions?

Notes

1. Robert D. Putnam, Community-based Social Capital and Educational Performance, in *Making Good Citizens: Education and Civil Society*, ed. Diane Ravitch and Joseph P. Viteritti (New Haven, CT: Yale University Press, 2001), 69–72.

2. Author's analysis of World Values Survey data.

3. Lewis A. Friedland, Communication, Community, and Democracy: Toward a Theory of the Communicatively Integrated Community, *Communication Research* 28, no. 4 (August 2001): 360.

4. Joseph P. Marchand, Suzanne Metler, Timothy Smeeding, and Jeff Stonecash, *The Second Maxwell Poll on Civic Engagement and Inequality* (New York: Syracuse, 2006), 13, 15.

5. American Political Science Association Task Force on Inequality and American Democracy, *American Democracy in an Age of Rising Inequality* (Washington, DC: American Political Science Association, 2004).

6. Harry C. Boyte and Nancy N. Kari, *Building America: The Democratic Promise of Public Work* (Philadelphia: Temple University Press, 1996).

7. Amy Gutmann and Dennis Thompson, *Democracy and Disagreement* (Cambridge, MA: Harvard University Press, 1996).

8. Seminal definitions of deliberation as rational talk include Jürgen Habermas, *The Structural Transformation of the Public Sphere*, trans. Thomas Burger (1962; Cambridge, MA: MIT Press, 1991), 54; Joshua Cohen, Deliberation and Democratic Legitimacy, in *The Good Polity*, ed. Alan Hamlin and Phillip Pettit (Oxford: Blackwell, 1989). For a critique, see Iris Marion Young, Communication and the Other: Beyond Deliberative Democracy, in *Democracy and Difference*, ed. Seyla Benhabib (Princeton, NJ: Princeton University Press, 1996).

9. Alexis de Tocqueville, *Democracy in America*, translated by Henry Reeve and Phillips Bradley (New York: Vintage Books, 1954), vol. ii, book iii, chapter xvii, p. 239.

10. Peter Levine, Creative Use of the New Media, in *Youth Activism: An International Encyclopedia*, ed. Lonnie R. Sherrod, Ron Kassimir, and Connie Flanagan (Westport, CT: Greenwood, 2005); Peter Levine, Collective Action, Civic Engagement, and the Knowledge Commons, in *Understanding Knowledge as a Commons: From Theory to Practice*, ed. Charlotte Hess and Elinor Ostrom (Cambridge, MA: MIT Press, 2006).

11. Daniel W. Drezner and Henry Farrell, The Power and Politics of Blogs (paper presented at APSA conference, 2004). Retrieved May 25, 2007. www.danieldrezner.com/research/blogpaperfinal.pdf.

12. Yochai Benkler, *The Wealth of Networks: How Social Production Transforms Markets and Freedom* (New Haven: Yale University Press, 2006), 260.

13. Benkler, 247.

14. Benkler, 255.

15. Benkler, 251.

16. Benkler, 251.

17. Benkler, 248.

18. Benkler, 255.

19. *Broken Engagement: America's Civic Engagement Index*, a report by the National Conference on Citizenship in association with CIRCLE and the Saguaro Seminar (September 18, 2006).

20. Amanda Lenhart, John Horrigan, and Deborah Fallows, Content Creation Online, Pew Internet & American Life Project, February 29, 2004.

21. Amanda Lenhart and Mary Madden, Teen Content Creators and Consumers, Pew Internet & Public Life Project, November 2, 2005, 8.

22. Cliff Zukin, Scott Keeter, Molly Andolina, Krista Jenkins, and Michael X. Delli Carpini, *A New Engagement? Political Participation, Civic Life, and the Changing American Citizen* (Oxford: Oxford University Press, 2006).

23. John Dewey, *Democracy and Education* (1916; Carbondale and Evansville: Southern Illinois University Press, 1985), 52.

24. Karl Mannheim, The Problem of Generations, in *Essays on the Sociology of Knowledge*, ed. P. Kecskemeti (1928; New York: Oxford University Press, 1952), 298. For a good summary of recent literature, see Constance Flanagan and Lonnie R. Sherrod, Youth Political Development: An Introduction, *Journal of Social Issues* (Fall 1998). The period between age fourteen and twenty-five is identified as crucial in Richard G. Niemi and Mary A. Hepburn, The Rebirth of Political Socialization, *Perspectives on Political Science* 24 (1995): 7–16.

25. David O. Sears and Sheri Levy, Childhood and Adult Political Development, in *Oxford Handbook of Political Psychology*, ed. David O. Sears, Leonie Huddy, and Robert Jervis (Oxford: Oxford University Press, 2003), pp. 62–108.

26. E.g., M. Kent Jennings and Laura Stocker, Social Trust and Civic Engagement across Time and Generations, *Acta Politica* 39 (2004): 342–79.

27. Nicholas Zill, Christine Winquist Nord, and Laura Spencer Loomis, Adolescent Time Use, Risky Behavior and Outcomes: An Analysis of National Data (Rockville, MD: Westat, 1995), available from the U.S. Department of Health and Human Services.

28. Evaluation by James P. Allen et al., summarized in Jacquelynne Eccles and Jennifer Appleton Gootman, eds., *Community Programs to Promote Youth Development*, a report of the National Research Council and Institute of Medicine, Board on Children, Youth, and Families, Committee on Community-Level Programs for Youth (Washington, DC: National Academies Press, 2002), 181–84.

29. U.S. Department of Education, National Center for Education Statistics, *Service Learning and Community Service in K-12 Public Schools* (September 1999), table 1.

30. Center for Human Resources, Brandeis University, *Summary Report, National Evaluation of Learn and Serve America School and Community-based Programs* (Washington, DC: Corporation for National Service, July 1999).

31. Shelley Billig, Sue Root, and Dan Jesse, The Impact of Participation in Service-Learning on High School Students' Civic Engagement, CIRCLE Working Paper 33, 26–27.

32. Alan Melchior and Lawrence Neil Bailis, *2001–2002 Earth Force Evaluation: Program Implementation and Impacts* (Waltham, MA: Center for Youth and Communities, 2003).

33. Center for Human Resources, 1–3.

34. Anderson, e-mail, July 17, 2006 (quoted by permission).

35. Joseph Kahne and Susan Sporte, Developing Citizens: A Longitudinal Study of the Impact of Classroom Practices, Extra-Curricular Activities, Parent Discussions, and Neighborhood Contexts on Students' Commitments to Civic Participation (unpublished paper, October 2006).

36. Future of the First Amendment, High School Profile component (544 schools). Retrieved May 25, 2007. http://firstamendment.jideas.org.

37. John M. Bridgeland, John J. DiIulio, Jr., and Karen Burke Morrison, *The Silent Epidemic: Perspectives of High School Dropouts* (Washington, DC: Civic Enterprises and Peter D. Hart and Associates for the Bill and Melinda T. Gates Foundation, March 2006), v.

38. American Youth Policy Forum, SOME Things DO Make a Difference for Youth, summary of Andrew Hahn, Tom Leavitt, and Paul Aaron, Evaluation of the Quantum Opportunities Program (June 1994) and Quantum Opportunities Program: A Brief on the Qop Pilot Program (September 1995); cf. Eccles and Gootman, 184–86.

39. National Alliance for Media Arts and Culture, Technical Assistance Grants Evaluation, 27.

40. For a sample of the theoretical literature, see Reed W. Larson, Toward a Psychology of Positive Youth Development, *American Psychologist* 55, no. 1 (January 2000): 170–83.

41. Rheingold, e-mail, July 19, 2006 (quoted by permission).

42. Global Action Project, Mission & History. Retrieved May 25, 2007. http://www.global-action.org/main.html.

43. McDermott, e-mail, July 27, 2006 (quoted by permission).

44. Educational Video Center, About. Retrieved May 25, 2007. http://www.evc.org/about/about.html.

45. Goodman, e-mail, July 11, 2006 (quoted by permission).

46. National Alliance for Media Arts and Culture, 12.

47. Walker, e-mail, July 12, 2006.

48. Lenhart and Madden, 8.

49. Jacquelynne S. Eccles and Bonnie L. Barber, Student Council, Volunteering, Basketball, or Marching Band: What Kind of Extracurricular Involvement Matters, *Journal of Adolescent Research* 14, no. 1 (January 1999): 31.

50. Bonnie L. Barber, Jacquelynne S. Eccles, and Margaret R. Stone, Whatever Happened to the Jock, the Brain, and the Princess? Young Adult Pathways Linked to Adolescent Activity Involvement and Social Identity, *Journal of Adolescent Research* 16, no. 5 (September 2001): 429–55.

51. Marshall van Alstyne and Erik Brynjolfsson, Electronic Communities: Global Village or Cyberbalkans? (1997), http://web.mit.edu/marshall/www/papers/CyberBalkans.pdf (accessed January 1, 2007); Markus Prior, Liberated Viewers, Polarized Voters: The Implications of Increased Media Choice for Democratic Politics, *Good Society* 11, no. 3 (2002): 10–16.

52. Probit analysis of the Knight First Amendment survey, details available from CIRCLE.

53. Dewey, *The Public and Its Problems* (New York: Henry Holt, 1927), 149.

54. Harry Brighouse, *On Education* (Abingdon and New York: Routledge, 2006), 87–88.

55. Dewey, *Democracy and Education*, 89.

56. Thomas Toch, *High Schools on a Human Scale: How Small Schools Can Transform American Education* (Boston, MA: Beacon, 2003), 7.

57. Christopher Berry, School Inflation, *Education Next*, fall 2004, 56 ff.

58. The Small Schools Express, *Rethinking Schools* 19, no. 4 (summer 2005): 4.

59. Friedland, 385.

Civic Identities, Online Technologies: From Designing Civics Curriculum to Supporting Civic Experiences

Marina Umaschi Bers

Tufts University, Department of Child Development

Scenario

Peter is a twelve-year-old boy. He connects to Zora, a virtual city built and inhabited by eleven- to fifteen-year-olds. His avatar has his own face. Peter is happy because he feels that the virtual home he created in Zora is almost finished. He put pictures of his favorite things and people, and wrote stories about his family and friends. Peter decides to go around the virtual city. He quickly navigates through Zora's different public spaces: the Baptist Church, the French Chateaux, the Sports Arena and the Jewish temple. Upon entering the Jewish temple a virtual rabbi welcomes him with a blessing. "This is clever!" thinks Peter, "I will program my soccer player to welcome visitors to the Sports arena." The temple is populated by Jewish symbols and characters created by other Jewish kids. At first sight, there is a map of Israel, Hebrew letters, and a picture of a man praying. Peter navigates around the three-dimensional space and encounters many different objects. Peter decides to add a television to the temple. Inside it, he puts a snapshot from the movie Schindler's List that he found in the Web. He associates the value "documentation" to the television and defines it in the Zora Collaborative Values Dictionary as "it is very important to remember history. That way, bad things won't happen again. Holocaust survivors are getting very old now, and if someone doesn't record their stories of what happened, we are doomed to forget and repeat the horrors."

As he is about to leave the temple, he finds a case placed by Elena earlier that week. It has a Web link to a news article about a shooting in a Jewish community center. Peter clicks on the case and learns more about what happened. He also sees that Elena has used the Zora values dictionary to create a new value, "tolerance," and link it to the case. As Peter is reading Elena's definition of tolerance, the Zora mayor invites him to join a meeting in the virtual city hall.

This scenario describes an actual engagement by young people participating in a virtual summer camp with a three-dimensional multiuser environment called Zora.[1] Zora provides easy-to-use tools for children to design and program their own virtual city and, in the process, learn new concepts and ways of thinking about identity and civic life. Children are put in the role of producers, instead of consumers, of information, knowledge, and habits of mind. The notion of youth as active cultural producers is a theme shared by most chapters in this

I am grateful to the following organizations that funded different aspects of the work presented in this chapter: Tisch College of Citizenship and Public Service at Tufts University, Academic Technologies at Tufts University, and NSF (NSF Career award "Communities of Learning and Care: Multi-user Virtual Environments That Promote Positive Youth Development," NSF IIS-0447166). The author is also thankful to members of the DevTech research group at Tufts University, in particular Clement Chau, Ashima Mathur, Daniela Mesalles, and Keiko Satoh, for their work on ACT. Finally, I'd like to thank Lance Bennett, the editor of this volume, for his constructive suggestions for improving this chapter, and the other contributors to this book for the wonderful exchanges and conversations we've had.

volume. In Zora, this takes a different meaning because the environment provides a safe "social laboratory"[2] for youth to experiment with some of the skills and attitudes needed to become good citizens. Zora is an example of a type of computational tool called identity construction environments (ICEs).[3] ICEs are developed in the spirit of the constructionist philosophy of learning, which asserts that children learn better by doing creative things with computers. Thus software and hardware should provide authoring tools to enable children to make, design, and create digital artifacts while participating in a community of peers. Zora provides tools for youth to explore self and community by encountering the challenges of democratic participation.[4]

As shown in the short excerpt above, Zora engages children in thinking about issues of identity by inviting them to construct their own virtual homes and populate them with their most cherished objects, characters, pictures, stories, and personal and moral values. The city metaphor invites children to explore their civic identities by building the city's public spaces and by participating in a forum for discussing civic issues, as it will be later shown. Zora allows youth to participate in the virtual community not only by engaging in discussions and arguments, but also by designing and making new objects and new places within the virtual city, as a response to the virtual world's civic needs. ICEs, such as Zora, engage youth in chatting as well as doing, discussing as well as creating, and thinking as well as producing.

This chapter first provides a rationale for the need of developing educational programs for promoting youth civic engagement that make use of new technologies. Then, it presents a typology to guide the design of Internet-based interventions, taking into account both the affordances of the technology and the educational approach to the use of the technology. To illustrate this typology, examples of technology-based civic educational programs are presented. Later, it briefly presents the design of the Zora virtual environment, highlighting the features that support civic learning, and two different case studies in which Zora was used. It concludes with future directions for how to develop and use on-line virtual environments to promote civic engagement experiences that might transfer to the off-line world; and with reflections on how to make the contributions of this chapter "timeless," as lessons can be useful regardless of the technology in vogue in a particular time and location.

The typology of different interventions and the case studies illustrate what is possible in terms of civic education when providing young people with technological and media literacy skills as well as civic habits of mind in the context of an immersive virtual intervention. The notion of media literacy is further explored in Rheingold's and Levine's chapters. Raynes-Goldie and Walker's chapter provide another example based on their extensive work done with the Web site TakingITGlobal.

Virtual Environments: New Opportunities for Civic Engagement

Today's youth are often criticized for their lack of civic participation and involvement in political life. Technology has been blamed, among many other causes, for fostering social isolation and youth's retreat into a private world disconnected from their "real life" communities.[5] However, current research is beginning to indicate that today's youth are indeed engaged in civic life, but in ways very different from previous generations. First, youth tend to choose activism, volunteerism, and community work, as opposed to well-established means such as voting in elections or participating in political parties, as has been stated in different ways by Coleman, Earl and Schussman, Montgomery, and Raynes-Goldie and Walker in this volume. Second, technology—specifically the Internet—has provided a new way for youth to create communities that extend beyond geographic boundaries. These virtual communities enable youth to engage in civic and volunteering activities across local communities and national frontiers, to learn about political life, and to experience the challenges of democratic participation.[6]

However, although there is a growing body of research indicating the educational and social potential of the Internet,[7] there have been few studies conducted to purposefully evaluate technology-based interventions in the area of civic engagement. Since virtual environments can provide quick access to a wide range of information and resources, communication mechanisms for engaging in critical debates,[8] and tools for supporting collaboration and for enabling new expressions of social life,[9] they can serve as powerful platforms for developing educational programs to promote civic education. In a test-driven educational atmosphere in which most public schools might not be able to devote resources and time to increase student's civic participation, the potential of new technologies is even greater for reaching those same students when they are outside of school and connecting to the Internet from their homes. Virtual communities, simulations, or interactive games specifically designed with civic education goals might offer a space for young people to become civically engaged—at least in the on-line world.

Although preliminary studies have shown the potential of new technologies to engage young people in on-line civic life, there is a need of more research looking at *how* technology-based interventions particularly aimed at fostering civic engagement can promote participation not only in the virtual world, but also in the face-to-face world.

While participation in virtual life does not replace traditional civic actions, research shows that adults are more likely to vote and be engaged in the civic sphere if, as youth, they were involved in community-based organizations or extracurricular activities.[10] As the Internet is becoming a new way for youth to form community-based organizations and to spend a big portion of their after-school time, it is plausible that future research will show that youth who are more active on-line will also grow into more engaged citizens.

For example, pilot work by Chau suggests that college students who possess high level of *interpersonal technological abilities* (i.e., who use technology to establish connections with others) may use the Internet in manners that are more conducive to building connecting and caring relationships with peers than would students with lower level of *interpersonal technological abilities*. Thus, youth who are low on *internal technological efficacy* may benefit most if provided first with educational opportunities to develop technological competence and a sense of confidence in their technological skills.[11] This early work indicates that it is important to understand and evaluate youth's technological competencies, before developing specific technology-rich educational interventions.

While technological competence is a prerequisite for youth to fully benefit from these programs, if the end-goal is to promote civic engagement, it is imperative to understand our philosophical and pedagogical stance regarding civic education. Do we want to use technology to design interventions that will help youth to develop civic skills, such as deliberation and decision making? Do we want to expose youth to opportunities that allow them to actively participate in community life through the use of technology? Or is our goal to provide technological environments in which youth can develop civic identities grounded on personal and moral values such as social justice? These different options are not mutually exclusive, and the best interventions integrate all of them.

From Civic Skills to Civic Identities

Once in the Zora City Hall, Peter joins a conversation about the case placed by Elena with a Web link to a news article about a shooting in a Jewish community center.

Elena says: It was very scary. I read the article and one of the things the man who committed this act said is that he wanted to remind people that all Jews should be killed. That sent serious shivers down my spine.

Kosho says: Nazis. A leader tells them that others are the cause of all their problems.

Peter says: Some people are just looking for someone to blame.

Janet says: People are gonna feel the way they want to feel and no one can really change their minds

Elena says: They are entitled to their opinions but it's their actions that need to be stopped. Janet, do you really think that? No one can change their minds? And if it's true that we can't change their minds, should we do something to limit their actions?

Peter says: There isn't anything we can do.

Nino says: This guy should be dragged out and flayed alive.

Kosho says: You just can't fix a wrong with a wrong.

Janet says: Yeah, violence is never the answer.

Nino says: If anybody deserves the death penalty, he does.

Peter says: But I think no one deserves the death penalty.

Carla says: He should just have life in jail.

Sheila says: He shouldn't be shot but helped, I really don't know how, but he just needs a way to get familiar with other cultures.

Nino says: That's not going to help. Death penalty.

Peter says: We don't have the authority to take a person's life. Death penalty is still not justified.

Sheila says: I think by killing him we show that we have given up and the only way to solve things is to kill somebody, and I know that is not right.

Matrix says: I read an editorial that said people should just be put in jail for life because, believe it or not, the death penalty cost more than letting him live for the rest of his life (30 yrs.).

Elena says: Answer my questions, should anyone who kills be killed? Or does intent matter? And if intent matters, does it matter more or less than the result of the action?

Nino says: Intent and result both matter.

Elena says: And once he is killed, assuming he is, what would be the repercussions of that? Would his family go after the government? Would he become a neo-Nazi martyr?

Janet says: Maybe there should be a boot camp for people like this.

Peter says: It wouldn't really work. The only prevention is at home. People need to be brought up knowing discrimination is wrong.

Sheila says: I think we can't do that much for adults, but the kids in school I know we can do a lot, so I think we should try to concentrate on making sure they know that this stuff is wrong.

While this on-line conversation continues, Ernie, one of the youngest and shyest children using Zora, who is very quiet "listening" but is too shy to participate, starts to make a new virtual place, the "Everyone's Temple," which he describes as a space for "all the cultures and religions to get along."

This example of the type of exchanges that happen in Zora points us in two different directions that this chapter follows.[12] First, the design considerations, both from a pedagogical and a technical perspective, that need to be taken into account when designing virtual environments that, beyond providing civic knowledge and information, afford opportunities for learners to engage in civic discourse and civic action. Second, the civic education approach used when developing these technologically rich interventions. On one side of the spectrum, civic education can take a behaviorist approach (i.e., providing skills and knowledge that might be useful for both living in a civil way and contributing to civil society). On the other side, it can take a psychological approach (i.e., focusing on helping children to develop civic identities by exploring personal and moral values deeply rooted in their own sociocultural and religious backgrounds). It is important to understand where in the spectrum we situate our educational programs so as to choose the best possible use of technology and the design features of the software.

The first question regarding pedagogical and technical considerations is addressed in the section "Educational Technologies and Civic Education," which looks at the different ways in which technology can be used to teach and to promote learning. A typology and examples are presented. The second question regarding approaches to technology-based civic education programs is addressed by presenting case studies of how a particular kind of technology, the Zora identity construction environment, was developed to integrate and combine both behaviorist and psychological approaches.

The goal of helping children to clarify their values as a first step toward civic engagement is not new in education, neither is it associated with the use of technology. However, new technologies such as multiuser virtual environments have the potential to amplify the experience by situating personal values in the context of a living community. When Lawrence Kohlberg, the well-known academic of moral reasoning, proposed the "just community" model as a safe educational space critical in shaping an individual's moral development,[13] he realized the importance of a community for advancing moral thinking and moral behaviors. Thus, as opposed to his most well-known work on moral reasoning (which focused, in the Piagetian tradition, on asking children to solve isolated moral dilemmas and assigning them to a particular moral reasoning stage), Kohlberg realized that a moral community was needed to breed moral individuals. In Kohlberg's "just community" program, students and teachers engaged in conversations about dilemmas and controversial issues similar to the ones described in Zora. However, members of these just communities could make decisions about all aspects of the community life, except curriculum decisions. This is a very important difference with the type of educational work that happens in virtual communities such as Zora.

There are three major differences between the just community educational approach and the experiences afforded by participating in Zora. Some of these differences are due to the choice of media (virtual environments vs. face to face) and others to the pedagogical stance. First, as shown by the examples presented earlier, community members do not follow an already-established curriculum specifying the activities they should engage in. They are empowered to decide what kind of projects and discussions they would work on. Thus, they engage in what Hart describes as one of the highest levels in the ladder of civic participation observed in children, child initiated and directed projects.[14] Second, Zora makes it easy for learners to observe the connections between what is said in the on-line conversations (i.e., discussion about discrimination) and what is done in the virtual city (i.e., creating the "Everyone's Temple"). An environment that offers the possibility of observing the relationship between *saying* and *doing* is powerful because in issues of identity and values, community and civics, concrete actions matter as much as analytical thinking.[15] In the real world, however, taking action would involve a long-term complex process for young children. Third, in Kohlberg's work, the tools people have to build a just community are words and their derivates such as meetings, sharing stories, discussing dilemmas, etc. In Zora, as shown by Eric's "Everyone's Temple," people can also engage in making concrete artifacts, such as virtual places, that can be used and inhabited.

Regardless of these major differences, Zora and the just community model share a similar educational purpose: the development of an educational approach to engage children in developing a community with the goal of learning about moral values, explore the civic aspects of the self and exercise civic skills by making decisions about community life. In the process, civic identities are developed and public voices, as discussed in Rheingold's chapter, start to emerge.

Educational Technologies and Civic Education

Kohlberg's just community is one of many civic education programs. I use it in this chapter as an example of what has been called praxis-based educational models. These are developed to give people the experiences through which they can become effective citizens.[16] Praxis-based models are in sharp contrast with knowledge-based models focused on what people should know and understand about citizenship.

These distinct approaches propose different pedagogies concerned with how best to support learning, and different epistemologies, concerned with the question of what is considered learning. While knowledge-based models pay attention to the teaching curriculum, praxis-based models are concerned with how young people can be given opportunities for engagement and decision making in their communities. The challenge is how to reconcile these models in the test-driven and politically confined environment of most public schools.

The distinction between knowledge and praxis permeates the world of education and is consistent with two different approaches for developing educational technologies, identified by Seymour Papert, pioneer in the field, as instructionist and constructionist. While the instructionist approach sees the effectiveness of a technology as situated in its instructional efficacy, and therefore its potential for transmitting knowledge and information, the constructionist approach conceives the computer as a tool to help learners have experiences that will support their own construction of knowledge.

Within the instructionist way of using technology for education, which is closely aligned with the knowledge-based model proposed in civic education mentioned earlier, two major paradigms have emerged: computer-assisted instruction (CAI) and intelligent tutoring systems (ITS).[17] While most of the educational technologies designed with the CAI paradigm serve as a new medium for the presentation and delivery of information to students in the form of drill and practice, the ITS paradigm aims at creating educational software that adapts itself to the user. Unlike static CAI applications, ITS educational software incorporates an interactive component, with each student receiving a different type of instruction based on skill level and ability.

While instructionism—and its two paradigms, CAI and ITS—focuses on the role of technology to do better teaching by providing better ways of transmitting information, constructionism asserts that computers are powerful educational technologies when used as tools for supporting the design, the construction, and the programming of personally and epistemologically meaningful projects that engage learners in new experiences. Constructionism is rooted in Piaget's constructivism, in which learning is best characterized as an individual cognitive process given a social and cultural context. However, whereas Piaget's theory was developed to explain how knowledge is constructed in our heads, constructionism, developed by Papert, pays particular attention to the role of constructions in the world as a support for those in the head. Thus, constructionism is both a theory of learning and a strategy for education. It offers the framework for developing a technology-rich design-based learning environment, in which learning happens best when learners are engaged in learning by making, creating, programming, and communicating.

Constructionism also has two major paradigms: the Logo-inspired programming languages for children, and the computer-supported collaborative learning movement. Constructionism views the programming of a computer as a powerful way to gain new insights into how the mind works and learns. Thus, it advocates for providing children with an opportunity to become computer programmers as a way to learn about different content areas (in particular mathematics and science) but, more important, to learn about learning. Papert argued that using a child-friendly version of the programming language LISP, called Logo or the language of the turtle, was an easy and natural way to engage students in programming. Logo allows students to actively create artifacts in a process of discovery-based learning—a process directly aligned with the praxis-based model of experiential learning. By now there is a long-standing constructionist tradition of authoring tools and programming environments that follow the Logo steps. Some of these technological environments are designed for children's learning about mathematics and science,[18] for creating virtual communities to foster peer learning and collaboration and for designing computational environments to promote positive youth development through storytelling.[19]

The other paradigm within constructionism is computer-supported collaborative learning. This most recently developed paradigm shifts the process of cognition as residing within the head of one individual to the view that cognition is situated within a particular community of learning or practice.[20] Therefore, educational technologies designed within this paradigm take seriously the need to provide tools for community building and community scaffolding of learning. Thus the focus is on creating social environments in which constructionist types of learning activities using technologies can happen. This pedagogical switch from learning as an individual experience, which was rooted in Piaget's theories, to learning as a social process, which is rooted in Vygostsky's theory, occurred concurrently with the fast-growing uses of the Internet in education and the development of virtual learning communities.

Aligning instructionist technologies with knowledge-based approaches to civic education, and constructionism to praxis-based approaches, provides a framework for thinking about the different ways in which new technologies, in particular the Internet, can be used for developing civic education programs and for distinguishing the pedagogical and technological affordances of the different approaches (see Figure 1). Both approaches can take a behaviorist or a psychological stance, or a combination of both, depending on the choice of primary learning outcomes, civic skills or civic identities.

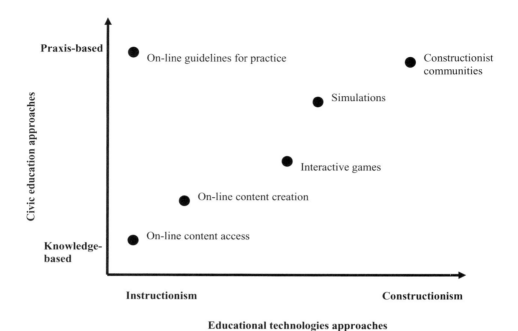

Figure 1
A typology for integrating approaches to civic education and educational technologies.

Figure 1 shows a typology emerging from intersecting civic education approaches with educational technologies approaches. By analyzing technology-based civic education programs, six distinct categories emerged in the typology. The first three categories refer to programs that provide opportunities for youth to access and create on-line content, as well as encounter on-line guidelines for practice. The other three refer to programs that provide learners with opportunities to immerse themselves in the civic realm by playing interactive games, participating in simulations, or developing constructionist communities.

Table 1 provides examples of technology-rich civic education programs within each typology. For a different kind of typology that looks at the content of the Web sites, regardless of the affordances of the technology regarding a particular stance toward civic education, refer to the March 2004 report "Youth as E-Citizens: Engaging the Digital Generation" by Montgomery et al.[21]

In the next sections I will present work done with Zora, an example of a constructionist virtual community, as a way to elucidate what represents for me the full potential of using technology to develop praxis-based programs that integrate behaviorist and psychological approaches to civic education.

However, although praxis-based programs are at the heart of what I consider powerful educational experiences using technology, this view is not always in agreement with current trends in the American educational system that tend to focus on knowledge-based programs in which students can be assessed using traditional means such as comprehensive multichoice exams.

The typology and the continuum of instructionist to constructionist approaches need to be problematized. For example, one of the reasons that programs such as Student Voices fall

Table 1
Examples of different online approaches to civic engagement and education

	Program	Web site	Description
On-line guide-lines for practice	Youth Voice. Net	http://www.indiana.edu/%7Eythvoice/socialtools.html	This Web site provides guidelines on how to be an advocate at the community level or in local or state politics. It provides resources for promoting civic engagement.
On-line content access	Student Voices	http://student-voices.org/	This Web site is aimed at engaging youth in politics. It provides discussion forums and educational links. It is well organized and clearly youth oriented. It includes ways to get involved in society both on the local and national level.
	Campus Activism.Org	http://www.campusactivism.org/	Interactive Web site aimed at college leaders. It offers networking with other college groups. Web site includes forums, online resources, calendars of events, e-mail lists, and lists of current and past campaigns.
On-line content creation	CholertonShand Online Consultation Platform	http://www.cholertonshand.co.uk/document.asp?id=15	This program, which mostly uses chat, e-mail, and interactive questionnaires, surveys and consults young people in political matters. It collects information about citizenship provided by youth.
	Taking ITGlobal	http://www.takingitglobal.org/	This highly interactive Web site presents an on-line international community aimed at getting youth involved at the local and global level. The Web site offers blogs, discussion boards, member profiles, and[22] links.

(Continued)

Table 1
Examples of different online approaches to civic engagement and education (*Continued*)

	Program	Web site	Description
Interactive games	DemGames	http://www.delib.co.uk/ knowledge_centre/ case_studies/ demgames	This series of games was developed with the purpose of teaching about democracy and citizenship through an interactive manner. The games are available online or through a CD. They include a teacher support pack. Demgames is being used in youth councils (twelve to eighteen year olds) to engage new participants and educate members. The technology is Blue-Tooth compatible and is being tested on mobiles.
Simulations	Smart/Sheffield	http://www.delib.co.uk/ knowledge_centre/ case_studies/ smart_connect	This textual-based interactive program promotes civic engagement by engaging youth in the discussion of citizenship-related issues.
Constructionist communities	Zora	http://www.ase.tufts. edu/devtech/ vclc/CHZora.html	3D multiuser environments that provides tools for youth to create and inhabit a virtual city, by creating virtual spaces, objects, characters, stories, and a values dictionary, as well as engage in debate over cases and real-time interactions.
	Quest Atlantis	http://atlantis.crlt. indiana.edu/start/ index.html	3D multiuser environment in which users undergo tasks or quests. Users are engaging in an already created world. Participants chat among themselves and with mentors. Quests have specific educational purposes and are associated with social or civic responsibilities.

in the left lower corner is that these programs are aimed at being realistically integrated with test-driven curricula. Virtual environments such as Zora provide flexibility regarding this. For example, if used in the context of public schools, the Zora curriculum can be strengthen thus taking the experience into a more knowledge-based model.

Zora: Developing Civic Identities

Zora is an example of a constructionist virtual community specifically designed to promote positive youth development. Positive youth development involves cognitive, personal, social, emotional, and civic aspects of adolescence, which researchers refer to as the six C's: *competence* (cognitive abilities and behavioral skills for being healthy), *connection* (positive bonds with people and institutions), *character* (integrity and moral centeredness), *confidence* (positive self-regard, a sense of self-efficacy), *caring* (human values empathy and a sense of social justice), and *contribution* (orientation to contribute to civil society).[23] Together, these characteristics reflect a growing consensus about what is involved in healthy and positive development among people in the first two decades of their lives.

Within this framework, the sixth C, contribution to civic life, plays an important role because it is a predictor of the positive direction toward which an individual is moving in his or her developmental trajectory. Zora has design features that promote each of the C's by providing tools for users to create and inhabit a virtual city and, in the process, learn new things about identity and civic life.

Zora's design and infrastructure provides a bridge between what I have called earlier behaviorist approaches to civic education, focused on helping children become better citizens by teaching them civic attitudes and skills such as respectful argumentation, debate, information literacy, and so on, and psychological approaches focused on internal motivation to support the development of morally responsible individuals who will shape a morally responsible and civically minded society. These can help children to discover their personal and moral values as inspirations and compasses for developing a civic self concerned with issues of equality, morality, and social justice.

In Zora, behavioral and psychological approaches are integrated by providing computational tools for children to create a virtual city with private and public spaces. They can navigate the three-dimensional space with their avatar of choice and chat in real-time. For example, each user creates his or her personal home and populates it with objects and characters. For each of them, children create a story to describe it and assign a value and its corresponding definition to indicate why the creation is personally meaningful and what moral message the object/character carries. For example, as shown in the example presented earlier, Elena had created a TV with the movie *Schindler's List* and had assigned and defined the value "documentation." All of the individual values and definitions created by children are updated into the Zora's collaborative values dictionary, which serves at least two different functions. First, it provides a way to understand the "moral climate" of the virtual city. Second, it engages Zora users in different activities to decide which of those values they want to keep as flagship for their city, which ones need some discussion because there is disagreement about their meaning (i.e., different users have entered a same value but define it in different ways), and which others will serve as the basis for developing the city's constitution, mission statement, and code of conduct.

As mentioned above, Zora's design supports both behaviorist and psychological approaches to civic education. In terms of promoting behavior changes, the most salient design features are "cases." A case is an object with a particular kind of shape and graphical image representing an event or a circumstance to be discussed and agreed upon by all community members. In the same spirit as a legal case, a Zora case requires community members to engage in debate and take action to resolve conflicts. This kind of participation in a learning environment might serve as a model for the larger political community in which children will participate as adults. Users can create new cases as new issues arise.

For example, in the scenario presented before, Elena had put a case with a link to a news article about an anti-Semitic incident. The fact that it was a "case," and not only an object, indicated to the Zora citizens that Elena wanted to have a discussion about it and prompted the Zora city mayor to call for a meeting in the City Hall. Once there, the exchange evolved from discussing anti-Semitism, racism, and xenophobia to debating about the fairness and usefulness of the death penalty, as well as preventive mechanisms for educating young people against hate crimes. While this case was about a current event reported in the newspaper, and thus engaged children in thinking about the impact on society at large, other cases are only relevant to Zora, such as those dealing with setting up the social organization of the virtual city, such as "I think that people should not change or put things in other peoples [sic] rooms. Unless they have permission," or "Anyone should be able to drop anything anywhere, but with a consequence. This should be like breaking a law, punishable by imprisonment of one hour."

Zora's design features that support a behaviorist approach, such as cases, are grounded on understanding civic education as a deliberative and argumentative process that helps children take on civic behaviors. Thus, the children's experience in Zora should serve them as a playground for experimenting with the ways of thinking and behaving needed to function in a community, in particular with the complexities involved in self-organization, government, and decision making, This is consistent with extensive research that suggests that the involvement in participatory democracy, social institutions, group decision making, and self-government are critical in shaping individuals' moral development.

Moral development is an important aspect of what I have called the psychological approach to civic education. Some of Zora's design features are developed with this in mind. For example, the collaborative values dictionary, which was described earlier, helps children to develop a sense of identity by asking them to think about their most cherished personal and moral values and how they have influenced their creations in the world. There is another type of object, called heroes and villains, which have special attributes and serve as models of identification and counteridentification. As the American psychologist Erik Erikson points out, "no ego can develop outside of social processes that offer workable prototypes and roles."[24] Thus, creating Zora's heroes and villains provides a way for children to engage in the dynamic process of identifying with and differentiating from others, which is essential to form a coherent sense of self. The values dictionary and the heroes and villains are the most notorious Zora's features explicitly designed to support building civic identities which are morally grounded and that invite children to explore, understand, and reflect about personal and moral values.

While some of these design elements are unique to Zora, they are also present in many of the technologies and tools mentioned in the typology of educational technologies for civic engagement presented earlier. For example, different forms of media production focused on civic engagement, such as the weblogs and the wikis presented by Levine's and Rheingold's articles and the on-line petitions described in Earl and Schussman's chapter can provide mechanisms for promoting collaboration, including comprehensive Web sites such as TakingITGlobal, described in Raynes-Goldie and Luke's article, which can offer opportunities for taking global civic action.

In the next section I describe an educational program, Active Citizenship through Technology (ACT), developed using the Zora environment, to help precollege students to develop civic identities, while forming a community of peers and social support network.

Using Zora to Create the Virtual Campus of the Future

Mike says: Anyone have strong feelings about the admission process?

Laura says: I think that peer review will be a better way at processing people. Maybe on a sub-personal level.

Caitlin says: To what degree?

Tom says: What do you mean by peer review?

Make says: Would peer review take the place of an essay?

Laura says: Like interviews.

Kim says: More like having admitted students read applications and give their feedback; the common applications with a supplemental essay.

This is a log excerpt from a real-time conversation in Zora by a group of Tufts University incoming freshmen who participated in the optional preorientation program, ACT, developed by Bers.[25]

ACT is both an educational and a research program. Students come together for three days to use Zora to create and inhabit a virtual campus of the future. At the end of the intensive program, they make a short digital video, or infomercial, about their virtual campus. During their first semester in college, students came together again in an open house to show their infomercials to the campus community. During their four years in college, ACT participants are asked to complete surveys and participate in focus groups in an effort to collect data regarding the impact of ACT in their academic and extracurricular experiences.

The ACT curriculum is designed so students, in the process of developing their campus of the future, can first learn about the real campus by interviewing faculty, students, and administrators and then discuss how they could improve its facilities, its policies and curricular offerings and, most important, what is the relationship between their campus and their surrounding community and what are student's civic privileges and responsibilities toward the local neighborhoods and international communities.

In the spirit of a constructionist community, the goal of ACT is to immerse youth in a high-tech playground where they can acquire civic knowledge and skills as well as experiment with civic behaviors and democratic participation. These will be useful not only for growing as committed citizens, but also for adjusting to their new community, the university campus.

During the first two years of running the ACT program, while most of the discussions in Zora were about building a stronger community within the campus, some started to explore how to build relationships between the campus and the surrounding neighborhoods. These discussions were supported by the creation of virtual exhibits displaying issues of concern in the Zora campus of the future.

The ACT intensive program, which takes place at the end of the summer just before participants' matriculation to the university, has several goals. First, to engage incoming freshmen in a fun activity that leverages on their interest on interactive games and virtual communities. Second, to help them to connect with each other and to find a social support network early on, before the stress of the academic year begins. Third, to promote civic engagement both at the campus and the community level.[26]

Some conceive civic engagement as being a good neighbor, obeying rules, and participating in the community; others think of it as engagement with political processes such as voting. In the work presented with Zora, the notion of civic engagement goes beyond a focus solely on the procedural aspects of democracy to one that embraces the many facets of a deliberative democracy in one's own environment, school, local community, or larger society. This includes the ability to engage in civic conversations, to develop civic knowledge, skills, attitudes and behaviors, and to participate in community service, activism, and advocacy. Since the ACT program is conducted with freshmen, civic engagement is primarily defined as all of the above in the context of college and campus community.

As mentioned before, ACT is part of an ongoing multiyear longitudinal pilot study in which two cohorts of students participate in the preorientation program using Zora and are followed through their academic career by collecting participant data via multiple means. First, the Zora environment readily provides a log of all online activities and conversations that happen throughout the program. Log files from the program are read and coded by orientation peer leaders and researchers. Second, exit focus group interviews and surveys to collect overall feedback about the program as well as suggestions for improvement of individual sessions and activities is requested from participants. Third, once a year, participants complete follow-up surveys, which are used to assess the carry-over effect of the program on participants' active involvement on campus and in the surrounding community. Data from a randomized control group (i.e., a randomized group of other students on campus of the same cohort who did not participate in ACT) are collected each year as comparisons. To date, two cohorts of students have participated in ACT. The first consisting of eighteen students, the second of twenty-one. Participants in the first cohort came back to the second group as peer leaders.

The first cohort of ACT participants chose to use Zora to develop a virtual campus very focused on student's own interests and needs. For example, they built the "Campus Safety Center," which offers "a shuttle service for 18 hours a day followed by a campus cab system that goes anywhere in a 5 mile radius of the campus, and the 'Jumbo Appetite,' a dining hall where themed meals are served and a suggestion box where requests for particular foods can be made."

During the three-day period each student created his or her own virtual dorm room. They downloaded favorite sports team images, pictures of famous singers, and other images

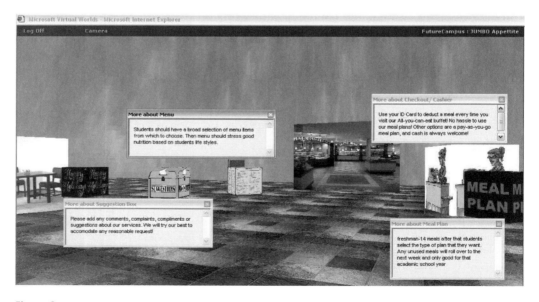

Figure 2
Jumbo Appetite, the restaurant in the virtual campus.

to decorate their virtual walls. Overall, they created sixteen public spaces, such as the Mike Jonas Student Center, the Sports Center, the Math and Science Building, the Orwell Language Hall, the Winifred Mandela Library, and so on. After on-line brainstorming about some basic houses that were needed, students began working alone. For example, one student created a computer room for the campus as he is planning on being a computer science major. He described it as follows: "The computer spot is a computer lab where all activity is subject to surveillance in order to protect against illegal actions. There is also a university Cellphone Network. The university will provide each student with a free cell phone and will have its own network, where all students and faculty can call each other for free."

As individual locations started to appear, and not everyone agreed on the purpose and facilities offered, the group decided they needed to come together and finalize a plan to complete their campus instead of working separately without discussing what they are doing. They discussed several cases as a group and divided up tasks. Students assigned each other rooms to create, and deadlines for completion were agreed upon. The group decided that the content presented in each house was more important than its aesthetic appearance; therefore, they focused on developing well-written descriptions, stories, and values associated with objects. For example, they chose the following values in their collaborative values dictionary as the most important to guide behaviors in their virtual campus: Academic Curiosity, Cooperation, Tolerance, Perseverance, Respect, Integrity, Leadership, and Respect.

The beginning of self-organization and self-governance started to appear on the second day of the program. They discussed issues such as student life, policies/rules for graduation, Internet, administration, and student services. Following is an excerpt of a conversation in which students discussed funding for students' clubs.

Peter says: Are we going to have fun student clubs? Do clubs have to give back to the community?

Melanie says: If you are giving back to the community, should you get more money?

Alan says: Should we fund the clubs?

Peter says: Every year, they give their proposal... then they decide... and get their permission.

David says: If you are giving back to the community, you should get money. Why put money into clubs ?

Peter says: If it lasts then that is good; but if you are new, you start-off with the minimum amount.

As shown in this excerpt, most of the on-line discussions focused on internal issues to campus life. Civic engagement was conceived as a process of becoming involved with the civic life of campus, such as assigning internal budgets or developing policies that would be best for students. While this was one of the goals of the ACT program, in this first experience, students did not explore the relationship between campus and community. Data from focus groups showed that since students were just entering into a new community (the college campus) they first needed to understand and master it, and then venture out of the hills of the university. As the ACT curriculum was focused on giving students the freedom to pursue their own interest in an effort to give them ownership over their virtual campus, the lack of connection between college civic life with the broader community is not surprising.

Figure 3
A virtual exhibit about the importance of art education programs in schools.

Based on this finding, the next year, the second cohort of ACT participants was exposed to a curriculum that focused on developing a civically engaged virtual campus with strong connections with the surrounding community. For example, students were asked to investigate the living conditions and the educational and health situation of the campus neighborhoods and propose recommendations of how their future virtual campus could have an impact on this.

For example, some students chose to focus on the relationship between the local town police and the university police. They conducted research to analyze if and how both groups interact and they interviewed police officials to understand better if and how the surrounding community benefits from the campus police. Other students chose to focus on the role of the universities, in particular the education, child development, and psychology departments, to provide child care and educational opportunities for members of the surrounding community.

Some students chose to do research about issues of public interest such as the impact of comprehensive exams in the learning environment and state-mandated curriculum, and the positive impact that athletics programs and art education programs can have on a local community (see Figure 3). Instead of writing their ideas and results of their research in a paper or action plan, they used Zora to develop a virtual exhibit to teach others about their findings. The interactive nature of Zora allowed participants to use the tool for both the process and the product, as well as to invite contributions from other ACT participants who did not choose to work on these issues.

In the ACT experience described above, two cohorts of incoming freshman used Zora to design and inhabit a virtual campus of the future. As one of the participants in the first group said, "I did not really learn much about civic engagement . . . well . . . actually if I wanted to become a senator ACT would have been very useful."

This student realized that through his experience in ACT he started to gain the skills needed to participate in public life, such as making decisions that might have a broad impact and engaging in thoughtful debate and argumentation. But most important, he started to develop a civic identity that prompted him to look beyond his own interests and to take into consideration the public's best interest.

However, this student did not understand that, although the skills he learned in ACT are useful for becoming a senator and participating in the civic life of the country as a leader, they are also useful to becoming a positive contributor to civic society from many other roles. Even more important, while ACT might have been useful to this particular student, skills and identities do not develop in three days, but over time. Research has shown that engaging young children in civic activities from an early age is a positive predictor of their participation in later civic life. This explains the effort to work with young children, as I did in the context of a summer program for children aged eleven to sixteen who used Zora to develop their virtual city, from which excerpts of the scenario presented at the beginning of the paper were taken.[27]

Future Directions: From Online to Offline Experiences

Zora is one of the many tools available today to provide children with experiences that will help them develop civic skills and attitudes as well as build their civic identities by helping them find a moral compass that will lead them to civic action. As technology rapidly changes, new tools will be developed and new possibilities for developing civic education programs will emerge. Thus, the question is what will not change even when everything else changes?

People, and our inclination to learn by doing, rather than by being told, won't change. A short answer to this complex question is the need to focus on technologies that allow young people to experiment with "what if" situations, by making, creating, developing, discussing, debating. In the continuum of instructionist to constructionist approaches to civic education programs using technology presented in the earlier typology, I suggest that the focus on constructionist types of experiences should remain. Even when there is a strong push toward knowledge-base approaches that are best suited to test-driven curriculum. The advantage of constructionist and praxis-based models is that they are open-ended. For example, in Zora, teachers can create their own public virtual spaces to directly educate students about civic facts and process. But they can also design an experience in which students will take the lead.

Open-ended technologies allow different kinds of learners to use them in the way it suits them best. For example, some might choose to display content (as the ACT participants did in their virtual exhibits), others to engage in storytelling (as those who used Zora to write stories or values definitions), while others might choose to engage in debates (as those who discussed cases), or to use technology to create or program artifacts as alter egos that represent their point of view through a graphical interactive object (such as the little boy who created the "Everyone's Temple").

Technological tools also need to be open ended to enable different kinds of teachers or after-school coordinators to best integrate them with their own teaching style, curriculum, and state and federal mandates. For example, some teachers might choose to design an experience with unstructured activities, such as the case of the summer camp with young children, while others might like to develop a more structured curriculum, as it was done in ACT. For example, one of the activities was designed to help students evaluate if the campus they designed could handle a real-life, controversial community-related issue (e.g., bias incident, cheating). Actual news articles from a college's student newspaper were posted in Zora for students to read and discuss. After discussing the articles, students were asked to present their responses and thoughts somewhere in their virtual campus (e.g., the campus center). In addition, students could go back to their virtual campus and make changes, such as revising or adding services, classes, committees, or resources. Teachers have different styles and curricular needs. Thus the technology needs to be flexible enough to enable all of them to appropriate it.

In sum, the work presented in this chapter shows a concrete example, with a particular kind of technology called Zora, of a praxis-based civic education program with a constructionist use of technology. This work opens up new lines of inquiry to explore questions regarding the impact of on-line civic learning experiences, such as the ones both young children and incoming freshmen had with Zora, on the off-line "real life." For example, is participation in virtual communities affecting youth's civic engagement in face-to-face communities? Are standard on-line technologies (such as e-mail and Internet portals) of value, or do we need specifically designed technologies to promote civic engagement, such as Zora or similar constructionist communities?

If we are going to allocate resources to the development of technology-based civic education programs, we also need to understand the role of adults and mentors. A lot is known about the role of mentors in both on-line communities and face-to-face programs, but what characteristics do mentors need to have to be versatile in both worlds? Do mentors need to be themselves civically engaged to serve the function of role models?

Finally, technological fluency—defined by Seymour Papert as the ability to use and apply technology in a fluent way, effortlessly and smoothly, as one does with language—involves mastering not only technological skills and concepts but also the ability to learn new ways of using computers in a creative and personally meaningful way. During the process of using the technology in a creative way, people are also likely to develop new ways of thinking; therefore the computer's role goes far beyond being an instrumental machine. Thus, we need to understand what level of technological fluency students need to have in order to benefit from technology-based interventions to foster civic engagement?

It is not the goal of this chapter to answer these questions, but simply to pose them. As new research involving new media and civic engagement starts to emerge and the field is establishing itself as an important area in both civic education and educational technologies, the hope is that these questions will illuminate some possible directions for academic research, policy decision making, and practical implementation. While a growing amount of research and educational programs show the benefits of the Internet to gain knowledge about politics and therefore make use of instructionist technologies and knowledge-based approaches, this chapter focuses on how the Internet can provide a safe space to experiment with civic life, by forming on-line communities that extend and augment the possibilities of young people to engage in face-to-face civic conversations, attitudes, and behaviors. This is a less explored terrain that makes use of constructionist technologies and praxis-based models, as presented by Zora.

Notes

1. Zora is a three-dimensional virtual environment first designed by the author as part of her doctoral work at the MIT Media Lab using the Microsoft Virtual Worlds platform, and later reimplemented and

extended by Bers and her team at Tufts University using ActiveWorlds. Zora provides tools for youth to build and inhabit their virtual city. Research on Zora can be found in Marina Bers, Identity Construction Environments: Developing Personal and Moral Values Through the Design of a Virtual City, *The Journal of the Learning Sciences* 10, no. 4 (2001): 365–415; Marina Bers, Joseph Gonzalez-Heydrich, and David Ray DeMaso, Use of a Computer-based Application in a Pediatric Hemodialysis Unit: A Pilot Study, *Journal of the American Academy of Child & Adolescent Psychiatry* 42, no. 4 (2003): 493–96; Marina Bers and Clement Chau, Fostering Civic Engagement by Building a Virtual City, *Journal of Computer-mediated Communication* (2006), http://jcmc.indiana.edu/vol11/issue3/bers.html.

2. Sherry Turkle coined the term *social laboratory* when analyzing the first experiences of adolescents using the Internet in the early nineties in her book *Life on the Screen* (Sherry Turkle, *Life on the Screen: Identity in the Age of the Internet* [New York: Simon & Schuster, 1995]).

3. The term *identity construction environments* (ICE) was coined by Bers to refer to technologies and technologically rich psychoeducational programs specifically designed to support positive youth development (Bers, Identity Construction Environments; Marina Bers, The Role of New Technologies to Foster Positive Youth Development, *Applied Developmental Science Journal* 11, no. 1 [2006]: 200–19).

4. Seymour Papert, pioneer precursor of the use of technologies to promote learning developed the constructionist theory of learning based on his work with Jean Piaget. See Seymour Papert, *Mindstorms: Children, Computers and Powerful Ideas* (New York: Basic Books, 1980); Seymour Papert, *The Children's Machine: Rethinking School in the Age of the Computer* (New York: Basic Books, 1993).

5. Research by Molly W. Andolina, Krista Jenkins, Scott Keeter, and Cliff Zukin, Searching for the Meaning of Youth Civic Engagement: Notes From the Field, *Applied Developmental Science* 6, no. 4 (2002): 189–95; Nakesha Faison and Constance Flanagan, *Youth Civic Development: Implications of Research for Social Policy and Programs*, vol. XV, *Social Policy Report* (Ann Arbor, MI: Society for Research in Child Development, 2001); Grantmaker Forum on Community and National Service, *The State of Service-related Research: Opportunities to Build a Field* (Berkeley, CA: The Grantmaker Forum on Community, 2000); Erik Michelsen, Jonathan Zaff, and Elizabeth C. Hair, *Civic Engagement Programs and Youth Development: A Synthesis* (Washington, DC: Child Trends, 2002); Robert Kraut, Sarah Kiesler, Bonka Boneva, Jonathan Cummings, Vicki Helgeson, and Anne Crawford, Internet Paradox Revisited, *Journal of Social Issues* 58, no. 1 (2002): 49–74; Robert Kraut, Michael Patterson, Vicki Lundmark, Sarah Kiesler, Tridas Mukophadhyay, and William Scherlis, Internet Paradox: A Social Technology That Reduces Social Involvement and Psychological Well-being? *American Psychologist* 53, no. 9 (1998): 1017–31; Norman H. Nie, D. Sunshine Hillygus, and Lutz Erbring, Internet Use, Interpersonal Relations and Sociability: A Time Diary Study, in *Internet and the Everyday Life*, ed. Barry Wellman and Caroline Haythornwaite (Oxford: Blackwell, 2002), 215–43; and Robert Putnam, *Bowling Alone: The Crumbling and Revival of American Community* (New York: Simon & Schuster, 2000) has extensively looked at the decreasing trends in youth civic participation and have, in some cases, blamed technology for this.

6. Interesting work can be found in J. Cassell, "We Have These Rules Inside": The Effects of Exercising Voice in a Children's Online Forum, in *Children in the Digital Age: Influences of Electronic Media on Development*, ed. Sandra L. Calvert and Amy B. Jordan (Westport, CT: Praeger/Greenwood, 2002), 123–44; Justine Cassell, David Huffaker, Donna Tversky, and Kim Ferriman, The Language of Online Leadership: Gender and Youth Engagement on the Internet, *Developmental Psychology* 42, no. 3 (2006): 436–39; and Neil Howe and William Strauss, *Millennials Rising: The Next Great Generation* (New York: Vintage Books, 2000); Jay G. Blumler and Steven Coleman, Realizing Democracy Online: A Civic Commons in Cyberspace, *IPPR/Citizen Online Research Publication* 2 (2001); Emory H. Woodard IV and Kelly L. Schmitt, Political Socialization in the Digital Age: The "Student Voices" Program, in *Children in the Digital Age: Influences of Electronic Media on Development*, ed. Sandra L. Calvert, Amy B. Jordan, and Rodney R. Cocking (Westport, CT: Praeger, 2002), 83–99.

7. See work by Sasha Barab, James G. MaKinster, Julie Moore, David Cunningham, and the ILF Design Team, Designing and Building an Online Community: The Struggle to Support Sociability in the Inquiry Learning Forum, *Educational Technology Research and Development* 49, no. 4 (2001): 71–96; Jodi Clarke and Chris Dede, Making Learning Meaningful: An Exploratory Study of Using Multi User Virtual Environments (MUVES) in Middle School Science (paper presented at the American Educational Research Association Conference, Montreal, April 2005); Kurt Squire and the Games-to-Teach Research Team, Design Principles of Next-Generation Gaming for Education, *Educational Technology* 43, no. 5 (2003): 17–23; Constance A. Steinkuehler, Learning in Massively Multiplayer Online Games, in *Proceedings of the Sixth International Conference of the Learning Sciences*, ed. Yasmin B. Kafai, William A. Sandoval, Noel Enyedy, A. S. Nixon, and Francisco Herrera (Mahwah, NJ: Erlbaum, 2004), 521–28.

8. See Chip Morningstar and Randy Farmer, The Lessons of Lucasfilm's Habitat, in *Cyberspace: First Steps*, ed. M. Benedikt (Cambridge, MA: MIT Press, 1991), 273–302; S. Jones, *Cybersociety 2.0: Revisiting Computer-mediated Communication and Community* (Thousand Oaks, CA: Sage, 1998); Marlene Scardamalia and Carl Bereiter, Adaptation and Understanding: A Case for New Cultures of Schooling, in *International Perspectives on the Design of Technology-supported Learning Environments*, ed. S. Vosniadou and E. De Corte (Hillsdale, NJ: Erlbaum, 1996), 149–63; M. A. Smith and Peter Kollock, eds., *Communities in Cyberspace* (London: Routledge, 1998).

9. See Marina Bers, A Constructionist Approach to Values Through On-line Narrative Tools, *International Conference for the Learning Sciences* AACE (1998): 49–55.; Marina Bers, Joseph Gonzalez-Heydrich, and David Ray DeMaso, Use of a Computer-based Application in a Pediatric Hemodialysis Unit; M. Bers, G. Gonzalez-Heydrich, and D. DeMaso, Identity Construction Environments: Supporting a Virtual Therapeutic Community of Pediatric Patients Undergoing Dialysis, in *Proceedings of Computer–Human Interaction*, ACM (2001), 380–87; Amy Bruckman, Community Support for Constructionist Learning, *Computer Supported Cooperative Work* 7 (1998): 47–86; Randy D. Pinkett, Bridging the Digital Divide: Sociocultural Constructionism and an Asset-based Approach to Community Technology and Community Building, The 81st Annual Meeting of the American Educational Research Association, New Orleans, LA, 2000; Mitchel Resnick, Amy Bruckman, and Fred Martin, 1996, Pianos Not Stereos: Creating Computational Construction Kits, *Interactions* 3, no. 6 (1996: 41–50); A. Shaw, Neighborhood Networking and Community Building, in *Ties That Bind: Building Community Networks*, ed. S. Cisler (Cupertino, CA: Apple Computer Corp, 1994), 134–37.

10. Some of this research can be found in Jeffrey Youniss, James A. McLellan, and Miranda Yates, What We Know About Engendering Civic Identity, *American Behavioral Scientist* 40, no. 5 (1997): 620–31; Sidney Verba, Kay Lehman Schlozman, and Henry E. Brady, *Voice and Equality: Civic Voluntarism in American Politics* (Cambridge, MA: Harvard University Press, 1995).

11. This pilot work can be found in the unpublished thesis by Clement Chau (Associations Between Online Civic Engagement and Personal Technological Characteristics Among College Students [unpublished master's thesis, Tufts University, Medford, MA, 2006]).

12. An extended version of this excerpt was first published in Marina Bers, Identity Construction Environments.

13. See work on the just community approach in Donald Reed, *Following Kohlberg: Liberalism and the Practice of Democratic Community* (Notre Dame, IN: University of Notre Dame Press, 1997) and Lawrence Kohlberg, The Just Community Approach to Moral Education in Theory and in Practice, in *Moral Education: Theory and Application*, ed. Marvin Berkowitz and Fritz Oser (Hillsdale, NJ: Erlbaum, 1985), 27–89.

14. R. Hart, *Children's Participation: From Tokenism to Citizenship* (Florence: UNICEF, 1992).

15. For discussion on civic identities see Augusto Blasi, Moral Cognition and Moral Action: A Theoretical Perspective, *Developmental Review* 3 (1983): 178–210; Augusto Blasi, Moral Identity: Its Role in Moral

Functioning, in *Morality, Moral Behavior and Moral Development*, ed. William Kurtines and Jacob Gewirtz (New York: Wiley, 1984).

16. Helen Haste, The New Citizenship of Youth in Rapidly Changing Nations, *Human Development* 44 (2001): 375–81, has developed this dual model of civic education. See also Judith Torney-Purta, Rainer Lehmann, Hans Oswald, and Wolfram Schulz, *Citizenship and Education in Twenty-Eight Countries: Civic Knowledge and Engagement at Age Fourteen* (Amsterdam: The International Association for the Evaluation for Educational Achievement, 2001).

17. For an informative discussion of the different paradigms and the history of educational technology, see Timothy D. Koschmann, Paradigm Shifts and Instructional Technology: An Introduction, in *CSCL: Theory and Practice of an Emerging Paradigm*, ed. Timothy D. Koschmann (Mahwah, NJ: Erlbaum, 1996), 1–24.

18. Many constructionist environments for learning math have been developed following the Logo tradition.

19. Amy Bruckman and Marina Bers have pioneered the development of constructionist virtual communities.

20. See Jean Lave and Etienne Wenger, 1991, *Situated Learning: Legitimate Peripheral Participation* (Cambridge, UK: Cambridge University Press, 1991).

21. Elizabeth Montgomery, Barbara Gottlieb-Robles, and Gary Larson, Youth as E-Citizens: Engaging the Digital Generation, Center for Social Media, School of Communication, American University, March 2004.

22. While as an organization Taking ITGlobal could be an example in the constructionist community typology, as it can be learned by reading Raynes-Goldie and Walker's chapter in this volume, the Web site itself does not provide an environment that meets the constructionist standards.

23. For a description of the Positive Youth Development framework and the six C's, see Richard M. Lerner, Jacqueline V. Lerner, Jason Alermigi, Christine Theokas, Erin Phelps, Steinunn Gestsdottir, Sophie Naudeau, Helena Jelicic, Amy E. Alberts, Lang Ma, Lisa M. Smith, Deborah L. Bobek, David Richman-Raphael, Isla Simpson, Elise D. Christiansen, and Alexander von Eye, Positive Youth Development, Participation in Community Youth Development Programs, and Community Contributions of Fifth Grade Adolescents: Findings From the First Wave of the 4-H Study of Positive Youth Development, *Journal of Early Adolescence* 25, no. 1 (2005): 17–29; and Lonnie Sherrod, Constance Flanagan, and James Youniss, Dimensions of Citizenship and Opportunities for Youth Development: The What, Why, When, Where, and Who of Citizenship Development, *Applied Developmental Science* 6, no. 4 (2002): 264–72.

24. Erik Erikson, *Childhood and Society* (New York: Norton, 1950).

25. For a paper about the ACT program see Clement Chau, Ashima Mathur, and Marina Bers, Active Citizenship through Technology: Collaboration, Connection, and Civic Participation, International Conference of the Learning Sciences, Indiana University, Bloomington, IN, 2006.

26. For more information on ACT, please visit http://www.ase.tufts.edu/devtech/vclc/ACTHome.html, accessed July 2007.

27. For a complete description of this experience with younger children, see Marina Bers and Clement Chau, Fostering Civic Engagement by Building a Virtual City.

Our Space: Online Civic Engagement Tools for Youth

Kate Raynes-Goldie and Luke Walker

TakingITGlobal Research

Introduction

The Internet is quickly becoming an integral part of life. The embedded role of the Internet in everyday life is perhaps most prevalent for youth, particularly in developed countries: in 2005, the PEW Internet & American Life Project found that 87 percent of American teens go online, and half of them report going online every day.[1] Many "real world" activities can now take place online—including many social-networking and community-building tasks that go well beyond traditional uses of information and communication technologies. Civic engagement, as other authors in this volume have presented, is one of the areas of activity that has made the transition to the online realm, with varied forms of implementation and varying degrees of success.

There is currently no established methodology for evaluating the effectiveness of online civic engagement sites, for youth or other segments of the population. We believe a shift in perspective of what civic engagement is and how it could occur online is necessary to evaluate the sites, methodologies, and tools that promote civic engagement among youth. Just as Jimmy Wales, founder of Wikipedia, argues that social software should empower rather than replace traditional forms of interaction, we see the role of online civic engagement tools as enhancing and empowering real-world action:

A lot of programmers, seem to me to think that the whole point of *social software* is to replace the *social* with the *software*. Which is not really what you want to do, right? Social Software should exist to empower us to be human ... to interact ... in all the normal ways that humans do.[2]

Preliminary research points toward this paradigm shift. Research conducted by Michael Delli Carpini,[3] of the Annenberg School of Communications, as well as research conducted by TakingITGlobal for the J. W. McConnell Family Foundation,[4] have found that efforts in the online civic engagement space are often more strongly suited for enabling or more deeply engaging young people who are *already* civically minded. MySpace and digital youth expert danah boyd has blogged[5] and written extensively about the importance of the latest generation of online spaces for youth in developed countries who, for various reasons, have low access to physical hangout spaces, such as the mall or the park.[6] MySpace is so popular, she argues, because it acts as a digital public space where youth can hang out online with

We thank Jennifer Corriero, Michael Furdyk, Xingtao Zhu, and Nick Moraitis for their assistance throughout the development of this chapter, with special thanks to Jo-Anne Raynes and Emily Kornblut, as well as John Horrigan from the Pew Internet & American Life Project, for their indispensable feedback.

their friends. So, providing civic engagement opportunities online—where youth already spend their time—has great potential. It is accessible, familiar, and does not ask youth to change their habits or step outside their comfort zones to get involved.

We have found that interactive Web sites and online communities aimed at promoting civic engagement, activism, or community involvement among youth are generally facilitators of the civic engagement that occurs in the offline world, but not necessarily the places where that engagement occurs. Our initial research shows that this role of online civic engagement tools is a valuable precursor to engaging young people in their physical communities.

Drawing on the work of Montgomery, Gottlieb-Robles, and Larson,[7] we define civic engagement as any activity aimed at improving one's community. Our initial findings point to online civic engagement sites as primarily facilitators of action, rather than places of action. While actions such as writing to an official or signing a petition are positive actions that do occur online, the majority of civic engagement activities resulting from online engagement actually happen in the offline world. Online engagement sites are facilitators of these offline activities, providing access to three keys of change: information, people, and tools to organize. These sites enable youth to access information about issues, other relevant organizations, and how to take action effectively. They can connect with their peers to get feedback and support, and organize around issues important to them. Armed with the support of like-minded individuals, tools to organize, and the right information, youth are empowered by these Web sites to step out into the offline world to volunteer, raise awareness, educate others, and start their own organizations.

This chapter consists of three parts. First, we present an overview of TakingITGlobal (TIG), where we are both employed. TIG runs TakingITGlobal.org, one of the largest and most sophisticated civic engagement sites in the world. Its purpose is to develop the capacity of young people to effect change in their communities. TakingITGlobal.org was one of the first of a growing number of interactive and social online engagement sites. Over five million people from around the world have visited since it was launched in 2000.

Second, we present initial findings from a survey we conducted to discover how young people are using TakingITGlobal.org and other online civic, community, or activist sites. Our aim was to find out how youth are using online tools and to determine what civic engagement activities they are involved in.

Finally, we look at these survey findings in the context of online community theory to create a snapshot of the current landscape of online youth civic engagement. We then conclude with a discussion of key learnings and areas for improvement. We hope our findings will be useful in guiding future developments of online civic engagement sites.

TakingITGlobal: New Tools for Youth-led Engagement

TakingITGlobal.org grew from the recognition that youth are not apathetic about social issues; rather they lack access to appealing forms of engagement. Working with this concept, Jennifer Corriero, Michael Furdyk, and a team of other young people launched TakingITGlobal.org in 2000. In its early iterations, the site had member and organizational profiles and discussion boards. Other tools, from blogs to an online art gallery, to project planning tools followed.[8] The site has evolved into a complex platform tying together the core tools that young people use so readily—blogs, discussions boards, podcasts, and instant messaging—combined with collaborative action-planning tools, background information

Table 1
TakingITGlobal members by region (as of January 10, 2006)[a]

North America	43,354	30.36%
Africa	31,624	22.14%
Asia	28,895	20.23%
Europe	17,572	12.30%
Middle East North Africa	9,285	6.50%
Australia and New Zealand	5,255	3.68%
South America	4,486	3.14%
Central America and the Caribbean	1,749	1.22%
Pacific Islands	598	0.42%

[a]TakingITGlobal, Membership Update (January 10, 2007).

on a broad area of social issues, and connections to relevant organizations, groups, and their peers.

The development of the TakingITGlobal.org platform has been driven by user feedback and feature requests. TakingITGlobal.org registered its 100,000th member in the fall of 2005 and at the time of writing had over 130,000 members from two hundred countries (see Table 1). Through the efforts of a global team of volunteers, TakingITGlobal.org is available in English, French, Spanish, Russian, Dutch, Italian, Portuguese, Romanian, Turkish, Chinese, and Arabic. The site is further localized with country sites, or portals to country-specific information. The average member is twenty-two years old and spends an average of thirty-four minutes per session on the TIG site.[9]

The TakingITGlobal.org online community is accessible and available to anyone with an Internet connection, anywhere in the world. The site supports learning, dialogue, collaboration and action on key topics, including:

- Arts and media
- Culture and identity
- Human rights and equity
- Learning and education
- Environment and urbanization
- Work and economics
- Health and wellness
- Peace, conflict and governance
- Technology and innovation

Social, Organizational, and Informational Tools

TakingITGlobal.org provides many tools similar to those of commercial social networking or online community sites, but it does so within the context of civic engagement. In their book *Wikinomics*, Don Tapscott and Anthony D. Williams describe the key difference between TakingITGlobal.org and its commercial counterparts:

Like MySpace and Facebook, TakingITGlobal harnesses all of the latest tools, such as blogging, instant messaging, and media sharing. But it promotes a decidedly different kind of social networking. Rather than list their favorite movie stars and music tracks, members list information about the languages they speak, the countries they have visited and the issues they're most concerned about. Members link to other members' profiles when they share similar interests, and those links create social connections that lead to new friendships and projects.[10]

The other key difference between TakingITGlobal.org and its commercial counterparts is that TakingITGlobal.org embeds its social-networking tools within the context of civic engagement and activism by providing relevant resources and informational tools (organization databases, issue directories, etc.). These tools allow members to find and share the information they need to create change in their communities. The information and resources found on the site are created by members and by TakingITGlobal staff or partners. The benefits of integrating tools that connect people with informational tools are twofold. First, it provides access to two key ingredients for action: people and information. Second, in providing youth-friendly social tools such as blogs and profiles, youth are engaged on their own terms and with the same types of tools they are already familiar with and use everyday. Providing youth with access on their own terms means they are more likely to engage.

TakingITGlobal.org's social tools consist of standard Web tools (see Table 4): blogs, profiles, and social-networking tools, a Web messenger and discussion forums, all of which help members to find, connect, and network with each other. TakingITGlobal.org also provides tools for organizing, such as Projects and Groups, which its commercial counterparts such as MySpace and Facebook, lack. These tools help members to organize around an issue or project. The informational tools on TakingITGlobal.org revolve around member content and include Understanding the Issues, the Global Gallery (photography), Member Stories, Panorama (creative writing), Intersections (mixed media), and *TIG Magazine*. Members also have access to extensive directories of events, organizations, and professional opportunities, to which they can add as well as search. These directories help members find volunteer opportunities, youth-serving organizations or events focused on various social issues and decision-making processes, such as the World Summit on the Information Society. TakingITGlobal.org also provides downloadable resources such as the Workshop Kit, Guide to Action, and information on running Open Forums.

All of the social, organizational, and informational tools on TakingITGlobal.org are tightly integrated and linked. For example, most of the items that are listed on a profile page are clickable, leading to related resources or lists—so clicking a name of a project on someone's profile will direct you to the Project page. This makes it easy for members to move between informing themselves on a resource page and taking action through a community tool. It also makes it easier to find other members interested in the same issues.

Bridging Offline and Online Engagement

TakingITGlobal consists of two intertwined yet distinct areas—TakingITGlobal's online community (TakingITGlobal.org) and its offline engagement areas. Most of TakingITGlobal's offline engagement activities are strongly linked or supported through the online components. Reflecting the generation it serves, TakingITGlobal does not strongly distinguish between online and offline engagement.

TakingITGlobal's offline engagement focuses on increasing the collaboration between youth-serving organizations both regionally and globally, and mainstreaming youth involvement into international processes, such as United Nations summits. Creating Local Connections (CLC) provides local staff support to youth-serving organizations. Their role is to facilitate the effective use of TakingITGlobal.org tools to better collaborate and overcome some of the barriers specific to youth-led organizations.[11] The CLC program served to build a body of high-quality content and inspirational member stories within the TakingITGlobal.org community, enhancing the experience and appeal of the site for all members.

In 2004, Microsoft Russia funded the CLC pilot, which won an award for best youth Internet project for youth at Russia's Festival of Youth Non-Commercial Projects.[12] The Russian CLC project began with the translation of the site into Russian (http://ru.takingitglobal.org), one of TIG's first multilingual efforts. By the end of the yearlong project, TIG's Russian membership had grown by nine hundred individuals and eighty organizations.

In 2006 the J. W. McConnell Family Foundation funded a three-year cross-Canada version of CLC. The program placed a coordinator in each province and territory, and engaged Francophone and Aboriginal Engagement Coordinators to meet the needs of these populations. In 2007, the West African version of CLC will implement the program in several countries in the region. In each country, local TIG staff works within partner organizations, reaching out to local organizations in their region, and building a substantial body of locally relevant content on the TakingITGlobal.org site.

International political or economic events present a set of participation barriers for young people. While critical decisions affecting the lives of young people are often made through major international policy processes, there is frequently little or no opportunity for youth engagement. Even if there is no formal barrier to youth involvement, such as registration restrictions, there are often logistical or financial obstacles. The UN World Summit on the Information Society (WSIS) in 2005 was a major opportunity for TIG, as it addressed the digital divide, a major area of interest for many TakingITGlobal.org members. Working with a coalition of youth-led and youth-serving organizations, TIG facilitated the youth caucus, mainstreaming youth participation into the Summit. Through the coalition's work, not only was there a prominent youth presence at the Summit, but hundreds of young people attended the WSIS preparatory meetings, running and speaking on high-level panels and lobbying delegates.[13] Throughout the process, young people were able to use TakingITGlobal.org's tools throughout the process to learn how to contribute and to share experiences with each other.

The XVI International AIDS Conference, held in Toronto in August 2006, presented TIG with another opportunity to mainstream youth participation. TIG and its partners Family Health International, the Global Youth Coalition on HIV/AIDS, along with several other organizations, worked together as the Toronto Youth Force. Representatives of the Youth Force were involved in all aspects of conference planning, including the development of an official Youth Program for the conference. TIG developed the Youth Program site (http://youth.aids2006.org) and ensured that the content created by over a thousand youth delegates would be sustained well beyond the short life of the typical conference Web site. By tying the conference's youth site to TIG's existing tools and user system, it ensured that youth media and networks created at the conference would exist simultaneously both online and offline, and continue to exist once the conference organizers shut down the main site.

Through the organization's work with networks like the Global Youth Coalition on HIV/AIDS (GYCA) and the Youth Employment Summit (YES), TakingITGlobal.org has, in many ways, become a network of networks. This precedent was set early on, when Nation1, an outgrowth of the MIT Media Lab's Junior Summit, decided to move its network to the TakingITGlobal.org site, rather than launching its own.[14] Work with groups like YES has drawn groups of active youth into the TakingITGlobal.org community, who can then serve as valuable mentors and sources of inspiration for other members.

TakingITGlobal.org's Tools in Action

Bossman Boakye, a TakingITGlobal member from Ghana, provided us with this story of how he used TakingITGlobal's tools to start a civic engagement organization in his country:

I got in touch with a friend who happened to be a member of TIG three years ago and he introduced me to this great site.

At first, what I used to check on the site was events and opportunities. I had a great zeal to travel to any youth programme so I found this site very interesting and worthy of links to youth events around the world.

During one of these searches, I came across an information on World Assembly and I decided to write to them to ask for more information. I was replied with the information that a new initiative known as Student World Assembly was in the pipeline to be introduced and that I could join and make inputs. Basically, this initiative seeks to promote democracy and civic participation globally.

I presented a proposal to the officials of Student World Assembly on the setting up of the organisation in Ghana. I must say that this is where TIG became of immense benefit to me. I had to visit the discussion board (English section) to discuss my idea with other people. I also read more on democracy and other issues the SWA was discussing on their website www.studentworldassembly.org on Understanding Issues. It is during one of my visits

Figure 1
A TakingITGlobal member blog.

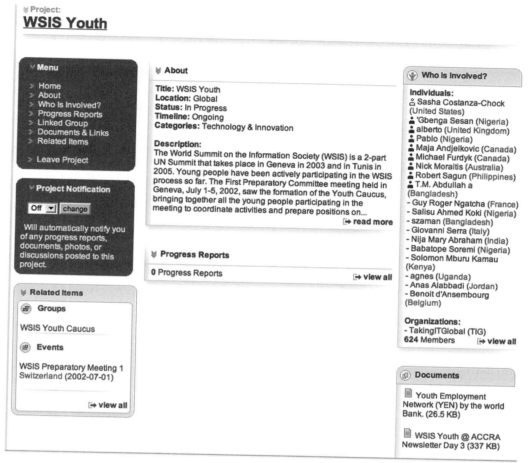

Figure 2
A TakingITGlobal project page.

to this site when I met a friend who also shared in my initiative and visions and who also happened to be a Ghanaian.

We met and he took me on a visit to very beneficial links at TIG website for me where I got to know how to write proposals, start up youth and students NGOs, fundraising, etc.

I must say that, TIG has helped me a lot in setting up Student World Assembly in Ghana which can now boast of over 10 established chapters in tertiary institutions in Ghana.

I am now the programmes and growth officer for the organization and I link up my success and excellence to TIG; I must say that it is a great site for youth endeavours.

This type of story provides insight into how youth are actually using different online tools, such as those of TakingITGlobal.org, to engage and make positive changes in their communities. This and similar anecdotes provide evidence of the efficacy of TakingITGlobal.org's role in assisting youth in making positive change.[15] Several project areas are working on implementing evaluation structures, including the education program and CLC Canada. Results of these more systematic research efforts will be available in late 2007.

Figure 3
A TakingITGlobal member profile.

Funding and Sustainability

TakingITGlobal operates on a budget of approximately $1 million. Its education and local engagement programs are funded by grants from the J. W. McConnell Family Foundation, Walter & Duncan Gordon Foundation, Royal Bank Financial Group, Microsoft, and the Canadian International Development Agency (CIDA). Though critical, grant funding has limitations especially when most grants occur on a one-time basis and offer no guarantees for renewed commitment. Project-based funding has been accessed from the UN Millennium Campaign to create campaign kits on the Millennium Development Goals, and from UNESCO to run a project on urban violence and youth.

TIG's other major source of funding is technology development work. TIG leverages the customized platform it has created for its own online community to build similar tools for other organizations, ranging from the Digital Divide Network (http://www.digitaldivide.net, which has since become an internal project of TakingITGlobal) to Greenpeace, Oxfam

Figure 4
The TakingITGlobal.org Home Page.

Figure 5
Bossman's steps to action.

Canada, and the Adventure Ecology. This strategy provides partners with excellent online tools that would otherwise be unaffordable, while simultaneously giving TakingITGlobal access to new tools to incorporate into its own online community. A project with the Youth Employment Summit (http://www.yesweb.org/), for example, led to the development of TakingITGlobal's project pages, now a core offering that allows any TIG member to create, manage, and promote an action project.[16]

Increasingly, TakingITGlobal's education program (http://www.TIGed.org) is a source of membership growth and financial sustainability. TIGed is a virtual classroom system combined with educational materials developed from TakingITGlobal.org content, allowing educators to create authentic learning experiences about global issues by using tools students are familiar with. Reaching out to teachers helps to involve those students who are *not* already engaged or civically minded, in addition to appealing to those who are looking to become *more* or *better* engaged. TIGed has created new opportunities for TIG to generate revenue from users: whereas individual membership is free, teachers, schools, and districts are charged for the additional tools that TIGed provides.

Youth Survey Findings

Presently, no methodology exists for evaluating the efficacy of online civic engagement sites. This lack of framework and standardized metrics are a barrier to funding and delivering the best tools for facilitating the offline civic engagement of youth. In deciding to conduct a survey of both TakingITGlobal members and online youth generally, we wanted to take the first steps toward discovering and assessing the offline impact of online engagement. We know anecdotally that youth are using TakingITGlobal.org's tools to better their communities, but we have not been able to map the connections between the online tools and offline youth engagement. We wanted to uncover TakingITGlobal.org's role in facilitating the outcomes our members have reported, and find out more specifically which tools TakingITGlobal.org members were using and how. We also wanted to know more about how youth—both TakingITGlobal.org members and others—were using other online tools and sites, and what actions they might be taking as a result.

For two weeks in the fall of 2006, we conducted an exploratory survey, promoted through TakingITGlobal.org and several other blog sites, to uncover how young people use online tools for the purposes of civic engagement. The survey solicited 769 responses from both members of TakingITGlobal.org and youth who found our survey through a number of other blog sites (classified as "Other Respondents" in Tables 2 and 3): 46.6 percent of respondents were male and 50.5 percent female (the remainder did not indicate their gender); 18.3 percent of respondents were under the age of twenty-one, 75.16 percent were between twenty-one and thirty, and 1.95 percent were thirty-one or older. The remainder did not indicate their age. The survey received responses from 111 countries. The top ten countries with the most respondents were Canada (146), the United States (50), Philippines (45), Australia (44), Nigeria (42), Pakistan (33), the United Kingdom (32), Kenya (24), Turkey (22), and India (21).

We learned that young people who are interested in civic, community, or activist issues are looking to the Internet for information about causes important to them, connections to like-minded peers and organizations, and for ways to organize and mobilize. When these needs are met, youth report in our qualitative section that they are able to make positive change in their lives and in their communities, demonstrating that the action or result of online engagement is occurring offline.

The youth survey consisted of two sets of questions: one set focused on the uses of online tools for civic engagement and the other on TakingITGlobal.org's toolset. As the responses indicate (Tables 2 and 3), young people who responded to our survey are interested in civic issues, and that interest can lead them to take offline action.

Survey respondents were asked to characterize their behavior as *NA/Never*, *Rarely*, *Sometimes*, and *Often*. The tables below summarize the percentage of *Often* responses for the two survey groups: TakingITGlobal.org members and general online youth respondents.

While this is a sample of young people who are more likely to be engaged according to their online activities, we note that the participation rate in voting is 64.7 percent and those likely to attend events aimed at effecting change is 43 percent. Yet there is room for improvement in the other action areas.

Several other researchers in this field, including Montgomery, Gottleib-Robles, and Larson,[17] have noted that while young people for the most part seem to have an interest in the issues affecting their communities, this interest is only modestly translated into action. In his chapter in this volume, Bennett points to the "withering away of civic education in schools"[18] as a possible factor. Corriero and Furdyk, TakingITGlobal's founders,

Table 2
Interest in the issues—percentage responding "Often"

	TIG Members	Other Respondents
I use Web sites, online communities, or online tools (IM, message boards, etc.) to discuss current events or issues of importance to me with my friends.	47.54%	40.56%
I make it a priority to stay informed about current events or issues important to me.	78.95%	58.89%
When I am with my friends, I discuss current events or issues of importance to me.	60.44%	48.33%
I read news online.	67.74%	46.11%

Table 3
Action on the issues—percentage responding "Often"

	TIG Members	Other Respondents
I attend protests or rallies.	10.02%	5.56%
I create media online (podcasts, videos, blogs, etc.) to get the word out about an issue.	12.05%	6.67%
I attend events or gatherings aimed at affecting positive change.	43.12%	15.00%
I participate in online protests.	15.45%	9.44%
I vote in elections.	67.40%	56.11%
I contact politicians, governments, or authorities about issues important to me.	16.64%	3.89%

offer a different explanation for this low participation rates in other action areas than voting and attending events. They believe there is a disconnect between the available opportunities for engagement and the spaces where young people spend their time. In other words, civic institutions and initiatives are simply not keeping up with the times.[19]

Our survey findings indicated that TakingITGlobal.org's tools were primarily used for three purposes:

- Support and motivation

- Networking and information

- Mobilizing and organizing real-world action

In questions relating to the use of TakingITGlobal.org's tools for these purposes, 40 percent or more of TakingITGlobal.org respondents gave positive responses. They also provided numerous qualitative responses indicating their use of these tools for these three purposes.

Support and Motivation
Of the 501 TakingITGlobal.org members who responded to the survey:

- 73.9 percent agreed that "through my experience with TakingITGlobal, my perception of the ability of youth to affect change in the world has improved;

- 63.5 percent agreed that "I have been inspired by a young person I have read about and/or communicated with on the TakingITGlobal site."

Qualitative responses further confirm that the online presence of a large network of youth leaders is in and of itself a great value to many TakingITGlobal.org members. As we discuss in our landscape survey in the next section, having the right people engaged in an online community is just as important as its functionality. Allan, from the United Kingdom, mentioned that "the key [motivator] was reassurance that there were other people out there trying as well—we are not alone."

Networking and Information

Beyond finding inspiration, many TakingITGlobal.org members reported finding information and networks to help them take steps toward action:

- 41.9 percent of respondents agreed that they "had contacted an organization listed in TakingITGlobal.org's database."

- 54.1 percent of respondents agreed that "the site has helped them become more informed about issues important to them."

In their qualitative responses, TIG members mentioned their ability to connect with peers through the site as a key factor in their projects:

I liaised with another TakingITGlobal member to produce a 30-second TV commercial that was shown on the local community cable TV channel and on YouTube. That commercial drove 10,000 people to our non-profit community event and was the key influence in driving 179,000 hits to the Web site.—Ginger, Canada

Some of the young people have been contacting me through TakingITGlobal and we have been connected from that time until now and sometimes it results to a project where we develop program exchanges in 2 countries.—Albert, Rwanda

Clearly, networking and information are some of TIG's key value-adds. The organization operates on the assumption that through the opportunity to connect easily and efficiently with young leaders in their areas of interest, more active members will inspire less active members to take action. This has been a key driver in the organization's decision to work with networks like the Global Youth Coalition on HIV/AIDS. TakingITGlobal.org gives any approved, youth-serving organization the opportunity to quickly, and freely, publicize their work to tens of thousands of daily visitors to TakingITGlobal.org.[20] This dissemination feature has proven to be of particular benefit to smaller organizations that have less capacity to create their own highly visible Web sites. Members of these smaller organizations can also take advantage of free project pages and mailing lists to organize and mobilize.

Mobilizing and Organizing to Real-World Action

- 44.1 percent of respondents agreed that "the information, networks, and tools to mobilize and organize found on TakingITGlobal.org have helped them make change in lives or community."

- 49.5 percent of respondents indicated that "TakingITGlobal.org had helped them to change something in their own lives."

While this survey has only begun to probe the changes that young people are making in the "real world" using TakingITGlobal.org's tools and online community, many respondents attribute the decision to engage or refocus their engagement projects to their involvement with the site. George, a respondent from Malawi, reported, "One of the very first inspirations I got from my involvement with TakingITGlobal was to set up an information centre (www.cridoc.net) on child/youth rights issues in Malawi." Other members had similar stories, ranging from an education campaign around Hepatitis B vaccinations in Ghana to the republication of an article about forced migration in a major Ugandan newspaper.

While these anecdotes are just that, they do provide a positive indication that involvement in TakingITGlobal.org is producing a more engagement-oriented attitude among youth. These findings should not be surprising, given that YouthNoise, a similar site reviewed in the next section, reports similar findings: "Studies have shown that YouthNoise participation has led to a 25 percent increase in volunteering and a 90 percent increase in the global awareness of users from modestly aware to highly aware."[21]

Putting TIG in Context: A Look at Other Sites

TakingITGlobal.org and the sites we look at in this section all use varying combinations of a standard set of online tools. These tools are used in a variety of contexts for a range of purposes and are all popular with youth. Not only are these tools important for engaging youth on their own terms—they have all been shown to be useful for finding and sharing information, networking with peers and organizing. The Pew Internet Report on Teens and Technology also confirms that American teens are using these tools in other contexts, such as finding health information or socializing.[22] Table 4 provides a summary of these standard online tools and how they are used in the context of youth civic engagement:

Landscape Survey Methodology   The initial results of our youth survey suggest that youth are using TakingITGlobal.org as a source of information and people through its informational tools, resources, and social networking features. They are also using the site to mobilize and organize, which leads to action in their offline communities. Based on these findings, we believe that the most important goals of civic engagement sites should be to facilitate these online activities. With this in mind, we set out to examine the current landscape of online civic engagement and report on best practices and areas for improvement. We hope that this will inform future online civic engagement projects and improving existing ones.

In order to create a snapshot of the current online civic engagement landscape we developed two screens. First, a screen to identify the sites for inclusion in our survey and, second, a screen to tease out the strengths and areas for improvement in the strategies and toolsets of the sites we examined.

To ensure that we examined comparable sites, we established a set of minimum criteria to determine which sites would be included in our survey. Specifically, a social networking or online community site must

- Be aimed at youth, or have a relatively large youth membership
- Have an interactive Web-based social tool at its core that allows members to interact
- Be current and operational (site is accessible and usable)
- Be available in English
- Be aimed at encouraging and supporting positive social change.

Our initial survey universe consisted of twenty-three potential sites. These sites were identified by experts in the field of online civic engagement, links from popular sites, and sites

Table 4
Standard online tools in the context of civic engagement

Tool	Description	Networking with peers	Finding and sharing information	Organizing
Blogs	▪ Journal-style entries made in reverse chronological order ▪ Created by an individual or group ▪ Readers can comment on entries	Blogs say a lot about their authors. Browsing peers' blogs makes it easier for youth to find allies and helpers.	Blogs are a great place to find and disseminate information. Their power and reach has been demonstrated in several high-profile situations. A survey respondent from Nigeria observed: "The discussion boards and blogs [on TakingITGlobal.org] helped access people's opinion on diverse issues."	Group blogs are a good collaboration tool for small groups. Members can share updates and launch discussions. Successful larger group blogs exist on LiveJournal, where members organically organize around specific topics.[a]
Discussion Forums	▪ A centralized collection of conversation threads ▪ Often moderated to some degree ▪ Members can start new or reply to existing threads	Youth can use forums to find: ▪ Support ▪ Feedback ▪ Volunteers for an initiative	Posting links or information to popular discussion boards is a good way to promote an issue.	Not very good for organizing as it is a public space used by many people – akin to holding a meeting in the middle of a party.
Web messaging	▪ Members can send private text messages to other members of the same site	A simple way to converse with a peer who might assist with a project. It also provides an easy entry point to the community. A survey of respondents from Australia reported: "TakingITGlobal.org instant messenger really helped me make the transition from Web site user to community member."	Web messaging can be used to send information to one person at a time, making it useful for targeted messages.	Good for organizing a small group, but as it is designed for one-to-one communication its use is limited.

(Continued)

Table 4
Standard online tools in the context of civic engagement (*Continued*)

Tool	Description	Networking with peers	Finding and sharing information	Organizing
Social networking tools	• Members create public profiles; contents vary by site • Standard details include personal and contact information, photos, location, etc. Some services show recently created content. • Members can list their friends. This list is public and browse-able. • Members can often leave comments, which are shown publicly on a profile.	Public profiles make it easy for youth to learn each other's interests and goals. Youth can also browse other's friend networks, increasing the number of other people they can connect with. Respondents to our survey mentioned that the profile page on TakingITGlobal.org was the way they found out about another member with whom they later collaborated.	Youth can post links or information about issues, current events, or ways to get involved on their profiles. Other youth are more likely to get involved or take action if they find out about something from a friend.	Youth can mobilize their networks of friends through their profiles. The efficacy of this was demonstrated in 2006, when American youth used their MySpace profiles to organize a countrywide walkout in protest of new immigration laws.[b]

[a] K. Raynes-Goldie, Pulling Sense out of Today's Informational Chaos: LiveJournal as a Site of Knowledge Creation and Sharing, *First Monday* 9, no. 12 (2004), http://www.firstmonday.org/issues/issue9_12/raynes/index.html (retrieved January 8, 2007).
[b] d. boyd, Identity Production in a Networked Culture: Why Youth ♥ MySpace, American Association for the Advancement of Science, St. Louis, MO, February 19, 2006, http://www.danah.org/papers/AAAS2006.html (retrieved January 8, 2007).

examined in other surveys.[23] We examined each one by signing up and systematically trying each feature. Out of the twenty-three sites, only six met our minimum criteria to be included in our survey. The top two reasons for exclusion in our survey were that the site was no longer operational or that the site did not include an interactive social component and was simply a static Web page. The six sites we surveyed were YouthNoise, CampusActivism, UNICEF Voices of Youth,[24] Youth Action Net, Zaadz, and BattleCry.[25] We also included TakingITGlobal.org, which we more thoroughly analyzed in the previous section.

Because there is currently no established methodology for evaluating online civic engagement sites, we adapted a survey methodology from an online community evaluation framework created by Clarisse De Souza and Jenny Preece.[26] De Souza and Preece define communities and social networks as combinations of two key elements: technology (usability) and sociability (policy, purpose, and people). Blogger Sarah Pullman noted the same element in her analysis of Zaadz: "there are two things that determine the value of social networking tools: (1) the functionality of the tools themselves, and what they allow people to do, and (2) the people who are using the service."[27] Having the most sophisticated and easy-to-use online community platform does not guarantee success, nor does having access to a large number of members. A site has to be relatively usable and have appealing technology so that people can easily accomplish their goals, just as it has to have a critical mass of the right kind of users. If the tools are frustrating, or there are very few members, a site is not likely to be used. As MySpace demonstrates, successful online communities do not necessarily have to be the best designed, but at least have the right people.

The functionality and type of tools on a site matter for two reasons. First, the site has to have tools that are appealing, familiar, and useful enough so that youth will use them. Second, the site has to facilitate activities that help youth reach their civic engagement goals. These activities, as we found in our youth survey, are finding the right information, organizing, networking, and collaborating. For this reason, we examined not only what types of tools were on the sites examined (profiles, blogs, tags, and so on) but also how sophisticated those tools were. For example, the blogging tools across the sites we examined varied greatly in terms of features and functionality and thus their appeal, familiarity, and usefulness to youth.

We also kept in mind the influence of commercial services. Although not aimed at civic engagement, MySpace and Facebook set the tone and expectations for many youth (especially those in developed countries). If these expectations are not met, they are not likely to use or keep using a site. Keeping all this in mind, we based our survey on three key areas: usability, people, and purpose and policy.

In usability, we looked at technology and design issues, such as

- What tools are used and how
- Ease of use
- Level of interactivity
- Level of maintenance.

With people, we were concerned with

- Size of membership
- Demographics of the members

- Languages spoken by membership.

  In purpose and policy, we were interested in

- Funding
- Who runs the site
- The openness of the community
- Rules and moderation
- Focus and purpose of site.

Overview of Web Sites Reviewed
In Table 5, we summarize the history and key features of the seven sites we reviewed in depth.

Landscape Survey Findings Usability   Despite vast differences in the tools offered by the sites surveyed, five of the seven had discussion forums. Forums were the primary means of communication on UNICEF Voice of Youth and Youth Action Network, while the others used a suite of communication tools including forums. Forums are among the oldest communication styles online, and operate in a manner similar to e-mail lists, which are popular in low-connectivity situations. As a result, discussion forums are more familiar and accessible to youth with limited connectivity. Sites that only offer discussion forums may however discourage youth with more sophisticated Internet literacy, as this group expects the latest innovations from the sites they use. Anything less may inadvertently imply that the site's makers "don't get it." The two sites with the most members (TakingITGlobal.org and YouthNoise) offered multiple modes of communication to members. This way, few users are directly excluded, and youth have access to the tools they are most familiar with.

Only two of seven sites featured formal collaboration tools to help youth organize around their goals. TakingITGlobal.org and YouthNoise both offer project pages that allow groups to publicize and coordinate their projects, using mailing lists and a shared online workspace. Youth Action Net offers project pages for displaying information, but does not provide collaboration features.

Problems with site design and usability were common. Many sites deviated from the standard conventions of usability as recommended by experts such as Steven Krug.[28] Navigation and findability were—in varying degrees—a challenge. On YouthNoise, for example, the navigation menu, visual queues and naming conventions all change from one part of the site to the next, which can be confusing for users. We noticed a similar problem with Youth Action Net, whose navigation menu inconsistently featured a prominent yet broken link to an essay contest. The navigation menu also appears on the left side of the front page, even though it is oriented on the right side everywhere else. Usability was also a problem for TakingITGlobal. In our youth survey, a number of TakingITGlobal members mentioned that the site was becoming overwhelming. Getting an idea of the goals or features of many of the sites was not easy, with most sites offering a complicated and jargon-filled mission statement to inform. These design and usability issues can not only harm a site's image but, more important, can make it harder for youth to find the necessary information and people to affect change in their communities. If a site is too difficult to use, less savvy Internet users will be discouraged and potentially excluded.

Table 5
Summary of basic site information and features

Site	Mandate and distinguishing features	Tools	Year launched and project details
Activism Network activismnetwork.org	The Activism Network is essentially an interactive database of activists, activist organizations, and events provided to facilitate networking and communication for those involved in activist causes. The goal of the Activism Network is to "strengthen progressive social movements around the world through the sharing of contacts, event information, ideas and resources."[a] A large part of the site's mandate is to provide connections and the resources that groups and individuals need for their offline events and initiatives.	• Searchable directories and lists (events, email lists, resources, campaigns, contacts etc.). Members can add items to any list • Simple profiles of members with contact information, issues of interest and campaign involvement	2002 **Size (as of January 2007)** 3700 **Demographic** Originally for college- and university-aged activists in North America, now for everyone. **Language(s)** English **Platform** Custom open source. Currently being ported to Drupal. **Creator/Funder** Aaron Krieder, who also funds the project with his own time and money. Additional revenue generated by Google Adsense
BattleCry www.battlecry.com	BattleCry is a social networking site and resource "for Christian teens, churches, youth groups, and leaders." The site was also dubbed as the "Christian alternative to Myspace" and the site featured the tagline "Let MySpace be His space."[b] Battlecry.com is part of a larger and older initiative by Teen Mania of offline stadium events, gatherings and demonstrations which use the BattleCry brand.[c] The offline activities are heavily promoted on the site.	• Basic blogging functionality • Social networking tools (profiles, ability to list friends, ability to leave messages on other people's profiles) • Resource section with videos, documents, and guides to help youth spread the word about their movement • Discussion forums at forums.battlecry.com, which were locked in May 2006 and new posts were disallowed. • Task progress tools.	Early 2006 **Size (as of January 2007)** 36,000 members (according to user profiles page—http://www.battlecry.com/x_search.php) **Demographic** Primarily American Christian (Evangelical) youth, some Canadian members **Language(s)** English **Platform** Custom closed source solution **Creator/Funder** Teen Mania Ministries

(Continued)

Table 5
Summary of basic site information and features (*Continued*)

Site	Mandate and distinguishing features	Tools	Year launched and project details
	BattleCry is the only site we looked at that had created a tool based on offline action. Members are given a set list of tasks (such as praying more often) that they can complete to further the goals of the initiative. The progress of these tasks are shown on a member's profile for other members to see and be inspired by.		
Youth Action Net youthaction-net.org	Youth Action Net is an interactive webpage with resources and a discussion forum. According to their site, "YouthActionNet is a program that invests in the power and promise of young people to create positive change. Through its dynamic Web site, awards, customized training programs, and peer-to-peer learning opportunities, YouthActionNet offers young change makers ideas, resources, and connections to like minds around the world."[d]	▪ Simple static Web page building tools (personal and project pages) ▪ Discussion forums ▪ Information and resource section ▪ Opportunities database that members can add items to	2001 **Size (as of January 2007)** 290 members' Web pages and 371 member project pages. Note: this number has not changed since October 2006 **Demographic** Global youth **Language(s)** English **Platform** Closed custom solution **Creator/Funder** International Youth Foundation. Funded by Nokia
TakingITGlobal takingitglobal.org	TakingITGlobal is an online community with social networking features aimed at providing a virtual space for cross cultural understanding, expression, dialogue and collaboration among youth.	▪ Social networking tools (profiles, ability to list friends) ▪ Customizable blogs (individual and group)	2000 **Size (as of January 2007)** 130,000 **Demographic** Global youth

(*Continued*)

Table 5
Summary of basic site information and features (*Continued*)

Site	Mandate and distinguishing features	Tools	Year launched and project details
	TakingITGlobal also runs many offline programs which are strongly integrated with the Web site, online tools and site members.	▪ Discussion forums ▪ Searchable events, organization and opportunities database where members can add to ▪ Resource and information sections ▪ Simple image galleries ▪ Podcasting tools ▪ Web messenger (TIG messenger) ▪ Interactive collaboration tools (mailing lists, project workspaces etc.)	**Language(s)** English, French, Spanish, Russian, Dutch, Italian, Portuguese, Romanian, Turkish, Chinese, and Arabic **Platform** Closed custom solution **Creator/Funder** TakingITGlobal Funded by various corporate and NGO donations and partnerships.
YouthNoise youthnoise.org	YouthNoise is an online community with social networking features that is designed as "a place for teens to talk about various issues, raise money for different causes, and many other things. The issues discussed range from economy, government, education, animal rights, tolerance, media, environment, health, poverty, war, peace, violence, spirituality, and more."*e* The mission of YouthNoise is "to inspire and empower young people everywhere to catapult their passion and idealism into movements to sustain the planet."*f*	▪ Discussion forums ▪ Social networking tools (profiles, ability to list friends) ▪ Basic blogging functionality (built into profile page) ▪ Collaboration tools (project page with project information and members involved) ▪ Information and Resource Section ▪ Videoblogging tools (through veeker.com) ▪ Legislative Action Centre (interactive tools to find and contact elected officials in the United States)	2001 **Size (as of January 2007)** 113,000 **Demographic** Originally aimed at American Youth, recently refocused to global youth audience. **Language(s)** English **Platform** Closed custom solution **Creator/Funder** Save The Children, now spun off as own entity. Funded by various corporate and NGO donations and partnerships.
UNICEF Voices of Youth unicef.org/voy/	Voices of Youth is a Web site with a discussion forum at its core.	▪ Information and Resource Section ▪ Discussion forums ▪ Chat	1995 **Size (as of January 2007)** 20,000

(Continued)

Table 5
Summary of basic site information and features (*Continued*)

Site	Mandate and distinguishing features	Tools	Year launched and project details
	Voices of Youth was originally founded in 1995 so that youth around the world could send messages to world leaders at the World Summit for Social Development which was held that year in Copenhagen.[g] Today, the goal of the site is "To offer all children and adolescents, including the hard-to-reach, a safe and supportive global cyberspace within which they can explore, discuss, and partner on issues related to human rights and social change, as well as develop their awareness, leadership, community building, and critical thinking skills through active and substantive participation with their peers and with decision makers globally."[h]		**Demographic** Global children and youth, with an emphasis on children and youth in developing countries **Language(s)** English, French, Spanish, Arabic **Platform** Closed custom solution **Creator/Funder** UNICEF
Zaadz zaadz.com	Described by critics as a being a site for "new agey, hippie, tree-hugging freaks,"[i] Zaadz is a social networking site with the aim of helping people to "change the world" though spirituality and "conscious capitalism." The Zaadz mission statement: "We're gonna change the world. Our math goes like this: you be the change + you follow your bliss + you give your greatest strengths to the world moment to moment to moment + we do everything in our power to help	▪ Podcasting tools ▪ Basic blogging tools ▪ Discussion forums ▪ Sophisticated social networking tools (profiles, ability to list friends, and ability to find, create, and join groups) ▪ Searchable database of books, events, businesses, and quotes that members can add to ▪ Tagging and tag clouds	2006 **Size (as of July 2006)** 33,000 **Demographic** "Spiritual activists"—not necessarily aimed youth, but site has large membership of youth (20% of members are aged 18–25 and 37% aged 26–35. Only 1% of members, however, were under 18).

(*Continued*)

Table 5
Summary of basic site information and features (*Continued*)

Site	Mandate and distinguishing features	Tools	Year launched and project details
	you succeed + you inspire and empower everyone you know to do the same + we team up with millions like us = we just affected billions = we (together) changed the world."[j] Unlike the other sites we looked at, Zaadz is entirely a social utility like Facebook and as such, has no significant static informational or resource components. In other words, Zaadz is more like an application than a Web page because it is more interactive than all the other sites we have examined. Zaadz was the only site we looked that is for profit. It was also the most sophisticated and well designed of all the sites and the only one to use AJAX, a new programming technique that makes Web sites act more like applications than static web pages.		**Language(s)** English **Platform** Closed custom solution **Creator/Funder** Brian Johnson and Aaron Eisenberger. Zaadz is for profit.

[a] Activism Network, Our Project, n.d., http://www.activismnetwork.org/ourproject.html (retrieved January 8, 2007).

[b] Wikipedia, BattleCry: Programs, Activities and Methods, 2006, http://en.wikipedia.org/wiki/Battle_Cry_Campaign#Programs.2C.activities.and.methods (retrieved January 8, 2007).

[c] J. DeFao, Evangelical Christian Concert Draws 25,000, *San Francisco Chronicle*, March 26, 2006, http://www.sfgate.com/cgi-bin/article.cgi?f=/c/a/2006/03/26/BAGRLHUDM81.DTL (retrieved January 8, 2007).

[d] YouthActionNet.org, Who We Are, 2004, http://www.youthactionnet.org/who (retrieved January 8, 2007).

[e] YouthNoise, Wikipedia, 2006, http://en.wikipedia.org/wiki/Youth.Noise (retrieved October 15, 2006).

[f] YouthNoise, About YouthNoise, 2006, http://www.youthnoise.com/page.php?page_id=2312 (retrieved January 8, 2007).

[g] UNICEF, Voices of Youth: About This Site, n.d., http://www.unicef.org/voy/about/about_261.html (accessed January 8, 2007).

[h] UNICEF. Voices of Youth: About This Site, Mission Statement, n.d., http://www.unicef.org/voy/about/about_255.html (retrieved January 8, 2007).

[i] Coolmel, C4Chaos: B-Scan with Brian Johnson (a.k.a. CEO+Philosopher of Zaadz), 2006, http://coolmel.typepad.com/iblog/2006/02/bscan_with_bria.html (retrieved January 8, 2007).

[j] Zaadz, "Zaadz: Connect. Grow. Inspire. Empower." 2006, http://www.zaadz.com (retrieved January 8, 2007).

We noticed maintenance issues on some sites. Like other software, Web sites often break due to updates, bugs, hacking, spam, or other user interventions. Even outgoing links must be updated regularly to avoid broken links, a common problem among the sites reviewed. While broken links are annoying, lack of proper site maintenance can prevent youth from getting involved entirely. We received an error when trying to sign up with UNICEF Voices of Youth, which prevented us from proceeding, and an e-mail to the technical support address went unanswered. This sort of experience can be frustrating for users and can cause them to lose interest or avoid the site in the future.

Ensuring that the systems behind a site are running smoothly is vital. Many of the sites we surveyed have implemented some degree of moderation. For example, Youth Action Net requires approval for member-created Web and project pages. Our submission to the Youth Action Net was still unapproved after four months, and the overall number of project and member pages listed had not changed during that time either, indicating a problem in the process. In this case, a lack of maintenance actually prevents members from using a core feature of the site. As we discuss in the next section on key learnings, these maintenance problems relate to issues of sustainability and funding, common challenges for NGOs.

The only sites free of these particular problems were Zaadz and BattleCry, both of which appear well funded. The former is the for-profit creation of two successful entrepreneurs[29] and the latter is operated by a large evangelical parachurch organization, with an in-house marketing department and guidance from top interactive advertising agency Tocquigny.[30] Also, BattleCry and Zaadz were created in the past year, whereas the rest emerged between 1995 and 2002, an entirely different era of Web design and functionality.

Purpose, Policy, and People   All of the sites we examined focused on civic engagement, community involvement and improvement, or activism. Within that lens, a wide spectrum of purposes emerged. BattleCry aims primarily at recruiting American youth to Evangelical Christianity. UNICEF Voices of Youth aims to give a voice to underserved children and teens around the world and provide rights education. Zaadz, a social-networking site for "spiritual activists," is not explicitly youth-focused, but the majority of its members are aged eighteen to thirty-five.

Despite the range of audiences and goals, five of the seven sites use a very similar strategy to engage and empower youth: a focus on providing information and facilitating connections and networking. Similarly, almost all the sites connected their online tools with offline action—some, such as Youth Action Net or TIG, with very explicit offline programs. This aligns with the initial findings of our youth survey, that youth use online tools to get what they need to make change offline: information, people, and organizing.

The exceptions were BattleCry and Zaadz, both of which use slightly different strategies than the remainder of the group. Zaadz has no static resource sections, unlike the other sites examined, nor does it make a clear connection between online tools and offline action. Rather, it is a sophisticated social-networking tool focused solely on helping people find and connect with each other. Beyond that, its strategy to help its members make positive change is unclear.

BattleCry stands out for an entirely different reason. BattleCry, like Zaadz, is primarily a social-networking site and less an informational resource. However, the similarities between the two sites stop there. Zaadz, and the other sites we examined, facilitated and encouraged bottom-up organic organization and communication among their members, focusing on enabling and guiding youth. Using Coleman's terminology from the following chapter, they are all examples of relatively autonomous citizenship. BattleCry, in contrast, took a very top-down or managed approach with a focus on instructing youth. The site's suggested strategies for individual and community improvement reflected this methodology, as did the tools it provided. The strategies are rigid and narrow, with little room for interpretation. The same is true of the site's tools: BattleCry only allows one-to-one or small group communication between members. The only group functionality is linked to church membership, and each member is limited to association with one church, limiting any individual's potential reach. The only one-to-many communication tool on BattleCry was a discussion forum, which was locked shortly after the site launched in 2006.

BattleCry is the only site that has created an online tool to direct and measure offline action. The tool allows members to list their "warrior disciplines" and "battle tactics" on their profiles, with a meter indicating their progress. Examples of the predetermined options include "I will recommit to be submissive to my parents" and "I will read BattleCry for My Generation [a book published by BattleCry itself] and give it to others in my youth group to read." While innovative, the tool fits with the rigidity of the site.

The number of members on the sites varied greatly. The most populated sites, TakingIT-Global and YouthNoise, each had well over 100,000 members, while the least populated, the Activism Network and Youth Action Net, had 3700 members and 400 member pages, respectively.[31] While TakingITGlobal and YouthNoise both have large memberships, when considered in relation to MySpace (which hit the 100-million membership mark in late 2006), it is evident that the online civic engagement space still has a largely untapped potential audience.[32]

Part of our criteria for inclusion in the survey was the availability of the site in English, so it was no surprise to find that most of the members of the sites we examined were English speakers. It is notable, however, that there are very few multilingual civic engagement or activist sites. Only two of the sites we examined (including those not included in the final survey) were available in multiple languages; the rest were only in English. TakingITGlobal is available in eleven languages and UNICEF Voices of Youth in four. This lack of linguistic diversity restricts the accessibility of these sites for many youth globally, and even in North America, where languages other than English are spoken.

Despite these overarching similarities, we noticed a great deal of difference among users, no doubt the result of the differing purposes of each site. BattleCry consists of American Christian youth, while UNICEF Voices of Youth caters to underserved children and teens from around the globe. Zaadz, aimed at a very specific crowd of "spiritual activists" has a large number of young members, but only 1 percent are under eighteen.

Learnings and Improvements

The results of our landscape survey can be summarized as follows:

- Most sites had maintenance, design, and/or usability issues, which made them less accessible and appealing for youth

- All the sites but one were nonprofit and NGO-run, and relied primarily on donations, volunteers, or sponsorships for their funding

- Robust and sophisticated collaboration tools were lacking

- Within the overarching goals of engaging and empowering youth by providing them with information and networking with their peers, there was still a diversity of purposes, policies and members
- Very few sites are offered in multiple languages
- There was a range of membership levels

Sustainability

Given the problems we identified with site maintenance, design, and usability, funding and sustainability is clearly a challenge for all the sites surveyed. Dynamic Web sites are like plants: they need nurturing and care. Deliberate and ongoing care is even more important considering the high expectations created by well-funded and maintained commercial sites. Therefore, the people and organizations behind online activist, community, and civic engagement sites must develop revenue streams to ensure their sites receive appropriate support and maintenance.

LiveJournal presents an interesting alternative solution. LiveJournal is a large community blogging site popular with youth, founded by early blogger Brad Fitzpatrick while he was still in college. Before Six Apart purchased it in early 2005, LiveJournal was supported by a large group of volunteer members who provided technical and community support as well as technical development. Member suggestions for improvements and features also factored heavily into the development of the site. By involving their members in the day-to-day management of the site, LiveJournal not only created a large, strong, and loyal membership but was also able to stretch their minimal resources. Compared to the sites we examined in our landscape survey, LiveJournal has had very few maintenance, usability, or design issues. Although LiveJournal is not focused on civic or community engagement, it has nonetheless empowered and engaged many of its young users in a meaningful way, and has given them the ability to influence the development of their online community. Unfortunately, the involvement of the community has diminished since Six Apart took control of LiveJournal and brought in more paid staff.[33]

LiveJournal is the only example we have seen of members being so heavily involved in the day-to-day operations of an online community. We contrast this with BattleCry, a site that had almost no member input or involvement. Activist, community, and civic engagement sites could benefit greatly from involving their members as LiveJournal has. They could potentially increase their membership by providing better tools and features to facilitate networking and information access, and by creating a sense of ownership and loyalty. Creating better tools and increasing membership is not only good for the organizations, but good for youth as well. The greater youth's access to people, information, and organizational tools, the easier it is to accomplish civic engagement or community improvement goals.

Tools

Almost across the board we observed usability and design issues, and a lack of robust collaborative tools. None of the sites we examined, except for the well-funded Zaadz and BattleCry, met the level of sophistication or usability of their commercial counterparts. It is vital that sites keep up with the state of the art set by commercial sites to ensure that youth are engaged in a way that is not only appealing but also highly effective. TakingITGlobal benefits from having multiple in-house staff members dedicated to technology development. YouthNoise, and to a lesser extent BattleCry, have both begun to take resource-saving measures to keep up with the latest Internet trends. YouthNoise has begun to feature embedded videos about current events and issues from the popular video sharing site, YouTube, on its front page. BattleCry now asks members for submissions via YouTube and provides banners that members can include on their MySpace profiles. This sort of integration with commercial services allows sites to easily add new features for their members, while also reaching out to youth who are sole users of commercial services.

Languages

Despite the global mandate of several of the sites we examined (including those not included in our final landscape survey), only two were available in more than one language. Given an increasingly global world, it is important for activist, civic, and community engagement sites to provide access in multiple languages, especially in countries with more than one official language. In so doing, these sites will be better able to provide youth with access to their peers in their most comfortable and functional linguistic environment. The importance of having the right people using a site was demonstrated by the success of MySpace—youth want to be where their friends are. Increasing the number of languages will not only increase membership but also help youth find the people they need to connect with to make the change they want in their communities.

Translating a site into other languages can be a good way of getting youth directly engaged with a site. TakingITGlobal was able to translate its site into eleven languages largely because of the help of volunteer members. In many cases, these translation volunteers have also taken on the role of promoting the site to build a local audience and locally relevant content. TakingITGlobal has been successful in reaching a global audience and has the largest membership of all the sites we examined. LiveJournal used the same strategy for their site translation, and as a result, has become a very popular blogging site in Russia (their second-largest member base after the United States is Russia).[34]

Conclusion

Throughout this chapter, we have presented examples and possibilities of a growing movement of youth who inform and organize themselves online, and then proceed to take action in their communities. We have also seen a growing movement of interactive online civic engagement sites based around social tools, such as TakingITGlobal.org, aimed at facilitating youth engagement by providing access to peers, information and tools to mobilize and organize. Yet, just like the movement, the research and feedback mechanisms are young and in need of further development.

The most burning research question revolves around the development of an evaluation methodology that assesses the efficacy of online civic engagement sites, specifically the connection between online and offline preparation and action. We recommend further exploration of the initial findings from our youth survey: specifically more detailed investigations into the use and potential improvements to online civic engagement sites for networking with peers, finding information, and organizing.

We are excited about the potential of well-executed online civic engagement sites. When youth are engaged on their own terms, we strongly believe that the future of young people and positive change in the world will be bright.

Notes

1. Amanda Lenhart, Mary Madden, and Paul Hitlin, Teens and Technology: Youth Are Leading the Transition to a Fully Wired and Mobile Nation, Pew Internet, 2005, http://www.pewinternet.org/report_display.asp?r=162 (retrieved January 8, 2007).

2. Joseph Hall, Jimmy Wales' Talk at SIMS, Not Quite a Blog 2.0, 2006, http://josephhall.org/nqb2/index.php/2005/11/03/jimbo (retrieved January 8, 2007).

3. Michael Delli Carpini, Gen.Com: Youth, Civic Engagement and the New Information Environment, *Political Communication* 17 (2000): 341–49.

4. Ayla Khosroshahi, Jennifer Corriero, Svetlana Taraban, Sarah Richardson, Franziska Seel, and Clarisse Kehler Siebert, TakingITGlobal, 2006, Cross Canada Mapping of Youth-led and/or Highly-engaged Initiatives: Final Report, http://about.takingitglobal.org/d/publications?view=17 (retrieved January 8, 2007).

5. danah boyd, Friends, Friendsters and Top 8: Writing Community Into Being on Social Network Sites, *First Monday* 11, no. 12 (2006), http://www.firstmonday.org/issues/issue11_12/boyd/index.html (retrieved January 8, 2007).

6. danah boyd, Identity Production in a Networked Culture: Why Youth ♥ MySpace, American Association for the Advancement of Science, St. Louis, MO, February 19, 2006, http://www.danah.org/papers/AAAS2006.html (retrieved January 8, 2007).

7. Kathryn Montgomery, Barbara Gottlieb-Robles, and Gary O. Larson, Youth as E-Citizens: Engaging the Digital Generation, Center for Social Media, 2004, http://www.centerforsocialmedia.org/ecitizens/youthreport.pdf (retrieved January 8, 2007).

8. Jennifer Corriero and Michael Furdyk, Interview by Kate Raynes-Goldie and Luke Walker, Mp3 Recording, October 12, 2006, TakingITGlobal Research Archives, Toronto.

9. TakingITGlobal, Annual Report, 2005, http://about.takingitglobal.org/d/publications?view=12 (retrieved January 8, 2007), 15.

10. Dan Tapscott and Anthony D. Williams, *Wikinomics: How Mass Collaboration Changes Everything* (New York: Penguin, 2006).

11. For more information, see Khosroshahi et al.

12. TakingITGlobal, Creating Local Connections: Russian Youth On-Line, 2005.

13. TakingITGlobal, Local Voices, Global Visions: A Compilation of Results From the 2003 WSIS National Information Society Youth Campaigns, 2003.

14. Corriero and Furdyk.

15. TakingITGlobal Member Impact Survey.

16. Ibid.

17. Montgomery, Gottlieb-Robles, and Larson.

18. Bennett, in this volume.

19. J. Corriero and M. Furdyk.

20. TakingITGlobal, 2005, http://about.takingitglobal.org/d/publications?view=12 (retrieved January 8, 2007).

21. YouthNoise, About YouthNoise, 2006, http://www.youthnoise.org/page.php?page_id=2312 (retrieved January 8, 2007); YouthNoise, The History of YouthNoise, 2006, http://www.youthnoise.com/page.php?page_id=2350 (retrieved January 8, 2007).

22. Lenhart, Madden, and Hitlin.

23. See Montgomery, Bers, in this volume.

24. UNICEF, Voices of Youth: About This Site, n.d., http://www.unicef.org/voy/about/about_261.html (accessed January 8, 2007); UNICEF, Voices of Youth: About This Site: Mission Statement, n.d., http://www.unicef.org/voy/about/about_255.html (retrieved January 8, 2007).

25. Wikipedia, BattleCry: Programs, Activities and Methods, 2006, http://en.wikipedia.org/wiki/Battle_Cry_Campaign#Programs.2C_activities_and_methods (retrieved January 8, 2007).

26. Clarisse Sieckenius De Souza and Jenny Preece, A Framework for Analyzing and Understanding Online Communities, *Interacting With Computers, The Interdisciplinary Journal of Human–Computer Interaction* (2004).

27. Sarah Pullman, Zaadz–Do We Need Another Social Networking Tool!? *SarahPullman.Com*, 2006, http://sarahpullman.com/zaadz (retrieved January 8, 2007).

28. Steve Krug, *Don't Make Me Think: A Common Sense Approach to Web Usability* (Berkeley, CA: New Riders Publishing, 2006).

29. Zaadz, Wikipedia, 2006, http://en.wikipedia.org/wiki/Zaadz (accessed January 8, 2007).

30. Tocquigny, Wikipedia, 2006, http://en.wikipedia.org/wiki/Tocquigny (retrieved January 8, 2007).

31. Activism Network, Our Project, n.d., http://www.activismnetwork.org/ourproject.html (retrieved January 8, 2007).

32. Pete Cashmore, MySpace Hits 100 Million Accounts, *Mashable! Social Networking 2.0*, August 9, 2006, http://mashable.com/2006/08/09/myspace-hits-100-million-accounts/ (retrieved January 8, 2007).

33. Livejournal: Demographics, Wikipedia, 2006, http://en.wikipedia.org/wiki/LiveJournal#Demographics (retrieved January 8, 2007); Livejournal: Community, Wikipedia, 2006, http://en.wikipedia.org/wiki/LiveJournal#Community (retrieved January 8, 2007).

34. Teen Mania, Wikipedia, 2006, http://en.wikipedia.org/wiki/Teen_Mania (retrieved January 8, 2007).

Doing IT for Themselves: Management versus Autonomy in Youth E-Citizenship

Stephen Coleman

University of Leeds, Institute of Communications Studies

"Don't mention the war"

In most contemporary democracies, significant energy and resources are being devoted to the project of cultivating, shaping, and sustaining the next generation of citizens. While everyone agrees that promoting citizenship is "a good thing," there is rather less consensus about the preferred forms or outcomes of civic behavior. A brief example from the recent experience of citizenship education in the United Kingdom will help to illuminate this contested terrain.

Citizenship education (the British equivalent of "civics") was introduced into the English and Welsh secondary school curriculum in 2001, following the recommendations of a report produced by a Commission headed by the political theorist Bernard Crick that called for "no less than a change in the political culture of this country."[1] Unlike U.S. civic education, with its emphasis upon an "adaptative and conditioned, rather than active and critical" approach,[2] the British model of citizenship education aimed explicitly to nurture young people who would be "individually confident in finding new forms of involvement and action among themselves."[3] An appendix to the Crick Report acknowledged the potential significance of digital technologies, stating that "the interactive character of the Internet provides opportunities for invigorating citizenship education."[4] The extent to which these lofty aspirations were translated into everyday pedagogies and activities was brought into sharp focus in Britain in the buildup to the U.S.-led war against Iraq.

Although the new citizenship curriculum requires schools to teach students about politically significant current events, as well as political structures and processes, a study of citizenship education teaching in English schools in the months before the invasion of Iraq found that teachers "were uneasy in dealing with the issues of Iraq or of terrorism" and "young people of all ages felt they were being sold short in terms of information and understanding."[5] The former chief inspector of schools for England endorsed this reluctance to engage school students in discussion about the war, arguing that

I worry a bit about encouraging young people to articulate judgements and feelings, however strongly they are held, when they haven't got the evidence, they haven't got the experience to really understand the full ramifications of what they are talking about.[6]

Thanks to my research assistant on this project, Julia Snell, for her diligent support. I would like to thank all of those who collaborated on this volume for the intellectually enriching experience of working with them.

A remarkable number of school students begged to differ and in the course of February and March 2003 Britain experienced an unprecedented wave of strikes organized by school students protesting against the British Government's support for the Iraq war. Libby Brooks, reporting for the *Guardian* newspaper on the protest by over a thousand school students outside the British Parliament, observed that

These young people were organising and leading their own protests, leafleting at school gates, organising email networks and expertly working the media. Their determination to be heard was palpable.[7]

Other sections of the British press were less positive about these demonstrations of political activism by young people, accusing them of not understanding the issues, being vulnerable to manipulation by sinister political forces, and engaging in illegitimate truancy.[8] Ironically, some British newspapers blamed the citizenship curriculum for these manifestations of dissent by young people. The reality was somewhat different: as Davies notes in her study of citizenship education, most schools failed to acknowledge, analyze or respond to the war, leaving young people with a sense of mystification and inefficacy in relation to one of the most consequential political events in recent British history; while those students who did take up "new forms of involvement and action among themselves" (as recommended by Crick) "faced disciplinary proceedings and suspensions."[9]

This failure to provide a democratic response to a momentous political event raises important questions about the capacity of a government-driven curriculum to address questions of conflict that potentially challenge its own power and legitimacy. It is a failure which supports Frazer's concern that the emphasis of the promoters of citizenship education upon generalized notions of values, rights, and duties conceals an underlying antipathy toward a more agonistic conception of politics.[10] The argument that I propose to pursue in this chapter is that the silence of citizenship education teachers about Iraq and the silencing of antiwar protesters by education authorities are indicative of a more deep-rooted tension between managed and autonomous citizenship. It is the aim of this chapter both to make theoretical sense of this tension and to explore its practical ramifications in the context of policy.

Two Faces of E-Citizenship

After Italy's unification in 1860, the Italian nationalist leader and novelist, Massimo d'Azeglio, remarked that "we have made Italy, we now have to make Italians." This project was pursued by exploiting a range of information and communication technologies (ICT), from the printing press to the mass circulation of patriotic songs. Contemporary governments seeking to promote sociocultural cohesion increasingly turn to ICT to cultivate and regulate norms, routines, and rituals of citizenship. But this grand project of "making citizens" entails an inevitable tension between liberal and communitarian ends. From a liberal perspective, citizens are free agents, and just civic norms are those that do not seek to impose upon individuals' collective notions of what is good. In contrast, the communitarian perspective places greater emphasis upon the common good than upon citizens' self-determination, and therefore justifies policies intended to shape civic behavior at the expense of individual agency. Any policy by government to promote civic engagement will be vulnerable to liberal criticism that its real intention is to encourage beliefs and actions consistent with its own values and interests, while marginalizing dissenting voices.

The British government has expressed considerable enthusiasm in recent years for the idea of promoting online political engagement, declaring that "ICT provides a means by which public participation can be increased, and we hope that with an active government policy the potential benefits can be maximised." The government's policy document on e-Democracy states that

One important target group for this policy is young people. All democratic institutions have a responsibility to ensure that young people are able to play their part. Evidence suggests that young people are among those least likely to see the democratic process as relevant to them. Young people are also among those most likely to be competent in ICT.[11]

The policy of "targeting" young people so that they can "play their part" can be read either as a spur to youth activism or an attempt to manage it. Indeed, the very notion of youth e-citizenship seems to be caught between divergent strategies of management and autonomy.[12] Although these two faces of e-citizenship represent ideal types, and should perhaps be understood as opposing points on a spectrum rather than mutually exclusive positions, they differ sufficiently in their contrasting conceptions of the status of young people, the affordances of digital technologies, and the authenticity of "actually existing democracy" to provide a useful theoretical context for assessing the projects discussed in the next section.

Youth as Apprentices or Catalysts

It would seem on the face of it that defining the status of youth would not be particularly contentious. Freeland, for example, constructs youth as a "stage of life between childhood and adulthood."[13] But what are the implications of this transitional status? Advocates of managed e-citizenship regard young people as apprentice citizens who are in a process of transition from the immaturity of childhood to the self-possession of adulthood. As apprentices, youth are in a state of dependency and becoming: to use Quovrup's wry phrase, they are human becomings rather than human beings. This means that they lack the powers of independent agency associated with self-determination. Civic apprenticeship entails learning the skills required to exercise responsible judgment in a risky and complex world.

In contrast to this conception of e-citizenship as socialization, proponents of autonomous e-citizenship refuse to see themselves as apprentice citizens, arguing that, despite their limited experience or access to resources, they possess sufficiently autonomous agency to speak for themselves on agendas of their own making. Autonomous e-citizens regard youth itself as a reflexive project in which narratives of emergence, socialization, and engagement can be renegotiated by each new generation. As Beck has argued, "The "biographization" of youth means becoming active, struggling and designing one's own life."[14] In this sense, not only the objective conditions facing youth, but the subjective experience of what it means to be a young person becomes a matter for politicized discourse.

The Internet as Anarchy or Enclave

Similarly contrasting perspectives characterize the ways in which the two faces of e-citizenship regard the Internet as a space for civic engagement. Managed e-citizenship starts from the assumption that the Internet, as an anarchic realm in which unknown nodes perpetually collide, is an unsafe place for young people, not only because their social innocence might be exploited by predators but also because they are politically vulnerable to misinformation and misdirection. For the Internet to become a useful locus of socialization, proponents of managed e-citizenship favor the establishment of safe, civilized, moderated enclaves in which youth can learn and have their say. As well as providing a safe environment in which young people can be heard and observed, a key objective of managed spaces of e-citizenship is to cultivate "responsibilized" citizens (to use Garland's term[15]) who are not only free to argue but to obey the rules of good argument; who are not only taught to be technically competent Internet users but self-regulating actors capable of surviving safely in a virtual world replete with real and imagined dangers.

It is precisely the anarchy of the Internet that appeals to autonomous e-citizens, who see it as a relatively free space in which untrammeled creativity and acephalous networks can flourish. With Bennett, they celebrate "the Internet's potential as a relatively open public sphere in which the ideas and plans of protest can be exchanged with relative ease, speed and global scope."[16]

While proponents of managed e-citizenship tend to be sanguine about the democratic characteristics of the Internet, autonomous e-citizens express concerns about "the ways in which citizenship norms, rights, obligations and practices are *encoded* in the design and structure of our increasingly digital surroundings."[17] They question what Luke has called the "hidden pedagogies of citizenship,"[18] fearing that citizenship is being molded and constrained by technological infrastructures that are designed to perpetrate a narrow, quiescent and consumerist model of civic action.

Democracy as Existing or Aspirational

From the perspective of managed e-citizenship, existing structures and processes of governance are essentially democratic, but are undermined by the failure of citizens to engage with them and of elected representatives to respond to those who do take the trouble to participate. Democracy is seen as suffering from a "deficit" that can be rectified by enhancing the voices of the public and the listening skills of politicians. Youth are regarded as a neglected social group whose political alienation from the democratic process can be addressed by making it more genuinely accountable and consultative. As the ministerial introduction to a cabinet office report entitled *Young People and Politics* puts it,

we must all take the action necessary to raise the levels of youth participation in democracy, and the numbers of young people who use their vote. If we say young people aren't interested in politics and voting, then we must strive to engage their interest. If we are to encourage them to express their opinions at the ballot box, we must listen to what young people are telling us, and then take the right action.[19]

Proponents of autonomous e-citizenship are more skeptical about the claims and limits of "actually existing democracy." Rather than engage with the established political process, they seek to generate new democratic networks that can circumvent established regimes of power. These might be compared to Bey's notion of the temporary autonomous zone, which he describes as being "like an uprising which does not engage directly with the State, a guerrilla operation which liberates an area (of land, of time, of imagination) and then dissolves itself to re-form elsewhere/elsewhen, before the State can crush it."[20]

The conflict between the two faces of e-citizenship is between a view of democracy as an established and reasonably just system, with which young people should be encouraged to engage, and democracy as a political as well as cultural aspiration, most likely to be realized through networks in which young people engage with one another. As ever, strategies of accessing, influencing, and reconfiguring power are at the heart of what might at first appear to be mere differences of communicative style.

Doing and Being Done For: Some Examples

Some e-citizenship projects are run for young people by adults; others are run by young people themselves. To understand this distinction, and the practical implications of managed and autonomous youth e-citizenship, six U.K.-based projects were selected for investigation. Two of the projects are government funded, one is funded by independent charitable foundations, and three do not receive any external funding. They are

- The Hansard Society's *Headsup* project (http://www.headsup.org.uk/content/), which describes itself as "a place where young people can debate political issues and current affairs. But it's not just about talking, it's about getting something done. The debates involve the U.K.'s top decision-makers from parliament and government who want to understand the views and experiences of young Britain." The project is funded by the U.K. government's Department of Constitutional Affairs.

- The English School Students' Association (ESSA) (http://www.studentvoice.co.uk/), which "aims to provide training, guidance and advice to empower students and equip them with the vital skills needed to become actively involved in the decision-making processes in their own school communities; and ... aims to work in partnership with other organisations to bring the views of secondary school students to the attention of local and national policy-makers, as well as the media, in relation to educational issues." The project is funded by charitable foundations.

- The Northern Irish project, *Where Is My Public Servant?* (WIMPS) (http://www.wimps.org.uk/), which describes itself as being "aiming to inspire and empower young people in Northern Ireland, giving them a voice in the decisions that affect all our lives, trying to get young people talking and influencing politicians and public representatives." The project is funded by the Northern Ireland Assembly and Executive.

- The *Students Against Sweatshops* campaign (http://www.studentsagainstsweatshops.org.uk/), which is "a student organisation which fights against the bosses of sweatshops worldwide—campaigning in solidarity with the exploited workers." The project is funded by the activists who run it.

- The George Fox 6 Campaign (http://www.free-webspace.biz/GeorgeFox/), which campaigns against the criminal conviction of six students for protesting during a conference at Lancaster University intended to promote the commercialization of research. The project is funded by the activists who run it.

- Educationet (http://www.educationet.org/) is a left-of-center news resource for students that describes itself as "the number one place to discuss the issues of the day concerning students, and of course to find out all the NUS gossip." The project is funded by the activists who run it.

The study of these six projects involved extensive semistructured interviews with key actors involved in running their online operations.[21] Interviewees were encouraged to articulate the political objectives of their projects; set out their reasons for using particular technologies and applications; reflect upon the governance of their projects, with particular reference to the regulation of online behavior; and consider the implications of having an actual or potential relationship with government. A thematic summary of their responses is set out in the following four sections.

Defining Political Objectives

There is a conspicuous difference between the political objectives of funded and nonfunded projects. The former exist to connect young people with powerful institutions that might otherwise ignore them. For example, the WIMPS project, which has been remarkably imaginative and successful in stimulating youth voices to intervene in the often opaque and tribal politics of Northern Ireland, was described as being

about young people engaging with public servants, mostly elected representatives, politicians at various levels and the reason we felt that was important was because there isn't a lot of engagement between young people and politicians here. (Smyth)

Likewise, the Hansard Society's Headsup project seeks to connect young people to parliamentarians. Described as being "a debating platform where essentially young people debate directly on a key topic" (Griffiths), a key criterion for the success of the site is the willingness of MPs to participate. Indeed, Headsup's project manager was eager to point out that "in the last year ... so that's only five debates ... we've actually had forty-seven MPs take part ... which is an average of about nine and a half per debate" (Griffiths). Young people are invited to vote on topics to be debated on the Headsup forum and, once a topic has been selected, the project manager sees it as his job to recruit politicians who are willing to listen and interact. This recruitment involves members of parliamentary select committees, all-party groups, and designated representatives of the main political parties. But what about unofficial voices: dissidents, the unelected, voices from excluded segments of society? The emphasis upon being heard by powerful people seems to exclude these counterconnections.

ESSA is also committed to connecting young people to power, but in their case it is educational authorities that they seek to influence:

We are working to give students between 11 and 19 a voice in education, because it was the realization that parents, teachers, governors, heads, in fact every single person in the educational sector, had a national body and had a way of having their voice heard, but the students who are the largest stakeholders didn't have such a body. (Dey)

The political objective of the funded projects seems to be to engender a form of witnessing, so that the voices of the less powerful are somehow acknowledged, respected, or even incorporated into the policy process. When asked to think about what would constitute success or failure for their projects, these interviewees were eager to return to this theme of the quality of democratic witnessing. For example, in the case of WIMPS, the battle seemed to be to drag recalcitrant politicians into a communicative relationship for which they were not fully prepared:

The average age of politicians is probably well into the 50s—and that's being generous—so what we are saying to them is you can't ignore this [the Internet], this is the way people communicate today. We did have one politician who had a meeting with the WIMPS team and was being very patronizing and saying "I don't take e-mail seriously. People should write a letter and if their grammar is not good I won't respond," but, interestingly, recently we noticed him responding to some e-mails on the site because they came from a group of young people at a special school who were complaining about education cutbacks and threats to their education, and I think he realized he couldn't afford not to respond to that. So that was really quite interesting. (Smyth)

The common claim made by interviewees was that being heard would make young people more active citizens in the future:

Research that shows if students are engaged in decision making in the schools and they feel more part of it they are more likely to do well and not want to truant, because they feel part of the system.. . . ESSA wants to engage youth in decision making with the view that if youth engage in decision making while at school they are more likely to vote as a side impact. (Dey)

Politics has disengaged from young people, not the other way around—and if we don't get that through to politicians, then I think the democratic veneer in our society is going to get thinner and thinner and people will become more skeptical about politics and politicians. (Smyth)

This attempt to rescue contemporary democracy from its own worst habits, by opening it up to hitherto neglected voices, is in stark contrast to the more pessimistic views of the political system expressed by activists within the unfunded projects:

I don't believe there is anything like a profound commitment to democratic principles within either government or wider society. I personally think one really big advance would be for people to simply stop calling the political system in which we live democratic. For example, people can say activists shouldn't use direct action, or break laws generally, because "we live in a democracy." They can't say we shouldn't do these things because "the government is responsive to demands from the public to stop arms deals, not go to war etc." because people know this simply isn't true. But with the shortcut of "democracy" they win—any further analysis and their point gets shown up for the sham it is. (Matt)

Regardless of the merits of this anarchistic argument, it is indicative of an approach to online communication that does not regard connecting to governing institutions as a valuable objective. Rather than tell government about perceived social injustice, the online campaign organizer of Students Against Sweatshops emphasized the importance of her site as a means of connecting the interests and experiences of students to those of exploited workers in other parts of the world:

There is a recognition by students that sweatshops are a Third World issue. It appeals to the students because they also have to work rubbish jobs, long hours for no pay and there has been a big movement, particularly in America, linking up sweatshop work with low pay on campus work and fighting for a living wage for workers and it's starting to take off in U.K. universities too, which we're hoping to feed into. (Buckland)

Rather than being witnessed by authority, the autonomous e-citizenship projects are seeking to encourage a collective consciousness of shared values:

We've had over two thousand people on the online petition and a lot of people contacting us.. . . Chomsky signing the petition boosted people's interest.. . . People from literally all over the world, which was really very nice; people from Asia, Australasia, and South America and so on. You can still see them online . . . all the different names, that was really inspiring. (Matt)

Both models of e-citizenship seem to regard the nature of political engagement as a form of witnessing: for managed e-citizenship this entails being witnessed by powerful elites; for autonomous e-citizenship the point is to bear witness to one another. The notion of citizens as witnesses is powerful, implying that democratic citizenship can only ever be realized through mediated communication. Such a conception is consistent with recent work by Zelizer, Peters, Ellis, and Sontag, each of whom has attempted to show how witnessing entails making the depth of original experience available to others.[22] As Ellis argues, the paradoxically distanced and involving nature of witnessing "implies a necessary relationship with what is seen."[23] An intriguing question for new media research is whether virtual communication enhances or undermines that relationship; whether the disembodied testimonies of faceless e-citizens can be more easily dismissed as ephemeral and ethereal or whether the force of the network might engender acts of what one might call collective witnessing.

Using Digital Technologies

Unsurprisingly, the most ambitious plans to use digital technologies came from the funded projects, which could better afford to invest in innovatory experimentation. For example, WIMPS is in the process of moving from solely text-based to audio- and video-based communications between young people and Northern Irish politicians:

One of the things we're doing is putting video on to the site, so, for example, a young person might pop up and say "Have you thought about this issue that you are working on and who the best person to speak to is—is this the kind of issue you might go to your MEP with?" so that there is an interaction between the people using the site. (Smyth)

WIMPS is also setting up opportunities for young people to produce and interact with blogs and iPods. Similarly, Headsup is "running a project in which young people can send in pictures and texts via mobile phone to the Home Affairs Select Committee" (Griffiths).

Interestingly, participants in these online projects seem not to be impressed by the more extravagant gimmickry of digital technology. In the case of WIMPS, the young people involved were highly critical of the original designs for the Web site produced by an external company:

The young people kept rejecting their designs. [The Web design company] has a very young staff, not much older than the people we were working with. They kept coming up with these sites flashy with bells and whistles on them which they thought would appeal to teenagers and we rejected about four different designs and one of the directors rang me up and said "We can't keep producing designs, time is money," so we sat the group down and talked it through and we realized was that they were trying to tell the designers was that they wanted something serious. They wanted the site to look serious. (Smyth)

Preconceived notions of "what kids want" are more than likely to be mistaken. The autonomous e-citizenship sites were equally unimpressed by digital gimmicks. Indeed, they seemed to subscribe to a fairly old-fashioned, broadcast model of how to use the Internet. For Students Against Sweatshops, the main function of the online project is to disseminate information:

It's an excellent way of getting information out to lots of people. We don't have loads of money. We can't afford to produce a newsletter that we send out to everyone. We can do it online basically for free and it can be updated instantly. People from all over the world can search for it. We get a lot of people. It's just really useful. (Buckland)

Similarly, the George Fox 6 Campaign saw their Web site as "just another resource," like putting up posters or handing out leaflets. Interviewees from the autonomous e-citizenship projects were very clear about the ways in which digital technologies has enabled them to compete in a fairer communication environment.

I think that activists like ourselves are playing on a remarkably unlevel playing field. I think the Internet gives us something. It's a positive thing. It gives you access to people that previously you wouldn't have contacted except through photocopied leaflets. You can be there in people's homes and they are on the computer and they can go to the Guardian Web site or Home Office Web site or they can go to our Web site, and in that sense we're on a slightly more even footing. (Matt)

The only way ESSA got where it has today is because of online communication. I wouldn't be able to get the word out there. Everything has happened via e-mails and newsgroups. (Dey)

Nonetheless, there was a recognition by most of the online activists that successful political relationships cannot be entirely virtual. As one interviewee put it, "I think technology is really effective where people already have a relationship and then they use the technology to enhance the relationship" (Smyth).

For the autonomous e-citizenship projects, it is the capacity to move from virtual communication to more tangible networks that held out the most alluring prospects:

If you look at the kind of activism that I'm involved in, it [digital communication] has been really beneficial for the people who have been involved because they can connect more easily and they can network within themselves more easily, which is definitely very useful . . . so I think definitely, for people who want to work in those ways, it can be helpful. (Matt)

I think social networks are really interesting. We've seen sites like Bebo or Facebook and MySpace becoming really popular amongst young people. So people do engage in these Web sites, but the question is, will they continue doing so in a political arena? (Dey)

For the editor of Educationet, the most useful function of his site is to facilitate journalistic networking, with him "digging up the raw material for other people to use" and "the people who are running student campaigns getting their information from Educationet" (Jayanetti).

Regulating Discourse

Interviewees from the managed e-citizenship projects communicated a strong sense that there is a particular way to talk about politics. Characteristics such as politeness, consensus-seeking, due respect for authority and rationality are encouraged. The manager of the Headsup project described participants in his forum as "very quick-tempered," but "in a constructive way, not ranting" (Griffiths). The manager of the WIMPS project was eager to explain that

Speaking publicly has a different implication to speaking privately. I think the young people have really learned that when they are putting stuff on the site—and this will be even more apparent when they are doing audio and video—they are speaking publicly and therefore they must use language that's appropriate. (Smyth)

This notion of appropriate speech was intriguing because of its echoes of Foucauldian notions of governmentality. According to Foucault, modern liberal governance is no longer based principally upon technologies of domination and coercion, but is increasingly concerned to cultivate habits of self-regulation, through which governable subjects are produced. The modification of talk about power among young people who are encountering politics for the first time provides an excellent illustration of this governmentalist process at work. There are three ways in which such regulation could be discerned. First, interviewees tended to subscribe to a risk discourse that emphasized the potential dangers of unrestricted online communication. Asked whether contributors to the Headsup debates could contact one another (perhaps to pursue a political argument or even to organize together on the basis of agreement), the project manager explained that

It's all done via the Web site really. They could always contact me and I'd act as a contact. But its quite tricky because of the data protection issues. You can't just pass people's identities very easily. You need to be very careful about that. (Griffiths)

While it is indeed the case that European data protection law is strict about the prevention of third-party distribution of personal information, that still does not explain why young people should not be able to contact one another directly, in the way that they surely can in the physical world.

Second, the need for debate between young people to be moderated by a supervisory presence was considered important:

In the initial stage it wasn't premoderated, which means that all the comments went on straight away. We quickly realized that the young people were very quick to cotton on to that and expose and exploit it and post lots of dodgy messages, so it's now premoderated, but the messages are of a really high quality now. (Griffiths)

The notion of "message quality" seems on the surface to be straightforward. One assumes it relates to messages that are reflective, evidential and tolerant. But these criteria are only ever implicit within the project. Nowhere on the Headsup Web site is quality either demanded or defined. What constitutes a "dodgy" message? (*Dodgy* is a British term, often used to describe improper or illicit activity.) In what ways, and with what intent, were young people "exploiting" opportunities to express themselves in inappropriate ways? There are too many unstated assumptions at play here to leave one sure that moderating techniques are politically neutral or inoffensive.

The third aspect of discourse regulation was encapsulated by official rules posted on some of the sites. The manager of the Headsup project was very candid about this:

I think with any online forum debate you need rules to help govern the participants really.... The thing is when you've got the rules it's easier to manage.... In my time of managing Heads-Up, which is about nine months now, I haven't had to refer or use any of them or say you've broken this rule etc. It's like a polite deterrent really. (Griffiths)

Again, this begs a question (which could perhaps have been pursued more energetically in the interview): what exactly are these rules deterring? The "obvious" answer associates youth with dangers of playful disruption, boundary testing, and irresponsibility. But what seems obvious is often no more than hegemonic prejudice. Sometimes deterrents never have to be used because they are not in reality deterring anything, but simply exist to reinforce institutional fear and authority. ESSA also favors guidelines for the peer discussions that it hopes to add as a key feature of its site:

I think we'd have guidelines as to what we would or would not accept. I don't think it would be very good if it became a ground for students to slag off each other or their teachers. That might not be very constructive and that might not be good for the site in general, so there would be guidelines about that. (Dey)

Each of these regulatory techniques raise questions about whose interests they are serving. Do they exist to maximize the benefits of democratic debate, or to promote a particular set of ethical principles, or to satisfy risk-aversive funders? And if there is a convincing democratic rationale for regulation, should this not be passed on to the autonomous e-citizenship projects that appear to have no guidelines regarding appropriate speech?

The Students Against Sweatshops campaign explained how they used technology to democratize decision making about appropriate content for their site:

We've got an e-mail list and sometimes before putting things up that might be contentious . . . we put them out on our open e-mail list and say, "Is this okay? What do people think about it?" So we've got shared editorial control over it. (Buckland)

The autonomous e-citizenship projects regarded the use of open-source software as an important principle of collaborative networking.

Relations With Government

Several interviewees expressed strong doubts about the British Government's genuine commitment to communicating with young people. As the editor of Educationet put it,

If the government wants more young people to be politically engaged, it should spend slightly less of its time carrying out policies that put not only young people, but pretty much all people, off having anything to do with politics and the political process. When the politicians say in their manifesto they will not introduce university tuition fees in the lifetime of the next parliament and then they go ahead and introduce tuition fees in the lifetime of the next parliament, the likelihood of people engaging positively in the way that *they want them to*, in terms of being good little citizens and voting and not making too much of a fuss about anything, that's not going to happen. What instead happens is people don't vote or they vote en-bloc in protest. People either disengage from the process or they get angry. (Jayanetti)

The WIMPS project manager was unconvinced by the listening postures of government:

Every government department is creating policies which they are supposed to consult with people on and they are sending out this gobbledegook that they want the youth workers to communicate to young people and then give feedback to the government departments. It was all on the terms of the department. It was mostly fairly uninteresting stuff to most people, let alone young people. But when young people even bothered to respond, at best they were invited to meet the Minister and shake his hand, but they were never really taken very seriously. (Smyth)

Nonetheless, government is a potential source of funding for projects that could help to realize democratic objectives that might not receive support from elsewhere. Headsup is funded by the Department of Constitutional Affairs, in return for which it is required to run at least one online debate on a topic selected by the DCA. WIMPS is funded by the Northern Ireland Assembly and Executive. To what extent are these projects constrained by government values? According to the WIMPS project manager,

The test will come when it [WIMPS] starts to raise issues that are really quite controversial and somebody in the government or electoral unit get a phone call saying, "Why you supporting this?" We need to be strong and robust enough to be able to stand up to them, providing what the team has done is legitimate and fair. So it needs to have journalistic independence. It's quite a tricky thing to establish the funding base that allows you do that. (Smyth)

ESSA, which has already received a good deal of moral support from people close to government, would consider accepting official funding subject to one condition:

If they could give us money with no strings attached, that would be ideal, but obviously we don't want to become a mouthpiece for the government. We want to do our own thing. If they see the value in what we were doing and gave us funding, that would be good. (Dey)

Other interviewees were more doubtful about the possibility of taking government money and being allowed to criticize its actions. Asked whether they would accept money if it came out of a government fund to encourage youth e-participation, the online organizer of Students Against Sweatshops explained that

I'm not sure that for our campaign we would accept that sort of funding. I think if it's a political campaign, regardless if you use the Internet or not, there's always the question of how much you can be influenced by taking money of that sort. Ours isn't just a campaign to get people engaged. There's a set of political objectives there. I guess we'd never come under the criteria for that. (Buckland)

The George Fox 6 Campaign was equally skeptical:

The strings that are attached, the stress that comes attached, the feeling of dependency that is created, the feeling that you can start to self-censor—it's a massive issue that once you've got money you start to think, "Am I going to piss these people off if we don't give them exactly what they want?" (Matt)

For WIMPS, the best way for government to avoid being seen as inauthentic and disingenuous in its commitment to e-participation is to support grassroots projects that are run by and accountable to young people:

The government coming out and saying we want young people to participate will probably put off significant numbers of the very young people that they want to reach. I think the success of WIMPS, to the extent that it's been successful so far, is that it's not a government site. It may have government funding, but it's most definitely not a government site. It's run by young people and I think young people coming on to it very quickly get a sense of that. (Smyth)

The editor of Educationet is less convinced by the British Government's recent enthusiasm for e-participation:

There hasn't been a fall in voter turnout because there aren't enough Web sites encouraging young people to get politically active.... We're coming from a period where there was no Internet. I don't vote because the parties are rubbish. I personally feel that they are going to go to Parliament to lie their backsides off—and that's based on experience. (Jayanee)

The relationship between government and the projects considered here seems to be problematic on two levels. From a pragmatic perspective, project organizers have to decide whether they can trust the government to support the principle of political engagement without seeking to manage it in practice. From a more overtly political perspective, there is the question of whether government is the provider of solutions or the cause of problems in relation to the atrophy of democratic engagement. If, as some of the interviewees argued, it is the performance—perhaps even the most basic institutional values—of governments (of various types and colors) that cause young people to turn away from politics, one might conclude that a more constructive role for them would be to provide resources for grassroots activists to use without political interference.

Supporting Youth E-Citizenship: Some Policy Proposals

The purpose of policy is to connect effective means to desired ends. Before arriving at strategic conclusions, there remains a need for clarity about the broader political objectives of youth e-citizenship. What exactly is it that the projects we have examined, and many others like them, are seeking to accomplish? As we have already seen, e-citizenship projects tend to fall into two categories. Those that have received external funding, from government bodies or charitable foundations, tend to be mainly interested in establishing "connections" between young people and institutions which have some power over their lives. Regarding youth as apprentice citizens who need to learn appropriate ways of engaging with encrusted structures of governance, they seek to promote habits of civility, while at the same time encouraging young people to think of themselves as empowered social actors whose (virtual) voices deserve to be heard. Autonomous e-citizenship projects tend not to be funded by government, and express strong reservations about having too close a relationship with the state. These projects are less interested in engaging with powerful institutions than in forming powerful networks of young people, engaged with one another to resist the power of institutions. Regarding youth as independent political agents, autonomous e-citizens expect less from the communicative potential of having their say; for them, empowerment entails an intimate relationship between voice and action.

Both of these approaches are open to critique. Managed e-citizenship can be criticized for promoting mainly vertical and bilateral communicative relationships between young people and power elites; for failing (often on spurious grounds of "risk") to facilitate horizontal networks in which young people cannot merely express themselves as individuals, but enter into collective activities; for circumscribing agendas of political debate, such as the neurotic avoidance of "sensitive issues" or any acknowledgement that most political debate is in reality of a partisan nature; and for placing too much emphasis upon talk and being heard and showing too little concern for the consequences of democratic expression and the capacity of organized opinion to influence political outcomes. Indeed, some might argue that managed e-citizenship, with its overriding interest in friendliness, deliberation and consensus, provides young people with a highly distorted simulation of the political world: a virtual community of well-trained democrats who would be lost in any real political party, trade union, or local council.

Critics of autonomous e-citizenship might point to its dislocation from structures and processes of effective power; its tendency to preach to the converted and to pay little attention to reaching opposed minds or entering into any kind of deliberative debate with the undecided; its emphasis upon single issues, at the expense of more generalized values or aggregated positions; and its reliance upon digital technologies that are encoded in ways that are bound to undermine its efforts.

I do not propose to conclude by subscribing to one or the other of these two approaches to e-citizenship. Rather than perpetuate this dichotomy, I intend to argue that there is a strong case for breaching this divide and seeking a productive convergence between these two models of youth e-citizenship. But before turning to such a creative policy synthesis, there is a little more theoretical work to be done, for, although we have distinguished the characteristics of managed and autonomous e-citizenship, we have yet to arrive at a satisfactory answer to the question, What is e-citizenship supposed to accomplish?

Following Foucauldian political theorists, such as Rose, Barry, and Cruickshank,[24] I want to characterize e-citizenship as a technology of governance. That is not to say that e-citizenship is about governing young people, in the traditionally coercive and dominating sense, but that it is about nurturing forms of conduct consistent with being a citizen. The function of e-citizenship is to conceive, create and sustain members of a political community. The emphasis upon membership is important, because, as citizens, young people are being invited into a community; they are being offered membership cards (IDs, passports); they are required to accept both rules and sanctions (law, morality; fines and prisons); they are urged to consider their responsibilities as well as rights as members; and they are expected to have regard for the specific nature of their community (Northern Ireland versus Ireland; Canada versus the U.S.A.; Iran versus Iraq). Members of a police force, an army, a football team or a dance troupe are expected to be trained. So are citizens. To be a nonmember of a community is to be a stranger, faced with all the risks and vulnerabilities of the outsider. But to be an insider carries with it sometimes onerous burdens. It is to prepare young people for these rites and rights of membership that e-citizenship, as one technology among others, is employed.

But the terms of citizenship are not static. A second function of e-citizenship is to contest those terms. Some of the projects examined above manifested a largely uncritical view of what it means to be a citizen in a contemporary liberal democracy, such as the United Kingdom. They operated on the basis that parliament represents the people; that voting is a key way of holding power to account; that the expression of public opinion is a key means of influencing policy; that the discussion of politics is best undertaken without the interference of partisan or class loyalties; that civil behavior entails particular norms and that uncivil behavior should be regulated. These assumptions reflect the values to be found in most textbooks on citizenship education. They do not emerge out of a sinister conspiracy to maintain the status quo, but neither to they encourage young people to think for themselves about the kind of democracy they want, at least until they have been socialized into the basic routines of the existing format. Other projects examined above tended to stretch the notion of citizenship beyond its textbook definition. For example, the George Fox 6 Campaign insisted that broadly conceived rights to protest against injustice should be protected for all members of any community; Students Against Sweatshops seek to extend rights of citizenship in two ways: by adding an economic dimension to them and by calling for such rights to be granted to "strangers" in the Third World whose exploitation is in some sense linked to that of students in the West.

Technologies of e-citizenship turn cyberspace into a locus for the contestation of claims about citizenship. Because entry into the virtual public sphere is cheaper and less burdensome than making one's presence felt in the conventional public sphere, it is particularly attractive to young people whose experiences and aspirations might otherwise be marginalized or forgotten. The inclusion of these voices and traditions in the development of e-citizenship is of the utmost importance, if there is a genuine commitment to cultivate a democratic culture of participation. This is the key policy question for governments: are they in favor of merely promoting participation on their own terms or are they prepared to commit to a policy of *democratic* participation? The latter will always be slightly uncomfortable for governments. Democracy should be disruptive to people in power. Why else would it be so cherished by the relatively powerless?

How, then, might a productive convergence between managed and autonomous e-citizenship be realized? The first stage entails combining in one policy the strongest democratic features of both models. A government wishing to promote democratic youth e-citizenship might start out, therefore, by signing up to the following six principles:

1   Government is willing to fund, but not directly manage or interfere with, common online spaces in which young people are free to express themselves as citizens, and about the terms of citizenship.

2   Online democratic spaces for young people shall include horizontal channels of inter-action, through which networks and collective associations can be formed, as well as vertical channels, providing dialogical links to various institutions that have power and authority over them.

3   It is up to young people to set the terms of their own political debate, without any external censorship.

4   E-citizenship involves both free expression and consequential political engagement. Young people are not to be expected to participate unless the scope and terms of their influence is explicitly outlined.

5   Among other aspects of e-citizenship, opportunities and resources will be provided to
     ensure that young people encounter others with whom they might disagree strongly,
     within various kinds of deliberative settings.

6   Young people are encouraged to mobilize online to counter social injustices and broaden
     the political agenda in any way that they see fit.

While the adoption of such principles would be promising, from a broadly democratic
perspective, it should be acknowledged that they merely synthesize the strongest democratic
elements of the two currently dominant models of youth e-citizenship. But policy is not only
constructed out of what people are already doing. Both current models of youth e-citizenship
can be accused of failing to transcend the historic limits that might be referred to as analog
citizenship.

In speaking of analog citizenship, I have in mind three broad limitations. The first concerns
ways of defining what is political. There is a curious similarity in the ways that both managed and autonomous e-citizenship projects conceive the political sphere. Whether as civic
apprentices or emergent activists, participants in these projects are mainly concerned with
traditional questions of power: being heard by those in authority; seeking the introduction of
just policies; facilitating forms of collective action. None of these political approaches are by
any means obsolete, but there are strong reasons for thinking that we are in a period of profound turbulence for the political sphere, in which hitherto neglected and affective concerns
about identity, personal relationships, and domestic space are invading areas of thought and
practice once occupied by instrumental and institutional political rationalism. The excellent
chapter in this volume by Earl and Schussman raises important questions about the porous
boundary between public affairs and private pleasures. The political is rooted in everyday
life and participatory practices are increasingly regarded as forms of shared experience rather
than mere aggregations of atomized interests. Democracy, which has often seemed to be
anesthetized by constitutionality, is rooted in expressive, cathartic, and carnivalesque practices that connect public policy to mundane culture. But the e-citizenship projects we have
explored tend to be characterized by an earnest solemnity: a language and aesthetic that
allows little room for the banal sociability and cathartic frivolity that has contributed to the
success of some of the most culturally radical social movements in the history of democracy.
By emphasizing rational deliberation, at one end of the spectrum, and collective solidarity,
at the other, the promoters of e-citizenship are in danger of perpetuating forms of symbolic
exclusion that have over the years led many young people to conclude that these institutional arrangements, this language of ideology and policy, these battles of winners and losers
are not for us.

A second limitation of the analog model of e-citizenship concerns the nature and use of
digital technologies. Since the early twentieth century, political communication has been
dominated by the broadcasting paradigm in which organized centers transmit messages
to mass audiences. In the early days of the publicly available Internet many politicians
saw what they thought was their chance to become their own broadcasters, preaching to
the public without bothersome interference from journalists. In reality, the Internet has
always been much more than a broadcasting medium. Yet the projects we have investigated
are remarkably unadventurous in their approaches to many-to-many communication. For
some, this potential was overwhelmed by an excessive sense of youth at risk; for others—
even those seeking radical objectives—the most valuable use they felt they could make of
digital technologies was to disseminate truth (or countertruth) more effectively than by any

other means. Digital technologies are good for more than the dissemination of neglected messages. The most innovative opportunities for political activity online involve specifically digital relationships to content, such as sampling, remixing, and social collaborations ranging from recommender systems to wikis.

Third, there has been a conspicuous absence in most of these youth e-citizenship projects to address key questions about what it means to be a youth. If, as Giddens, Beck, and others argue, life stages are increasingly encountered as reflexive projects, in which identities are constructed at least to some extent knowingly, why is there so little discussion of these choices and dilemmas within e-citizenship projects? Why do so few online "youth" projects challenge social definitions of childhood, adulthood, and transitions to maturity?

Transcending these limitations could entail the adoption of three further policy principles:

7   While e-citizenship embraces traditional questions of power, inequality, organization, and ideology, it does not exclude everyday political experience, such as the negotiation of feelings and sensitivities, the governance of spaces and relationships, and the many intersections between popular culture and power that affect life and lifestyle.

8   Young people are urged to use digital technologies innovatively with a view to utilizing and expanding their democratic features. (The chapters in this volume by Bers, Levine, and Rheingold offer some stimulating proposals in this regard.)

9   It is within the scope of youth e-citizenship to raise challenging questions about the nature and political status of children, adults, and youth, and to challenge condescending or stereotypical notions of youth identity.

We are coming closer to a coherent policy for youth e-citizenship, but still there is a major problem with the policy process to be addressed.

Thinking Democratically about Democracy: An Adventure in Policy Making

When governing institutions come to think about extending participatory democracy, it is remarkable how rarely they consult people about how they want to participate. The result is often a confused effort, in which policy makers decide how ordinary citizens should use their energies and citizens refuse to join in because they would rather be using their energies in other democratic ways. With policies for youth, there is all too often an even more profound dislocation between policy and public demand, for many young people do not yet have the vote, and therefore do not figure on politicians' radar screens, and those who do often speak a democratic language that does not easily translate into bureaucratic rationality. Ironically, therefore, much of the current emphasis by governments upon "giving the kids a say" amounts to little more than acting upon hunches about what will keep young people quiet.

If youth e-citizenship is to be more than a top-down exercise in bureaucratic management, a tenth policy principle needs to be added to complete this proposal:

10   All e-citizenship policy will be determined in partnership between official policy makers and young people themselves, using wikis and other forms of collaborative decision-making software.

The transition from an analog to a digital vision of youth e-engagement entails more than enthusiasm for the technocratic future. It calls for confidence in the self-determining ethos of what Lance Bennett has called "actualizing citizens" (chapter 1) and what I have referred to as "autonomous citizenship." It calls for a democracy in which citizenship is not merely inherited as found, but made through creative experience. It calls, most immediately, for an inclusive, transparent, global debate about how the digital mediasphere is reshaping the expectations, desires, responsibilities, and prospects of young people in democratic societies.

Notes

1. Qualifications and Curriculum Authority [QCA], *Education for Citizenship and the Teaching of Democracy in School. Final Report of the Advisory Group on Citizenship* (London: QCA, 1998), 7.

2. Henry Giroux, Critical Theory and Rationality in Citizenship Education, *Curriculum Inquiry* 10, no. 4 (1980), 329–66.

3. QCA, op. cit.: 1.5.

4. QCA, op. cit.: Appendix B: 67. For the sake of transparency, I should make clear that I was the author of this appendix.

5. Lynn Davies, Teaching about Conflict through Citizenship Education, *International Journal of Citizenship and Teacher Education* 1, no. 2 (2005): 19.

6. Chris Woodhead on *The Long View*, BBC Radio 4, 8 April, 2003.

7. Libby Brookes, Kid Power, *Guardian*, 26 April, 2003, 41.

8. Elizabeth Such, Oliver Walker, and Robert Walker, *Childhood* 12, no. 3 (2005): 301–26.

9. Steve Cunningham and Michael Lavalette, 'Active Citizens' or 'Irresponsible Truants'? School Student Strikes against the War, *Critical Social Policy* 24, no. 2 (2004): 264.

10. Elizabeth Frazer, Citizenship Education: Anti-political Culture and Political Education in Britain, *Political Studies* 48, no. 1 (2000): 88–103.

11. HM Government, *In the Service of Democracy: A Consultation Paper on a Policy for E-Democracy* (London: HMSO, 2002), 16.

12. This typology has much in common with Lance Bennett's Actualizing and Dutiful Citizens. Indeed, one might argue that managed citizenship tends to produce DCs and autonomous citizenship tends to produce ACs. One of the fruitful outcomes of collaborating on this volume is our intention to work further on exploring the theoretical and empirical connections between these concepts.

13. John Freeland, Education and Training for the School to Work Transition, in *A Curriculum for the Senior Secondary Years*, ed. Terri Seddon and Christine Deer (Hawthorn, Victoria: ACER, 1992).

14. Ulrich Beck, *The Politics of Risk Society* (Cambridge: Polity Press, 1998), 78.

15. David Garland, *The Culture of Control* (Oxford, Oxford University Press, 2001).

16. W. Lance Bennett, New Media Power: The Internet and Global Activism, in *Contesting Media Power: Alternative Media in a Networked World*, ed. Nick Couldry and James Curran (Lanham, MD: Rowman & Littlefield, 2003), 20.

17. G. Longford, Pedagogies of Digital Citizenship and the Politics of Code, *Techné* 9, no. 1 (2005): 68.

18. Robert Luke, Habit@online: Web Portals as Purchasing Ideology, *Topia: A Canadian Journal of Cultural Studies* 8 (fall 2002): 61–89.

19. Children and Young People's Unit, Cabinet Office (2002).

20. Hakim Bey, *T.A.Z.: The Temporary Autonomous Zone, Ontological Anarchy, Poetic Terrorism* (Brooklyn, NY: Autonomedia, 1991), 101.

21. The interviewees were Barry Griffiths of Headsup, interviewed on July 4, 2006; Rajeeb Dey of ESSA, interviewed on July 4, 2006; Paul Smyth and Tully Kewley of WIMPS, interviewed on July 28, 2006; Sofie Buckland of Students Against Sweatshops, interviewed on August 9, 2006; Matt of the George Fox 6 Campaign, interviewed on August 7, 2006; and Chaminda Jayanetti of Educationet, interviewed on August 10, 2006.

22. Barbie Zelizer, *Remembering to Forget: Holocaust Memory Through the Camera's Eye* (Chicago: Chicago University Press, 1998); John Durham Peters, Witnessing, *Media, Culture & Society* 23, no. 6 (2001): 707–23; Susan Sontag, *Regarding the Pain of Others* (New York: Farrar, Straus, and Giroux, 2003).

23. John Ellis *Seeing Things: Television in the Age of Uncertainty* (London: IB Tauris, 2000).

24. Andrew Barry, Thomas Osborne, and Nikolas Rose, eds., *Foucault and Political Reason: Liberalism, NeoLiberalism and Rationalities of Government* (London: UCL Press, 1996); Andrew Barry, *Political Machines: Governing a Technological Society* (London: Athlone Press, 2001); Nikolas Rose, *Powers of Freedom: Reframing Political Thought* (Cambridge: Cambridge University Press, 1999); Barbara Cruickshank, *The Will to Empower: Democratic Citizens and Other Subjects* (Ithaca, NY: Cornell University Press, 1999).